Virtual States

Virtual States challenges the idea that the nation-state is dead. In all the hype about the Internet, little thought has been given to the systematic inequalities being brought about by globalisation, and exacerbated by the global spread of the Internet. Jerry Everard argues that new disparities are emerging between the information 'haves' and the information 'have-nots'; between wealthy and poor states; and between the wealthy and poor in wealthy states. *Virtual States* systematically addresses these inequalities.

The book argues that there are two economies embodied in nation-states: the goods and services economy, and the identity economy. While the state's role in the first may be diminishing, its role in the latter is stronger than ever. In today's climate of change and uncertainty, people are turning to nationalism and engaging in regional conflicts over identity. Jerry Everard suggests that identity is the outcome of boundary-making processes: ways of identifying the Self from Other – 'us' from 'them'. The Internet's ability to cross borders with impunity challenges traditional, state-based identity structures. What is needed, he argues, is a theoretical framework within which states can be disaggregated into multiple sets of identities and this book provides just such a framework.

Structured in four parts, with detailed chapter summaries, *Virtual States* presents a compact – and easily accessible – theoretical and historical introduction to the Internet: its relationship to the developing world; the Internet in relation to the developed world; and the Internet and society. The book also covers issues such as war, censorship and the philosophical implications of hypertext, which is at the heart of the Net. Written for the general reader, this book is also a core resource for those interested in the implications of the Internet in cultural studies, international relations and international political economy.

Jerry Everard is in the Department of English and Theatre Studies at the Australian National University. This book was written while on secondment from the Department of Defence in Canberra and does not necessarily reflect official Australian government views.

Technology and the Global Political Economy
Edited by Michael Talalay
Principal Consultant, Butler Group

Chris Farrands
Principal Lecturer, Nottingham Trent University, Nottingham

Despite its evident importance in our daily lives, technology has too often been ignored as a critical factor in international affairs and in national and corporate policy-making. This series places technology at the centre of explanation in theories of international relations and international political economy, aiming both to alter the way in which scholars and students think about these disciplines and to provide guidelines for policy-makers in the face of ever-increasing technological change.

Editorial Board:

Dr Gary Acres OBE, retired Director of Research for Johnson Matthey; Professor Gerd June, University of Amsterdam; Professor Roger Tooze, University of Wales at Aberystwyth; Professor JoAnne Yates, Sloan School of Management, Massachusetts Institute of Technology.

Books in the series:
Technology, Culture and Competitiveness: change and the world political economy
Edited by Michael Talalay, Chris Farrands and Roger Tooze

Virtual States: The Internet and the boundaries of the nation-state
Jerry Everard

Virtual States

The Internet and the boundaries of the nation-state

Jerry Everard

London and New York

First published 2000
by Routledge
11 New Fetter Lane, London EC4P 4EE

Simultaneously published in the USA and Canada
by Routledge
29 West 35th Street, New York, NY 10001

Routledge is an imprint of the Taylor & Francis Group

© 2000 Jerry Everard

Typeset in Times by
Keystroke, Jacaranda Lodge, Wolverhampton
Printed and bound in Great Britain by
Biddles Ltd, Guildford and King's Lynn

British Library Cataloguing in Publication Data
A catalogue record for this book is available from the British Library

Library of Congress Cataloging in Publication Data
Everard, Jerry
 Virtual states : the Internet and the boundaries of the nation-
state / Jerry Everard.
     p.   cm. — (Technology and global political economy)
   Includes bibliographical references.
   1. Information society—Political aspects. 2. Internet (Computer
network)—Political aspects. 3. Internet (Computer network)—Social
aspects. 4. National state. I. Title. II. Series.
HM851.E94 1999
303.48'33dc21   99–20772
                                                                   CIP

ISBN 0–415–17214–4 (pbk)
ISBN 0–415–17213–6 (hbk)

For Sharon and Eve

These our actors,
As I foretold you, were all spirits, and
Are melted into air, into thin air:
And, like the baseless fabric of this vision,
The cloud-capp'd towers, the gorgeous palaces
The solemn temples, the great globe itself,
Yea, all which it inherit, shall dissolve,
And, like the insubstantial pageant faded,
Leave not a rack behind.
We are such stuff as dreams are made on
And our little lives are rounded with a sleep

William Shakespeare *The Tempest* IV: I

Contents

PART IV
Internet and society 119

Series editor's preface

Crossing from the United States to Canada takes you across the world's longest undefended border. You move from one English-speaking country to another. Sport and entertainment are much the same in both. Trade and tourism flow freely and massively between the two. Canada borders on no other country, the US only on Mexico. And yet, the two countries are fundamentally different. As a Canadian who has lived in the US, I certainly believe so. A Swedish colleague of mine visiting North America for the first time a few years ago felt exactly the same. Culture, society and individual behaviour all differ.

The border between Canada and the United States may be extremely permeable, but the boundaries are very distinct. They show no sign of fading away. It is just this phenomenon that Jerry Everard addresses in his study of the virtual state. He looks at the conflict between two apparently incompatible systems. On the one hand, there is the European nation-state system as symbolised by the Treaty of Westphalia, just over 350 years old. On the other, there is the concept of cyberspace epitomised by the rather more recent Internet and WorldWideWeb. Jerry asks what is happening as they meet. In his own words 'W(h)ither the State?'

The Internet is the ultimate in globalisation. It makes time and distance irrelevant. In an economy and society where information increasingly is the prime commodity, it really does signify what Frances Cairncross writing in *The Economist* called 'the death of distance'. To the Internet, borders and time zones are meaningless. I can 'jack in' (as William Gibson puts it in his cybernovel, *Neuromancer*) to the Web anywhere at any time and send and retrieve information to and from anyone around the globe – as long as that person is connected.

The state on the other hand depends on borders. Its *raison d'être* is to distinguish between 'us' and 'them' and to protect the former against the latter. In a sense, the existence of the state hinges on the condition of autarky. The more isolated and the less penetrated the state is, then the more it remains a sovereign, independent entity.

The Web challenges all of these conditions. It should herald the withering – with only one *h* – of the state. Many commentators argue that this is indeed bound to happen. But will it? Jerry Everard persuasively argues that the influence of the Web is likely to be far subtler. It will change the nature of boundaries, but it will not erode them. The state of the future might not be Westphalian, but it will certainly continue to exist. Philosophically, as long as identity – both individual and group – rests on the distinction between Self and Other, some old boundaries will persist and new ones arise. The state may change, but as the ultimate arbiter of these boundaries it is unlikely to disappear. Jerry goes so far as to pose the question of whether the totally deterritorialised state – the 'cyberspace' – could actually exist in the future.

Virtual States touches on a number of other very interesting topics. It gives a brief history of the origins of the Internet and its enabling technologies. It discusses the implications of information war – where electronic bytes rather than explosive bits decide battles and even campaigns. It looks at censorship on the Web, and it addresses the problem of the English language not as a facilitator of globalisation but rather as a barrier to those who do not speak it and cannot surf in it. It touches upon shifts in power from nation-states to transnational actors in the context of the Web. It talks about a new imperialism – that of domain names. Very importantly, Jerry Everard draws his examples from Europe, Australia, Africa and the Far East – and does not merely focus on the US experience.

He also addresses – in addition to the concept of Self and Other and the state – one further grand theme related to the Web. The distinction between haves and have-nots increasingly rests on access to information. In a global economy and society where email and e-commerce connect us socially and economically, how will the 'unconnected' fare? There will always be a role for the robber baron. The successful entrepreneur will continue to reap rewards for courage and boldness. The stars – be they in sports, music or film – will earn their millions and live in their tax havens. By and large, however, it is Peter Drucker's 'knowledge worker' for whom the future holds the well-paid jobs and the lifestyle that accompanies them. Where does this leave those individuals and those states that are unconnected, that cannot 'jack in', that can not surf the Web, that can not live and work in a world increasingly linked by intranets, extranets and the Web itself?

The theme of this series is the influence of technology on the global political economy. This book is a major contribution to this subject. It asks how the Internet – one of the most recent and least physically bounded technological innovations – will affect the nature and even the existence of the nation-state – one of the most long-lived and geographically fixed of the institutions in the global political economy.

Michael Talalay

Preface

Virtual States arose from a project on cyberpunk science fiction that I began in 1994. The dystopian visions within that genre led me to consider the influence of fiction on the reality of a computer-linked society. How real are the claims of writers like William Gibson (1984) that the nation-state will wither away under corporate pressures? How real is the threat of information warfare? How will globalisation affect the developing world? I was interested too in how identity was being constructed in cyberspace, and where the role of the body fitted. I presented two seminars at Lancaster University and at Nottingham Trent University during a visit to the UK in 1995–6, and by this stage my thinking had turned to the implications of the Internet for international security.

As an Australian I was conscious of writing from the margins of European consciousness, while at the same time living in the world's third most wired state. The tensions between these identities led to broader questions of the Internet, globalisation and the philosophical implications of hypertext.

As the Internet spreads around the globe new challenges arise for states. Quite abruptly, it seems, we are living in a borderless world with new opportunities and new challenges. Media views of the Internet seem to oscillate wildly between the 'den of iniquity' thesis and the 'global shopping mall'. Clearly there was room in the literature for a longer term and more considered view.

Acknowledgements

The impetus for this book came from a good friend, Adam Cobb, who convinced me to present a paper at Nottingham Trent University. It ultimately took the enthusiastic response of Michael Talalay of Nottingham Trent (and, as it turned out, commissioning editor for Routledge) to persuade me to put a formal proposal together, and to commission the book. My thanks, too, to Vicki Smith of Routledge, who showed great patience and understanding in dealing with me from half-way round the globe. The book is the product of an intellectual journey of several years, but the final sprint was accomplished during a period as Departmental Visitor to the Department of English and Theatre Studies at the Australian National University. I would also like to thank Mark Poster and Radhika Gajjala for their enthusiasm and comments on the thesis version of this work.

I could not have done it without the considerable support of my partner, Sharon, and my daughter, Eve.

I would like to thank the Australian National University for providing the resources for me to attend and contribute to the Cybermind96 and Deleuze conferences in Perth, Western Australia, and for the use of English Department resources during my stay.

I would also like to thank Alan Sondheim (co-moderator of Cybermind), Radhika Gajjala, Jon Marshall and Adam Cobb for their friendship, support and incisive criticism of ideas and arguments within this book. Thanks, too, to the collective wisdom of the Cybermind discussion list for their friendship, wisdom, humour and poetry.

Finally, I would like to thank Professors Horst Ruthrof and Michael O'Toole of Murdoch University, for their role in providing much of the intellectual equipment for this journey.

The responsibility for any errors is, of course, entirely mine.

Acronyms

ACM	Association for Computing Machinery
ACSnet	Australian Computer Science Network
AFP	Agence France-Presse
APEC	Asia-Pacific Economic Cooperation Conference
ARPA	Advanced Research Projects Agency
ARPANET	ARPA Network
ASEAN	Association of South-East Asian Nations
AT&T	American Telephone and Telegraph
BBN	Bolt, Beranek and Newman
BITNET	'Because It's Time' Network
C^2	command and control
C^2W	command and control warfare
CD-ROM	Compact Disc: Read-Only Memory
CDA	Communications Decency Act
CERN	Conseil Européen pour la Recherche Nucléaire (European Council for Nuclear Research) – a high energy physics laboratory
CIX	Commercial Internet Exchange
CMU	Carnegie-Mellon University
CoCom	Co-ordinating Committee on the Exports of Dual-Use Technologies
CSIROnet	Commonwealth Scientific and Industrial Research Organisation Network
CSNET	Computer Science Network (US)
CUNY	City University of New York
CWRU	Case-Western Reserve University
DARCOM	Defence Advanced Research Communications (Message Research Group)
DARPA	Defense Advanced Research Projects Agency
DFN	Deutsches Forschungsnetz
DNS	Domain Name Server
DoD	Department of Defense (US)
DoE	Department of Energy (US)

DSIRnet	Department of Scientific and Industrial Research Network (New Zealand)
EARN	European Academic Research Network
EFF	Electronic Frontier Foundation
EIN	European Informatics Network
EUnet	European Union Network
EW	electronic warfare
FTP	file transfer protocol
G7	Group of Seven: US, Japan, Germany, France, UK, Italy and Canada
HTML	hypertext markup language
ICCP	Information, Computers and Communication Policy (OECD Committee)
IDD	international direct dialling
IFF	identification – friend or foe
IMP	information message processor
INRIA	Institut National Recherche d'Informatique et d'Automatique (France)
INWG	Internetworking Working Group
IP	Internet Protocol
IRC	Internet relay chat
ISAD	Information Society and Development (Ministerial Conference)
ISP	Internet service provider
IT	information technology
ITU	International Telecommunications Union
IW	information warfare
JANET	Joint Academic Network (UK)
JUNET	Japan Unix Network
LAN	local area network
LEO	low earth orbit (satellites)
MAD	Mutually Assured Destruction
MILNET	MILitary NETwork
MIT	Massachusetts Institute of Technology
MOO	multi-user domain – object oriented
MSC	Multimedia Super Corridor
MUD	multi-user domain
NASA	National Aeronautical and Space Administration
NCP	Network Control Protocol
NGO	non-governmental organisation
NORDUnet	Nordic research network (Scandinavia)
NPL	National Physical Laboratories (UK)
NSA	National Security Agency (US)
NSF	National Science Foundation
NWG	Network Working Group

OECD	Organisation for Economic Cooperation and Development
PARC	Palo Alto Research Centre
PPP	purchasing power parity
PRnet	Packet Radio Network
RFQ	request for quotation
RIPE	Réseaux IP Européens
RMA	revolution in military affairs
SATnet	Atlantic Packet Satellite Network
SCADA	Supervisory Control and Data Acquisition
SDC	Stanford Defence College
SERCnet	Science and Engineering Research Council Network (UK)
SLORC	State Law and Order Restoration Committee
SRI	Stanford Research Institute
SUNET	Swedish Universities Network
TCP	Transmission (or Transfer) Control Protocol
TCP/IP	Transfer Control Protocol/Internet Protocol
UAV	unmanned aerial vehicle
UCLA	University of California at Los Angeles
UCSB	University of California at Santa Barbara
UIU(C)	University of Illinois at Urbana-Champaign
UNINETT	Norwegian academic network for research and education
UUCP	Unix-to-Unix CoPy
VRML	virtual reality markup language
WAIS	wide area information servers
WAN	wide area network
WTO	World Trade Organisation
WWW	WorldWideWeb

Introduction

As we journey into a digital future, whether bright with promise or dark with foreboding, it is time to take stock and ask ourselves: how global is globalisation? How much of the world is on the WorldWideWeb? We need to remind ourselves, too, that others before us have travelled similar paths – perhaps there are things for us to learn from them.

Just as Plato warned in his *Phaedrus* of the dangers of an information technology, so too does his work survive because of that technology – writing. He too raised questions about authentication, about commerce, about education, about the warping of young minds through their exposure to such technologies. Horace, too, in his *Odes* warned that travel, experience, call it what you will, inevitably render us monstrous to our own kind. But Plato still wrote, and Horace still travelled.

It is time to take a realistic look at the extent of the promises, and at the extent of the realistic dangers – not in order to take a Luddite's revenge, but rather to be able to plan ahead with knowledge and understanding of the real benefits and the real limitations of this awfully big adventure.

Through it all, some large themes emerge. Issues of access and of identity form a common thread throughout this book. The global spread of the Internet confronts us with new kinds of identity structures, defining communities of information 'haves' and 'have-nots'. *Virtual States* explores four intersecting surfaces or boundaries which broadly correspond to the four parts in this book.

Part I examines the theory and practice of virtual states. It begins with some thoughts about the nature of states, and shows how the Internet emerged from a particular set of historical conditions, and grew into something rather more and rather different from a particular solution to a particular problem. In that sense it is a narrative about a technology that became a cultural artefact and then a cultural medium.

Part II concerns the unwired states of the developing world, and the consequences for the developing world of remaining 'information poor' within the global economy. Part III concerns the haves and have-nots within the developed world, while Part IV concerns broader issues of the Internet and society. Who benefits? Who loses? Are media fears concerning the Internet justified? This part explores some philosophical and practical issues that have concerned people since the invention of the first great information technology, that of writing itself.

The book begins by sketching out some theoretical considerations with an examination of how states came about – what brought them into being, what is useful about such structures, and what makes them such powerful forms of community. The state, as a unifying idea, is an important part of the process by which people frame their own identity – this is the source of nationalism. But just as individual people present different facets of their identity in different situations, as parent, as lecturer, as diplomat, as lover, so too do states articulate different facets of their identity, through foreign and security policy, through agricultural and trade policy, through education and cultural policies and so on.

As a multifaceted structure, states may come under considerable pressure in one sphere, while they may become stronger than ever in others. This was clearly in evidence when, for example, in 1982 Britain's political leaders were struggling for political survival and national credibility until the Falklands War strengthened its support by appealing to the security identity of the state, building on public responses and opinion in ways that favoured the nation's political leadership. Thus at critical moments the economic considerations that some commentators would suggest underpin all political activity, can be sidelined where interests of national identity are foregrounded. Economics is not the sole determinant of people's lives, and it can be useful to keep this in mind in any discussion over the supposed 'fading away' of the nation-state.

As Dillon (1988: 14), following Wittgenstein (1983) and Foucault (1979), points out, language 'makes rather than (merely) reflects life', and this holds for all social discourses that shape and constrain the way people live their lives. In other words, 'to speak is to act and to act is to exercise power'. Information technology is therefore a medium for the exercise of power.

Globalisation is above all a social process, operating unevenly across and between societies. The resulting dynamism not only helps to maintain the drive for globalisation, but also serves to institutionalise structural inequalities.

If we are to analyse the impact of globalisation and the global spread of the Internet, it is important to trace three threads:

- the disaggregation of the unitary state
- the process of identity formation
- the interaction of these processes in maintaining social and economic inequalities.

Any notion of the 'decline' of the role of the nation-state needs to be tempered with the view that the world is simply becoming a more complex place. As with Kennedy's (1989) fallacious thesis of the decline of the US, we need to think rather in terms of a *relative* decline, as other actors emerge into the international sphere. This book is about one such 'actor'.

Part I
Virtual states
Theory and practice

1   W(h)ither the state?

Viewed from almost any perspective the world appears to be shrinking rapidly.
With the global spread of electronic telecommunications, epitomised by, but not
restricted to, the Internet, some commentators are suggesting that we are in the grip
of a change as radical as the industrial revolution, or even the Renaissance. As
markets become more time compressed and as money flows become increasingly
independent of state borders, it seems timely to ask: w(h)ither the state?

Unpacking this short question suggests immediately two possibilities: either
the state could wither away (without the *h*), or it could have a future that might be
a little different from what it seems to be today, hence whither (with the *h*). If the
latter, then what role will the state play in a globalised economy?

To address these questions I want to divide this chapter up into a set of themes.
To that extent I intend to frame this chapter more as a map for further development
elsewhere in the book. First, I want to examine the nature of the state-as-
information – a 'discourse formation' that will both allow for the operation of
history (the state's essential 'contestedness') and emphasise the contingency of the
state.

Second, I want to disaggregate the state into multiple facets, in order to show
why the idea of the decline of the state can be both evident and wrong depending
on which facet of the state is being considered. Finally, I want to examine the
globalisation of Internet in terms of its potential impact on the state's various
facets. In doing so I hope to counter some of the more extreme hype about living in
a 'wired' world, while examining some of the real changes that are occurring as I
write.

Don Tapscott, Chair of the Alliance for Converging Technologies and author of
The Digital Economy, opens with this claim:

> Today we are witnessing the early, turbulent days of a revolution as signifi-
> cant as any other in human history. A new medium of human communications
> is emerging, one that may prove to surpass all previous revolutions – the
> printing press, the telephone, the television, the computer – in its impact
> on our economic and social life . . . Such a shift in economic and social
> relationships has occurred only a handful of times before on this planet . . . A
> new enterprise is emerging . . . as different from the corporation of the
> twentieth century as the latter was from the feudal craft shop.
>
> (Tapscott 1996: xiii)

Certainly a shift is occurring, as it does with the widespread introduction of any new technology, but whether it will surpass the revolutions brought about by writing, or by movable type printing, or by railways, telegraph or telephone, is debatable. Perhaps we need to view the emergence of global telecommunications more as part of a continuing tradition of human (inter)networking.

In recent debates about globalisation and about the global spread of tele-communications, several themes are presented in sets of binary oppositions: sovereignty as against the borderless society; public access to information as against privacy; the state as against individual interests; the virtual as against the real (including the tension between states as software as against the real communities that exist as a product of that software); and so on. Such binaries, as we shall see, can lead to misunderstandings or overstatements.

The state as hyperreal

The state in many respects is like a piece of software – it seems stable enough while the power is on and it has not run into a major bug yet, but interrupt the power supply, or corrupt it, and it falls apart with startling rapidity. Such was the case with the collapse of the former Soviet Union, and with the break up of the former Yugoslavia, and many other state formations around the globe from Africa to the Baltic. States everywhere, it seems, are being transformed. Political spaces are being rearticulated to constitute new forms of community. Part of that challenge is coming arguably from the process of globalisation itself, and partly through the formation of new pathways to communication around the globe through electronic media, whether televisual or computer mediated. Part of what is at stake here is the issue of sovereign identity.

Traditional classical Realist approaches to the state have tended to articulate states as relatively unitary actors, espousing a Cartesian version of sovereign identity. Such a view is exemplified in Thomas Hobbes' view of the state as 'Leviathan'. That is to say that the state is seen as the social embodiment of the 'corpus' of the domestic polity. By analogy the Prince was seen as the captain of the ship of state, literally, the 'head' of state (see Machiavelli 1986). The functional social organs were, by extension, analogised into the arms/limbs of the state. With the rise in humanism, and its concomitant emphasis on the role of the individual, the humanist epistemology influenced the questions available to ask of the functioning of the social and political world of post-Renaissance Europe.

The Europe of the seventeenth century was a turbulent one. It was a Europe transforming itself from medieval to modern. It was doing so at a number of levels (Rosecrance 1986: 77ff) from trade within and between states, from a rearticulation of authority and of the balance between international loyalties (Church, the Holy Roman Emperor, and so on) and domestic loyalties (monarch, bishoprics, duchies, family, and so on). It is perhaps no coincidence that this epistemic shift coincided with the spread of movable type printing technologies to Europe.

Interestingly, the Korean invention of the movable type printing process, and the casting of type in metal two hundred years before Gutenberg, was not accompanied by the widespread social changes that occurred in Europe. Thus printing can be said only to be a factor that depended on a climate of social change to become an information revolution in its own right.

The Europe of the late seventeenth century was emerging from the Thirty Years War – arguably one of the great wars of identity, insofar as it represented the fundamental struggle of loyalties divided between the national and the international. From it emerged the Treaty of Westphalia (1648), a treaty that established the system of states we know today. That states are seen to have emerged so strongly from this turbulence is perhaps more a reading of a desire for stability than any reflection of the reality of the time (see Walker 1991: 128–163).

So we have a number of problems confronting traditional Realist approaches to the state and to the idea of the (inter)national. These problems have a lot to do with the location of identity in an increasingly globalised and wired world. Identity is arguably produced through practices of boundary making, practices that divide the idea of Self from the idea of the Other ('us' as against 'them').

States, under this rubric, might be viewed as 'symptoms', or outward signs of their boundary-making practices. From this it follows that the state will have a multitude of facets – each reflecting aspects of what it means to be a state from a particular point of view. The state therefore would need to be conceived in a disaggregated form, existing as a function of its differences and dispersions, rather than as the rational, unified originary actor of modernist realist discourse. States then consist of the narratives that are constructed about them.

The other side of this process is that the identity produced/invoked by practices of boundary making itself forms the locus for further boundary-making practices. Which came first historically is less important than the recognition that these processes occur. Moreover these processes become arguably one of the key mechanisms of history – if states sprang fully formed from some ideal type there would be no shifting of boundaries across time.

Collective identities in the form of states can be invoked for specific purposes, such as treaty making in international law, or the state setting of interest rates. But one aspect of this view of states as identities is that these identities themselves become visible where they are weakest – where they reveal a contested and contingent site of absence. The idea of statehood is arguably most strongly invoked when the place or importance of the state is placed in question by an Other identity, whether internal (insurgent) or external (from other states).

If states and other identity formations are at base produced through their boundary-making practices, then maintenance of those boundaries by those legitimised to act in the name of the state becomes a matter at least of credibility, and at the extreme, of state survival. So states (or more properly those who speak in the name of the state) are concerned to have internal policing and security mechanisms to ensure that those who are legitimised to speak for the state retain a monopoly on the power to do so.

So, whether about military or cultural violence, two points become clear: first, that nation-states have always been, in one form or another, about the prince or his analogue having a monopoly over the legitimate use of force. Such force has always been about policing and maintaining boundaries between Self and Other. It is no accident that the words 'policing' and 'policy' derive from the same roots.

Cognisant of this derivation, the Napoleonic-era strategist Carl von Clausewitz came to his now classic formulation of war as 'a continuation of policy by other means'. Clearly Clausewitz (1987: 119) was aware of the discursive nature of war. Thus the state as traditionally conceived in Realist accounts of international relations is perhaps more accurately termed the 'security state'. Given the genealogy of the Internet this account of the state is particularly pertinent. I shall consider other modalities of state (economic, cultural, political) later in the chapter.

Second, in the foundational texts of Realist discourse, the state has always been recognised as a discursive formation – a legal fiction – articulated to (re)present the will of the people as an overarching identity to which the domestic polity subscribes. It follows from this, that the state in Realist discourse (at least by the founding fathers – and I use the gendered term advisedly) has always been at its most visible at its moments of challenge, that is, at its boundaries (Dillon and Everard 1992: 281–312; Dillon 1995: 323). At the heart of this are sets of practices that speak the state. Indeed, as Dillon has argued, the constitution of what he terms (inter)national political order is, above all, a creation of power. And power can be seen as coterminous with knowledge.

Considering that the development of Internet arose from basic research at RAND sponsored by the US Department of Defense to improve computer processing performance through networked computers, and considering it was taken up as having almost coincidentally solved a potential military problem, the globalisation of the Internet continues to have a lot to do with nation-states and power. Indeed security – a term arguably at the core of what international relations traditionally has been about – is still most usually defined in terms of military security.

Against this, Charles Herzfeld (1995: 171), director of Advanced Research Projects Agency (ARPA) in the 1960s, asserts that the Internet was not developed to solve the problem of military command and control (C^2) in a nuclear warfare environment. Rather, it was developed by the US Defense Department's Advanced Research Projects Agency (DARPA) 'to link university computers and researchers to assist them in conducting basic research on computers and on communication nets and to use these networked computers for basic research'. In making this comment, Herzfeld glosses over the fact that this basic research was sponsored by the US Department of Defense, which gave its initial funding to DARPA, despite linking universities, companies and government.

Negroponte (1996: 236) asserts that: 'the role of the nation-state will change dramatically and there will be no more room for nationalism than there is for smallpox'. What Negroponte seeks to point out here is that with the globalisation of the Internet, there will be, as there are now, multiple sites of political activity, with increasing input into international affairs from non-state actors.

Along with many classical Realist theorists of international relations, Negroponte (1996) conceives of the nation-state as a unitary object. Something that, to use his terms, is tied to 'atoms rather than bits'. He refers to the state as being tied to 'space and place, geometry and geography'. In other words he sees states in terms of the physical traces – the manifestations in the walls, rivers, or mountains – of their boundaries or borders.

Rereading Machiavelli, Hobbes and Rousseau, one can locate a view along the lines that states are like software programmed to run in the wetware of the people who subscribe to the identity of the state. Like software the state exists while it is 'run' and maintained. It is a very complex piece of software written in a number of programming languages, such as economics, military security, environmental discourse and so on. These exist as articulations of a particular mode of defining Self and Other. It is about sets of relations between those who are included (us) and those who are excluded (them). It is about locating a sense of self and a sense of belonging – loosely and traditionally interpreted as a sense of place. It exists primarily as the result of a set of boundary-making practices that invoke and are invoked by the people subscribing to the idea of the state. This probably explains the emphasis placed on military security when terms like security and sovereignty are invoked. But security is broader than military security.

States are above all cultural artefacts. Another way of looking at this is to see states as information produced by and through practices of signification – from the writing of foundational documents (constitutions) to the discourses of smart bombs and the global spread of Coca-Cola. Sovereign identity, then, is comprised of bits rather than atoms.

Moreover, it is relations of power that have characterised relations within the domestic polity; between the domestic polity and the broader interests of the state; and between states within the global system.

We can begin, then, to construct a grid to illustrate something of the nature of the complex of relations between actors. Such a grid arises from the boundary-making behaviours in which people participate in order to articulate their relations as identifiable 'bodies' with respect to the issue areas they invoke.

On the one hand, we can look at issues of size or scale (individual, sub-state actor, state, system of states, transnational organisations or corporations, and the global). On the other hand, we can look at a set of issue areas, or arenas in which these identities are produced (security, economic, cultural, environmental, and so on). What becomes mapped as boundaries are those areas where relations between identities/actors come into conflict, collision or collusion with other actors at the individual, state, transnational corporation or non-governmental organisation (NGO) levels, or within and between issue areas, for example, where environment and economics conflict. Add to this the additional dynamic of economic first world/developing world and the extent of complexity becomes clearer. Under this rubric we can examine aspects of the globalisation of communications technologies epitomised by Internet in functional terms, rather than as an integrated set of over-hyped assertions.

In the process of disaggregating the state, it needs to be defined in terms of its relations with individuals and sub-state actors, with groups of states – such as the Asia-Pacific Economic Cooperation Conference (APEC) or the European Union

(EU) – its relations with transnational organisations and its relation to global issues, such as refugees, pollution and so on. The state is also defined in terms of its ability to mobilise its sub-state actors to provide for their safety, economic well-being, cultural identity and its environmental concerns, such as emissions controlled/regulated by domestic legislation, and by the agreements signed in its name with other states, such as, for example, the Biodiversity Convention.

When people start to think in terms of the death of the state – usually they are saying that one or another of the *facets* of the state is taking a more prominent role with respect to an issue area – that is, transnational corporations are becoming more prominent in the arena of capital flows around the world. That does not, of course, mean that the state is necessarily less powerful in other issue areas, such as military security for example. What should be becoming clear from this is that I want to treat states in Foucauldian terms, as *discourse formations*. That is to say, I want to treat them in terms of the sets of relations between those things and statements that serve to describe or invoke a state. This includes relations between those things that systematically define a state as different from something else, or from other states; in other words, its dispersions as well as its identities, for it is by the thousand small steps that an identity emerges from a set of practices.

Pollutants do not recognise national boundaries, as was shown so poignantly by Chernobyl in 1986. Narcotics traffic and organised crime seem to cross national boundaries with impunity. With the development of sophisticated technologies of communication, international economics has taken a quantum leap, rendering states seemingly increasingly powerless to control their own resources, and with the globalisation of Internet, even the cultural identity of individual nations is coming under threat. Pornography, transnational organised crime, dissidents and the spread of the English language raise legitimate concerns in the hearts and minds of the developing world. But I want to suggest that this is only part of the concerns of states, and part of what shapes their reaction to the globalising power of the Internet. Above all what concerns states is the power of the Internet to seem all-pervasive. So states see a need at least to be aware of, if not entirely in control of, the flow of information to their domestic polity. In a paternalistic way, it is about a power to protect the polity from the 'dangers' of an anarchical international system (Bull 1977).

This indeed seems to be the case, whether discussing the exercise of, or struggle for, power. This includes the sanctioning and continuation of inequalities displayed in and through war, even down to the narratives of peace that serve to institute and inscribe a status quo which in themselves are narratives about the effects of the conflicts. Such conflicts established these sets of relations through the inscription of boundaries by an arrangement of forces. Such a view becomes particularly evident when one analyses what various states have said about the growth of Internet and what it means for them as states. This latter issue will be taken up again in Chapter 5.

Chapter 2 provides a brief history of the Internet, in order to show how the development of the Internet was systematically related to the boundary-making practices of states, the process of identity formation, and the constitution (or maintenance) of the idea of Self as against the identity of the Other. In the development of what follows, I want to suggest that, as the Internet became privatised in the mid-1990s, other social formations began to emerge, to which states were responsive to the extent that they considered their own identity-making practices to be threatened.

Summary

- Unifying ideas, such as states, are important to the formation of identity. Such ideas allow the domestic polity of states to subscribe to the idea of a national identity in ways similar to those that draw people together in online discussion lists in 'virtual communities'.

- The state is not a unitary identity – it is multifaceted, so while it may be under pressure or erosion in one sphere of activity, it may remain strong in another sphere.

- The Internet may be seen as both a symptom of a broader philosophical shift in western society, and as a catalyst for the development of an ever more rapidly growing 'global' economy of information – at least for the west.

- There have been a number of models of the state, ranging from Realist state-as-actor models to so-called postmodern accounts of the state as occupying a number of possible subject-positions.

- The modern state is inherently tied to the rise of humanism in the west, and the subsequent dominance of western accounts of the state within the international system. The end of humanism as the driving philosophical principle in western society will inevitably lead to a shift in the nature of the state.

- States will remain important, if rearticulated, identity structures in the age of the postmodern globalised economy.

- Globalisation is above all a social process, and it operates unevenly across society and between societies. This differential quality provides the dynamism behind globalisation. It also promotes structural inequalities.

- The Internet's emergence within a military and security community has left it with an unbalanced demography that remains primarily western, Caucasian, young and male, although there are signs that this is changing slowly.

- Three processes are important in any analysis of the impact of globalisation and the global spread of the Internet. These are: the disaggregation of the state as actor; the Self/Other divide in the constitution of identity; and the operation of these processes in the maintenance of social and economic inequalities.

- International society is characterised both by the elevation of non-state actors, such as large multinational corporations and NGOs, as well as the continuing role of states. Any decline in the role of the state should thus be read more as a relative decline as other actors take up additional roles, rather than an absolute decline in state roles or powers.

2 internet@www.history.edu

The sky above the port was the colour of television tuned to a dead channel.
(William Gibson, *Neuromancer*, 1984: 9)

The history of the Internet can be written in two ways. First, as a history of communications networks, and second as a history of the enabling technologies which led directly to the Internet as we know it today. I want here to concentrate on the latter, rather than the former – for two reasons. First, in a book of this scope there is insufficient space to do more than gesture to earlier communications networks, and second, I want to focus on the modern Internet, albeit in a fairly non-technical way. This chapter will therefore present a generalist understanding of how it works through a history of the technology in order to deal with the broader issue of why it is the way it is today, and how it differs from almost any previous form of communication network.

There have been networks since people first organised themselves into groups. Technologies which supported these networks included organisations of runners, such as those, like Pheidippides, employed on the battlefield at Marathon; lines of fire beacons; smoke signals (still used by the Vatican to communicate the election of a new Pope); the passing of written messages, and so on. Later, more technological means were adopted, such as Chappe's 'optical telegraph' semaphore tower network in France, the electric telegraph, telephone, radio and television networks. In most of these cases, the networks were most highly developed in support of military ends. Thus it comes as no surprise that the Internet too began with military ends in mind. I want to argue that the reason for this is that the military forms the most visible of the state's identity-making mechanisms. It has the loudest mode of inscription, defining identity in terms of Self and Other through life or death. As Lyotard (1984) reminds us, to speak in these terms is literally to silence the Other.

Following the Second World War, the growing unease with the new world order gave rise to a stand-off between the then superpowers, in the shape of the Cold War. This was the first postmodern war insofar as it was a war based on the premise of non-use of the key weapons systems – nuclear weapons. Their awesome power was finally of a magnitude that their actual use was just short of unthinkable. Their power lay in their power as tokens of discourse. That said, in order to be believable as tokens of discourse, they had to be seen to be both functional (hence they were tested regularly) and usable, hence there had to be doctrines of use, including credible war-fighting strategies, such as Mutually Assured Destruction (MAD).

That a single bomb would be enough to destroy a city suggested to Cold War defence planners that with the land-line telephone system then in use, it would be only a short time into a nuclear conflict before communication was effectively cut off from the central command posts. By the early 1960s, when the former Soviet Union was perceived by the US to have reached or even exceeded parity in numbers of nuclear weapons, the problem became critical in the minds of some defence planners.

In the late 1950s the US Department of Defense established the ARPA within the US Department of Defense. This agency was established following the Russian launch of Sputnik to address issues of how to maintain the US technological edge in the emerging Cold War environment, fostered by perceptions of first a 'bomber gap' and later a 'missile gap' perceived to be in Russia's favour. Specifically, one of ARPA's tasks was to bring together US expertise in advanced computing equipment, in order to help develop more accurate and more powerful weapons.

In 1962, in the wake of the Cuban Missile Crisis, the US Air Force sponsored a study by RAND Corp on how to overcome the problem of how to maintain communications in the aftermath of a 'small' nuclear exchange. Given that scenario, it is not surprising that the answer, when it came, was couched in military terms. Paul Baran presented a paper prosaically entitled 'On Distributed Communications Networks' under RAND contract number AF 49(638) – 700 (Baran 1962). This paper laid the theoretical foundations for the architecture of what was to become the Internet.

In modelling the scenario, it was clear that the main telephone switching facilities would be destroyed in a nuclear conflict, as would the military command and control systems. Baran (1962) suggested a system that would have no centralised switches and could continue to operate even if many of its links had been destroyed. It considered the relative merits of a 'star-hub' system as against a matrix network, with modelling indicating that the latter would have greater survivability in the context of a nuclear conflict.

Baran also advocated splitting all the message data into equal length segments so that they could be sent as individually addressed packets that would find their own way through the network by any available route. If a node was blocked or damaged, the packet would be switched automatically to other nodes until an open one was available, continuing until the packet reached its final destination.

Each 'packet' would be of equal length, the bulk of it being taken up with the data to be transmitted, and then the remainder, at the top and tail of the message, would provide 'housekeeping' at each end of the packet. These end bits would indicate the start of the message, the routing address, the sender's details, the number of the packet in the chain, an error detection segment and the end of the message. When the packet arrived at its destination, it would be reunited with the other packets which comprised the message, and would display to the recipient as a complete message.

What is more, Baran devised a system whereby the network would 'learn' the shortest routes through which to switch message traffic, even if some of the nodes were destroyed. The system he described would attach numbers to the packet each time the message was relayed from one node to another. By reading the most recent number, and using this to update the numbers being added to the outgoing packets, the system would constantly adapt to find the shortest path-length between any two nodes on the network. This system as a whole became known as 'packet-switching' and is the basis for the digital telephone systems operating today.

Finally, Baran worked out that the benefits of redundancy diminished after a four-fold duplication of connections at each node. He was thus able to arrive at a robust, reliable network of relatively fixed cost, which would find the most efficient way for multiple users with different message loads to share a single net-work system, using 'store-and-forward' message relaying. In effect Baran's team solved virtually all the technological problems facing the design of a networked system. The rest of the story is about how his theories were implemented.

One way to read all this is that the state responded to the fundamental challenge posed to its sovereignty (by nuclear war) by seeking a way to maintain command and control following a nuclear first strike, in a way that would enable the state to retaliate with a second strike. Under deterrence theory, it was the fear of retaliation that would deter an adversary from making the first strike. Thus a robust network would ensure the maintenance of the identity of the state, while at the same time assuring the maintenance of peace. This is, of course, an oversimplification, because such practices operate at all levels of society, states being just one among many. The other levels of society come into play as the Internet moves outward into wider society, and I shall discuss the implications of this in the next section. Moreover, while concentrating on US developments, I want to show that parallel developments were taking place in Europe and parts of the Commonwealth, as the technology became increasingly internationalised.

ARPANET is born . . .

In 1965, a year after the US passed its Civil Rights Act, ARPA sponsored a study entitled 'A Cooperative Network of Time Sharing Computers', which examined how computers might be used from remote locations, in order to make efficient use of the still relatively few large computers then in existence. In the same year, Donald Davies, in the UK's National Physical Laboratories (NPL), conducted research into how best to break down data into packets for a storage and forwarding transmission system. Clearly, Britain was considering its options with an approach similar to that of the US, and under similar political conditions. Indeed, perhaps for the UK the situation seemed more critical, given Britain's lack of strategic depth in the face of the nuclear threat. At issue too, for the UK was the growing impetus towards European integration in the trade sphere with the establishment of the European Economic Community (EEC).

Then, in 1967, the Association for Computing Machinery (ACM, which was founded in 1947) held a symposium at which a plan was presented for a packet-switching network. ARPA brought together university and commercial (US defence contractors) experts to discuss proposals for a protocol for exchanging messages between computers. From this meeting came the concept for the ARPA Network or ARPANET packet switch, using the information message processor (IMP). That same year, in the UK the NPL published a proposal known as NPL Data Network, which outlined a network similar to the eventual ARPANET proposal.

A year later, ARPA released a request for quotation (RFQ) for a network of four IMPs with a possible growth to nineteen. The theory was quickly becoming a reality, and in 1969, the year of the first manned lunar landing, ARPANET was born. It began with a node at the University of California at Los Angeles (UCLA) and soon afterwards connected with the Stanford Research Institute (SRI), University of California at Santa Barbara (UCSB) and the University of Utah. It used IMPs developed by Bolt, Beranek and Newman (BBN) running on Honeywell 516 minicomputers with just 12K of memory. With a network finally up and running, a Network Working Group (NWG) was formed to develop host communications protocols; it was chaired by Steve Crocker. The host software was developed by his group, and in 1970 ARPANET began using a version of this software called Network Control Protocol (NCP).

Up until this time computer networks were seen almost entirely in terms of time sharing by running programs on remote computers. Eventually it became clear that more than programming data could be sent along the data channels. In 1969 Larry Roberts, of the Massachusetts Institute of Technology (MIT) Lincoln Laboratories, wrote the first email program as a TECO macro.

In 1970 the UK's NPL begin operating its Mark 1 network. Parallel developments were taking shape on both sides of the Atlantic.

By the end of 1971 the ARPANET had grown to fifteen nodes, all of which were conducting research funded by the US Department of Defense. The nodes were at the original four sites (UCLA, UCSB, SRI and the University of Utah) plus BBN, MIT, RAND, Stanford Defence College (SDC), Harvard University, Lincoln Laboratories, Stanford, University of Illinois at Urbana-Champaign (UIU(C)), Case-Western Reserve University (CWRU), Carnegie-Mellon University (CMU) and the National Aeronautical and Space Administration (NASA).

This same year, France began its prototype network. France was well aware of the benefits of an efficient communications network, having pioneered an optical telegraph system, using semaphore towers after the French Revolution. France was early to adopt the telephone and was just behind the UK in testing a computer network. Moreover, France was among the first to make such a network publicly available, while others still restricted theirs to military and academic use. There are historical, philosophical and political reasons for this.

Also in 1971, the NWG defined protocols for remote terminal access (Telnet) and for file transfer protocol (FTP). These two protocols are still in use today. Telnet, in addition to being a means for remotely operating a computer from one located elsewhere, is also the means for operating a real-time virtual space, such as a MUD or MOO (multi-user domain, or multi-user domain – object oriented). This means that people can communicate with each other via computer by holding a typed conversation without the in-between delays of electronic mail (email). It is the physical basis for some forms of online community. In essence, a group of people can dial into one computer (that hosts the MUD or MOO) and each person is able to type into that computer so that the others who are logged in can read what is being written, and type their responses for others to see. This was an outcome that was entirely unforeseen by those who developed Telnet as a means for running computer programs remotely.

FTP is still used today to download complete files from the Internet, or from remotely located computers.

The first public demonstration of ARPANET was in 1972 at an international conference on computer communication, held in Washington, DC. The demonstration was run by Bob Kahn of ARPA. By this time ARPANET comprised forty machines. Later in the year, as it became apparent that several networks were emerging, both in Europe as well as within the US, the Internetworking Working Group (INWG) was established to address the need for agreed upon protocols that would allow communication between separate networks. This working group was chaired by Vinton Cerf.

This was also a historic year as it saw the first electronic mail message sent via ARPANET, by Ray Tomlinson of Bolt, Beranek and Newman. Earlier email was sent on a direct computer–computer link, rather than via a distributed network. According to Tomlinson the first message actually read something like 'QWERTYUIOP' – a test message to himself. The next went to his colleagues explaining how to use the addressing system he developed (which incidentally appears to have been the first use of the @ sign). It was a demonstration of his email program which was designed to send messages across a distributed network. The @ sign was to distinguish between local messages to others on the same server, and those addressed to other hosts on the network. The message reputedly showed how to put an @ between the user's login name and the name of the host computer, so the message announced its own existence. Email quickly became the most used feature of the system. Also, the first email discussion list is reputed to have focused on discussion of *Star Trek*, and the Internet has maintained a close relationship with science fiction ever since (Cambell 1998).

The year 1972 also saw the birth in Australia of the Commonwealth Scientific and Industrial Research Organisation Network (CSIROnet) and the French Cyclades research network. Cyclades/Cigale is a packet networks research programme run by Louis Pouzin at the Institut Recherche d'Informatique et d'Automatique (IRIA). The latter is now known as the Institut National Recherche d'Informatique et d'Automatique (INRIA); it was designed to link several major computing centres in France together. Two other developments in that year were the introduction of the Intel 8008, the first commercially available eight-bit micro-computer, and the introduction of dial-up services for remote terminals. These latter were critical in the development of private bulletin boards, the forerunners of today's online communities, and were important in the later emergence of the 'hacker' phenomenon in the 1980s.

The following year saw the first international connections to the ARPANET, to England and Norway, the former having developed from the early work of the NPL. In June 1973, Vinton Cerf and Bob Kahn began work on Transfer Control Protocol/Internet Protocol (TCP/IP). In 1974 they published a paper, 'A Protocol for Packet Network Interconnections', which defined the TCP to allow computers to communicate across a system of networks. The Transmission (or Transfer) Control Protocol refers to the packet numbering system which 'hands on' the packet from one node to the next, and is a direct descendent of Paul Baran's work on shortest path routing. Up until this point, ARPANET was like a single intranet, or local area network (LAN), but from this point it was evolving into what would become an inter-net of multiple networks connected together.

By June 1974, there were sixty-two hosts on ARPANET. BBN developed the first high-performance packet switch for use on ARPANET in order to handle the increasing amounts of message traffic. In the same year there was a major revision to the Telnet protocol and 1974 also saw the inauguration of the Berlin Hominess research network (HMInet).

By late 1974 it was apparent that ARPANET would continue to grow, and that it would grow beyond US defence contractors and defence-funded academics in a few select institutions. As more academics heard about what could be done with networked computers, and with the prospect of greater information sharing possible via such networks, there was clear pressure for ARPANET to move beyond military circles. In an effort to stem this pressure, on 1 June 1975 the US Defense Communications Agency took over the operational management of ARPANET. A month later, BBN opened Telenet, a commercial version of ARPANET.

This development enabled the establishment of the Defence Advanced Research Communications (DARCOM) Message Research Group, one of the first email mailing lists. Parallel with this, AT&T (American Telephone and Tele-graph) aggressively licensed Unix to universities to establish a broad consumer base of 'open-system' computers. This was followed a year later by the introduc-tion of Unix-to-Unix CoPy (UUCP) which enabled file copying between Unix-based machines.

Also in 1975, BERNnet expanded HMInet to West Germany, and the European Informatics Network (EIN) began operations. Networks now existed in the US, UK, France, Germany, Netherlands, Norway and Australia. These were still largely separate networks, however, and were still held within the narrow confines of defence agencies and some universities.

The following year saw some developments in packet switching that moved into wireless media, such as Packet Radio Network (PRnet) and Atlantic Packet Satellite Network (SATnet). Now messages could be routed, not merely among land-lines, but along whatever medium was available, and whatever would suit the required bandwidth. Again this was envisaged by Paul Baran back in the early 1960s, but now it had become a reality.

By March 1977, ARPANET boasted 111 hosts. In addition, THEORYNET was established at the University of Wisconsin, providing electronic mail services to over 100 researchers in computer science. This system used UUCP technology.

Elsewhere in the world, New Zealand opened the Department of Scientific and Industrial Research Network (DSIRnet) and Canada opened its DATAPAC public data network (operated by Spender Corp, a company joint-venture owned by Canada's major telephone system carriers). A year later, France's TRANSPAC national public network began operations. (It is now part of France Telecom.) In Norway, the UNINETT academic network for research education was started for the Norwegian Science Research Council. In 1978 the Internet protocols become operational, as did the UUCP file copy protocols for Unix systems.

In 1979 Australia launched the Computer Science Network (ACSnet). Alongside this, Usenet newsreader services were launched using UUCP. It was set up first at Duke University, then at the University of North Carolina by Tom Truscott and Steve Bellovin. In the same year a meeting between the University of Wisconsin, DARPA, National Science Foundation (NSF) and computer scientists from several universities established the requirement for a Computer Science Department research computer network in the US (CSNET). In the UK, the Science and Engineering Research Council Network (SERCnet) developed what came to be known as the 'Coloured Book' protocols determining standards for packet length and window size. In 1981 BITNET ('Because It's Time' Network) was set up by IBM at City University of New York (CUNY) and Yale.

Within two years, the CSNET was built using seed money from the NSF, as was the UK's Joint Academic Network (JANET); so too were networks established among Sweden's universities (SUNET) and in Germany, with the Deutsches Forschungsnetz (DFN). Canada's NetNorth came online in 1983, just in time for MCIMail to begin its service.

On 1 January 1983 the NCP was discontinued on ARPANET – henceforth it would be based entirely on the TCP/IP standards. The INWG, in establishing TCP/IP as the standard for communications between networks, led to one of the first definitions of an Internet as a connected set of networks, specifically those using the now standard protocol. In addition, the US Department of Defense declared TCP/IP to be the standard for its own networks. Anyone wanting to connect to the department must thereafter use this standard or be locked out.

The Internet was beginning to open up. In that same year, concerned about security on the growing Internet, the military component of ARPANET split off to become MILNET (MILitary NETwork), a completely separate network that would henceforth be based purely on military communications networks. ARPANET became a primarily academic network, with a major component of its traffic still coming from commercial military contractors. In addition, ARPANET installed a gateway between ARPANET and CSNET. Corporately the need of the market was shifting from time sharing on large single computers, to inter-connections between whole LANs.

In Europe, the European Union Unix Group formed EUnet to provide email and Usenet services. In addition, the European Academic Research Network (EARN) was established along similar lines to BITNET in the US. One important development back in the US was the development by the University of Wisconsin, of a 'name server'. For the first time, users did not need to know the exact path to the destination systems in order to send email.

The year 1984 did not see the dystopian networked society predicted by George Orwell, but it did see the number of hosts exceed 1,000, and the establishment of the Japan Unix Network (JUNET) using the UUCP protocols. The Apple Macintosh was also released that year – the first personal computer to be Year 2000 compliant from its inception. Its graphical user interface made it the first personal computer to be truly 'user friendly'. In 1985 NORDUnet connected Scandinavian universities. (NORDUnet is the Nordic Internet highway to research and education networks in Denmark, Finland, Iceland, Norway and Sweden; it provides the Nordic backbone to the Global Information Society.) By this time amateur bulletin boards were being set up across the US. From these groups of enthusiasts came the hacker culture celebrated in William Gibson's (1984) novel *Neuromancer*, and the word 'cyberpunk' was applied to a group of US writers, whose work took various forms of hacking and computer culture as their themes.

That same year the fledgling Internet nearly broke under the strain of too much growth too quickly, and routing paths on ARPANET became gridlocked. The NSF saw a way around this and set about building a robust and fast backbone. In the process, in 1986, it established five super-computing centres to provide powerful computer facilities for anyone on the network. This led to a stand-off between ARPANET and NSF, the latter responding by setting up its own network with the aid of NASA and the US Department of Energy (DoE). This led to an enormous and rapid growth of connections.

In 1987 the National Science Foundation signed a cooperative agreement to manage the NSFnet backbone with Merit Network Inc., which included IBM and MCI (formerly Microwave Communications Inc.) involvement. Together they founded ANS (standing for Advanced Network and Services). In addition, UUNET was founded with Unix funds to provide commercial UUCP and Usenet access. The number of hosts exceeded 10,000. By this time almost 4,000 bulletin boards were linked by hobbyist networks. These networks provided a 'venue' for alternative culture views to be widely and inexpensively disseminated.

A year later was the Internet's 'plague year' as a virus in the form of a 'worm' was released accidentally onto the Internet, and more than 6,000 (around 10 per cent) of the internetworked computers across the US were crashed. The crash blacked out much of North America from telephone communication, as the virus caused cascade failures throughout the Net. In 1988 ARPANET began being dismantled – a process which took over a year to complete.

In 1989, the exponential growth of the Internet continued, as the number of hosts exceeded 100,000, necessitating an upgrade to the NSFnet backbone to be able to handle a quantum leap in the amount of traffic. Europe, too, was growing together, and RIPE (Réseaux IP Européens) was formed by European Internet service providers (ISPs) to put in place the administrative architecture and technical cooperation required to allow a pan-European network to function. The year 1989 also saw the first relay between a commercial electronic mail carrier (CompuServe) and the Internet through Ohio State University; 1989 was also the year in which China's fledgling democracy movement was violently crushed. News about the events in China was quickly circulated among dissident groups via the Internet, as well as fax machines and ham radio networks. This was an important event for the Internet as it showed for the first time its potential for publishing dissident views in ways that to this day remain virtually impossible to censor. This year was particularly meaningful to me as it was the year in which I first went online at the Australian National University. The use of email enabled me to co-author a paper with Mick Dillon (who was based at Lancaster University in northern England) via a series of exchanges lasting a mere two months.

By 1990 ARPANET had been dismantled, its functions taken up by other Internet providers. In response to increasing US government interest in regulating the fledgling Internet, the Electronic Frontier Foundation (EFF)was formed by Mitch Kapor. Its purpose was to promote the values of freedom of speech on the Internet, and to form a lobby group for electronic civil liberties.

In 1991 the Commercial Internet Exchange (CIX) was formed to provide commercial online services. Gopher was introduced by University of Minnesota as the first menu-based system for exploring the Internet. In addition, WAIS (wide area information servers) was released by Thinking Machines Corporation; this was a system for searching databases across the Internet.

As the number of hosts passed 1 million in 1992, the Internet linked more than 17,000 networks across 33 countries. Many of these countries, however, still had only basic email access. It was in this year that the WorldWideWeb (WWW) was launched. Tim Berners-Lee from CERN developed hypertext markup language (HTML) which enabled the development of the Web. A couple of graduate students, Tim Berners-Lee and Marc Andreesen, wrote the program Mosaic, the first truly graphical interface with the Internet.

The year 1993 saw the Internet become publicly political with US President Bill Clinton and Vice-President Al Gore going online (president@whitehouse.gov and vice-president@whitehouse.gov). This same year, the UN and World Bank (International Bank for Reconstruction and Development) went online. Having reached the highest levels in the US, Congress put in place legislation known as the US Information Infrastructure Act which launched the concept of the 'information super-highway'. This concept was taken up and given public prominence in a speech by Al Gore. The Act considered the political, economic and social issues relevant to the formation of a national information infrastructure. The media began to take an interest in the Internet from this point.

In 1994, commercial users for the first time outnumbered academics on the Internet – by a two-to-one ratio. In February, Hong Kong police set about isolating a hacker by disconnecting all but one of the colony's Internet providers. Later in the year, former plain dial-up services, such as America Online, Delphi, CompuServe and Prodigy, began to provide Internet access. In May, the Vatican went online, with its own domain name 'va'. In September, a US$50 fee was imposed for registration of domain names with the US Domain Name Server (DNS) system. In the same month, BBN supplied encryption technology to Financial Services Technology Consortium's electronic cheque program, to ensure secure financial transactions over the Internet. This was also the year of the electronic shopping mall, although at this time few would make money from physical sales over the Internet.

The following year saw NSFnet revert to a research network, offering fast service exclusively to researchers. By this time most of the US traffic was routed through interconnected network providers. By August 1995 several Internet-related companies went public. Netscape's launch was particularly spectacular, achieving the third largest ever NASDAQ share value. In October, more Internet technologies were released, including Sun's Java scripting code, and online virtual environments were made possible by virtual reality markup language (VRML). The military had been doing this since the early 1990s, using simulation technologies on high-speed dedicated lines. Using such technologies, military planners were able to rehearse some of their missions during the Gulf War. From 1995 NASA opened a website for the Shuttle missions, including an email address connected directly with the orbiting Space Shuttle, so schoolchildren could email astronauts with questions about their mission and what it was like to be in space. Astronauts for their part dedicated part of their orbital schedule to answering email.

In December 1995 soldiers sent to Bosnia on a UN mission could stay in touch with their families over Christmas through Operation Home Front, which connected soldiers in the field with their families via Internet.

In 1996 an element of consolidation came into the Internet, as more people came online, WWW addresses began to appear on paper advertising, and radio and television stations advertised their Internet sites. The year 1996 also saw Netscape's encryption algorithm cracked by a couple of enthusiastic amateurs – their efforts undermining confidence in fledgling financial transactions on the Internet. Although Netscape was quick to respond with a more complex encryption key, consumer confidence was shaken. The issue of privacy on the Internet and citizens' rights to strong encryption were widely discussed on and off the Internet.

At a 1997 conference on ASEAN (Association of South-East Asian Nations)/ Europe issues, the Internet was raised as a political issue, and members of ASEAN called for a greater presence of their own material, and material in their own languages to appear on the Internet, to counter what they saw as a growing domination of Anglo-American culture that spoke for them and described their countries only through culturally western eyes.

Vietnam and China took tentative steps onto the Internet, imposing heavy regulation on the few trial nodes installed by their governments. Censorship became a major issue in this year, as the media fed a frenzy over pornographic sites on the Internet. US strident calls to make the Internet 'safe' for children led to heavy-handed proposals for legislation and the introduction of a v chip intended to screen out 'adult' material.

On the issue of domain names, 1998 probably saw the end of US Department of Defense involvement with the domain name system. Amid moves to establish an international, privately funded consortium, Network Solutions, for so long the sole registrar of Internet domain names, was set to lose its Defense Department funded monopoly. This was accompanied by a further increase in the range of domain types, from .org, .net, .edu, .gov and so on.

The beginning of 1998 also saw the number of Internet users worldwide jump to over 100 million, slightly more than double the numbers for the previous year, maintaining the exponential growth rate established at the Internet's inception. Perhaps the biggest challenge for the Internet will come in the year 2000 (Y2K), when potentially non-Y2K compliant systems could cause widespread outages in the system. At that point, the resilience of Baran's packet-switching technology will be put to the test – the 'damage' ironically being caused by the use of programmers' shorthand listing date fields as two rather than four characters. T. S. Eliot seems to have been prophetic in his poem *The Hollow Men* where he says: 'This is the way the world ends, not with a bang, but a whimper'.

There is, of course, no special reason why the world should end on that date rather than any other, and I would be very surprised if the Internet itself failed completely in 2000. Indeed, its existence may well speed up the recovery process substantially in the way software patches, and test software are being distributed via the Net. There are likely to be reverberations from the year 2000 for some years to come, just as there are already early hints of what lies ahead. For example, a couple of years ago I received notification that I had a piece of academic writing due on 10 December 1900.

This chapter should at best be seen as a tentative outline of what was essentially a chaotic development of a technology that was driven by its users, certainly more than any single developer or designer. One way to describe this process is echoed in Gibson's words from *Neuromancer*: 'the street has its own uses for things'. I have put this here in order to situate the emergence of aspects of this technology, as there are cultural and historical reasons that led to its developing in the particular way that it did. Moreover, the history of its emergence in a military technological sphere goes at least part way to explain the demography of the Internet. Its users are still predominantly middle-class Anglo-Europeans, and above all male. The Internet emerged from historical need and military execution.

It is a story that can be viewed as a slow emergence over thirty-five years, or even thirty-five hundred years, tracing communications networks back to Sun Tzu, or it can be viewed as a phenomenon that hit the streets less than five years ago – all three views are correct. However it is read, it is clear that little about its development arose from female culture, or from a culture in which women participated to any great extent. Moreover little about its development came from or really addressed the needs of the poor within states, or poor states themselves. That this demography is changing is perhaps more due to the spread of Internet into wider society, so that it gradually begins to take on aspects of the demography of broader society. History will tell to what extent this continues to occur into the future.

The Internet continues to develop at a prodigious rate, and later chapters will deal with some of the issues of uneven distribution and cultural dominance, raised by the spread of Internet into Asia and the developing world. Later chapters will discuss the emergence of new forms of social division based on information wealth or poverty. Moreover these divisions are emerging, not merely within states, but between them. New forms of exploitation beckon as poor countries, such as the Philippines and India with English-speaking populations are hired for manual data inputting, and programming of legacy systems. There will continue to be a process of third-world-isation of parts of first world countries, and there will continue to be exploitation – people online are still people, and still take their cultural baggage with them into cyberspace.

There will be opportunities for those who are enterprising and educated, but it will take governments to apply to the Internet the social conscience of the 'rest' of society – the unwired. As I noted at the start of this chapter, despite the growing importance of private enterprise in infrastructure development, national governments still install much of the infrastructure (or manage the outsourcing contracts for such installation), set international connection standards, and raise in international fora those issues that pertain to relations between nations. So far, despite the burgeoning of online communities, and claims for the Internet as a democratising force, governments show every sign of continuing the process of governance, and forms of governance are being transposed from 'real life' into cyberspace, drawing lessons from international relations and international law, which of necessity operates by consensus. It is indeed, as Gibson notes, a 'consensual hallucination' but then so too are states.

Summary

- The history of the Internet can be written in two ways. First, as a history of communications networks, and second, as a history of the enabling technologies which led directly to the Internet as we know it today.

- Ever since people began organising themselves into groups, they have been forming communications networks. These range from fire beacons to road and sea networks, to optical and telegraphic networks, railways, telephone, radio and television and more recently digital communications, including between computers.

- The Cold War gave rise to the question of how to build nuclear-survivable communications networks. This problem was solved in a RAND paper by Paul Baran, who described a packet-switching distributed communications system in 1962.

- The US Defense Advanced Research Projects Agency developed the first distributed network, ARPANET, between four nodes in 1969.

- Telnet, developed in 1971, provided the software for multi-user environments, such as MUDs and MOOs.

- The year 1979 saw the first opening of the ARPANET to universities, but it was to take until 1994 before full commercial public access to the Internet enabled it to become a global cultural phenomenon. Until that time the Internet was essentially a government and university communications and research tool. From 1994 anyone with the means could have access.

- Despite huge growth in the number of Internet hosts, or nodes, the demography of the Internet remains primarily (75 per cent) American, young, Anglo-Saxon and male. While Asia is coming online with a faster growth rate, it is from a very small base figure, and it will be some time before there is any real approach to the numbers of English-speaking westerners.

- National governments still set connection standards, and still operate with a duty of care to their citizens, so there will remain a strong role for states to play, no matter how globalised the economy becomes. Issues remain for the least wired states, primarily in Africa, who seem destined to be marginalised from the global economic system. New forms of informational colonisation seem to be emerging.

Part II
The developing world

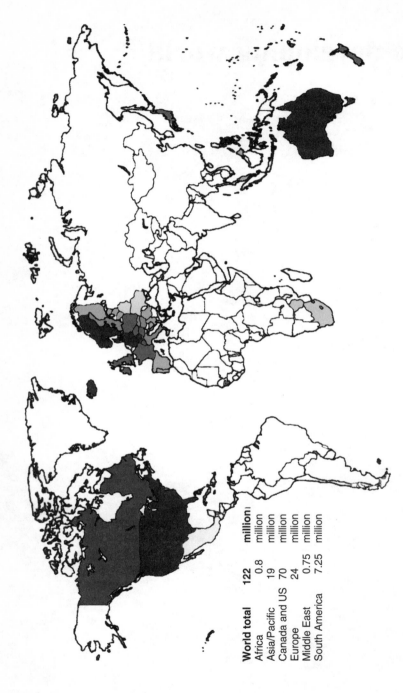

World total	122	million
Africa	0.8	million
Asia/Pacific	19	million
Canada and US	70	million
Europe	24	million
Middle East	0.75	million
South America	7.25	million

World Internet population June 1998
Source for figures: various – compiled by NUA Internet Surveys
http://www.nua.ie/surveys/how_many_online/index.html.

Map © 1999 J. L. Everard

3   Hungry, thirsty and wired

This chapter raises the question of the role of the Internet in the development of developing nations. It argues, along with Held (1991: 221), that 'the importance and appeal of the idea of the modern State lies in the notion of a common structure of authority, a circumscribed system of power, which provides a regulatory mechanism and check on rulers and ruled alike'. Clearly this is the practice and experience of relatively few states in the contemporary world. Nonetheless, the equality of states under international law resonates powerfully with Held's thesis. As the global economy comes to depend increasingly on a global electronic communications system, then systemic exclusion from such a source and market for information will continue to see significant inequalities, not merely of economic competitive advantage, but of access to the means to acquire the life chances necessary to aspire to effective political and economic participation in the global system.

This chapter is therefore concerned with what Held terms the 'nautonomic'. That is, in Held's view, the case where relations of power systematically generate the asymmetrical production and distribution of life chances that limits and erodes the possibilities for effective participation in the global economy. This will be considered at the state level.

This chapter will proceed along three lines. First, it will examine the issue of development as an aspect of globalisation. Second, it will examine traditional theories of development/modernisation. Third, it will examine the spread of Internet into the developing world, with an analysis of the thesis of democratisation versus the 'nautonomic' in relation to the spread of Internet. It will thus examine the question of appropriate technological development, while testing the extent of globalisation in poorer countries.

Along with this, the chapter will consider the growth of service sector industries among some poorer states. In the process it will consider who 'owns' the knowledge economy. Finally, the question is raised about new forms of (re)colonisation by examining the extent to which there are genuine shifts in the location of decision making from nation-states to transnational actors in an era of globalisation, over against the view that decision making that relates to the state sphere could in large measure be retained by the state, and that transnational actors would therefore form merely a complicating factor in the locus of power.

Autonomy and power

First and foremost, autonomy and power are issues of identity. They are about the ability (power) of individual entities, and this applies to all levels of subjectivity from the individual to the state, to enjoy the ability to pursue their goals as individuals and as collective subjects. It entails equality of rights and obligations to the structures that shape their lives and aspirations. This is what Held refers to as a common 'structure of action' (Held 1991: 222).

With economic asymmetries, however, clearly not all states, or those within states, enjoy such a common structure of action. One way to examine this process is to examine the interlinkages between levels of subjectivity across four levels (Waters 1995: 42):

* the individual
* national society
* the international system of states
* humankind.

One could argue that one of the differences between developed and developing states lies in the articulation of relations between these levels of subjectivity. These relations and their modes of articulation are closely allied to what Foucault (1970) terms *epistemes* – the dominant philosophical structuring principles by which members of a society identified the structures that shaped their lives and aspirations.

Foucault identifies the epistemic development of western society in four stages that he groups in broad historical terms as

* Renaissance
* Classical
* Modern
* Contemporary (postmodern).

While not wishing to imply that non-western states develop teleologically along the same lines as the developed west, I do wish to draw out some problems with development theories that seek to do so. Foucault proposes a taxonomy of each *episteme* which examines each 'period' in terms of its dominant philosophical concerns, as well as its economic and linguistic practices. Clearly there are difficulties presented in any attempt to 'periodise' developing countries without either patronising or assuming that all should conform to some western notion of what constitutes development. One can, however, examine some aspects (images) of developing countries (while recognising that this too is an oversimplification on the grounds that there are many forms and degrees of development – even in purely economic terms).

For Foucault, the Renaissance label is concerned with identity at a basic level, of primarily sub-state identities concerned with subsistence economy and philosophical concerns at the level of theology – received beliefs. The Classical is defined in terms of representation – identity making at a primary level as a nation of communities, and a basic material exchange economy. Philosophically the dominant mode is considered as rationalism. The Modern is characterised by self-representation (assertion of nationality), its dominant concerns being with material exchange and human development and at the philosophical level with 'anthropological' concerns. The schema represented by the Contemporary is defined in terms of self-reflexivity, its dominant mode of expression being oriented towards symbolic exchange.

These *epistemes* are organised by Waters into three basic modes of economy within the broader global economy. These are

- material exchanges (Modern, individual)
- political exchanges (Classical, national society and international system of states)
- symbolic exchanges (Contemporary/postmodern, human question)

with the Renaissance (perhaps more accurately termed pre-modern) subsistence economies not figuring beyond the local level.

In many ways this chapter is concerned with the interactions between these levels or forms of economy as the developed world becomes more dependent on increasingly globalised modes of production – including cultural production (symbolic exchange) as epitomised by the spread of electronic digital telecommunications. We are increasingly confronting a world of contact and influence between radically asymmetrical economies.

At one level such contact is not new insofar as the past has seen colonisation through the material economy bringing Modern western countries into asymmetric interaction through the material economy of goods. Increasingly we are seeing similar interactions in a post-colonial world in terms of interactions at the symbolic level, perhaps best represented by financial flows and global debt. This is the information economy.

The world as a whole is not as wired as the proponents of global telecommunications would like us to think. That some 80 per cent of the world's population has never made a phone call should give us pause to think through what this means in terms of the notion of globalisation. According to Nua (1996) Internet surveys, of the 20 per cent (or 1.2 billion) of the population who have made a phone call, about 100 million or less than 1 per cent have access to the Internet. Clearly while there are people in almost all countries who have some access to a telephone, one still needs to ask 'who, precisely, has access within these countries?'

Soroos (1986) makes this point in terms of the ambivalence with which developing countries enter the 'global' telecommunications system:

Third world leaders have been intrigued by the possibilities of using the new technologies as instruments for economic development, while expressing concern that they may perpetuate, if not increase the inequalities between rich and poor states.

(Soroos 1986: 324)

Some countries have sought to make the most of their geographical advantage, despite being poor states. Tonga, for example, a small Pacific island nation, found that it was beneath the ground-swathe of one of the key points for positioning a geostationary satellite for telecommunications. Thus it formed a joint venture partnership with a satellite manufacturer, and set about leasing transponder space on the satellites (TONGASAT 1&2) – effectively charging rent for the information traffic that was passing overhead. Even so, it was not until 1997 that the King of Tonga was able to make the first phone call from Tonga's own telephone exchange.

This is, of course, a rare and isolated case. Nonetheless, as Soroos points out, with the rise of the Non-Aligned Movement, developing countries have been able to exercise some authority in the International Telecommunications Union (ITU). They recognised early on that the developed countries were dependent upon geosynchronous satellites for navigation, telecommunications traffic and military purposes. Moreover the orbital slots available were limited, as were the wavelength bands, which, if overused, can cause interference with each other. To some extent these bandwidth problems are being addressed through the laying of terrestrial optical fibre cables between continents. Indeed the network is such that data may be switched freely between fibre-optic cables, microwave links and orbiting satellites on the basis of network demands at each step of the way.

A number of issues arise from the spread of such a communications network. As Soroos (1986) notes:

> Technologies that can transmit information over great distances have signifi-cant implications for the flow of communications across national boundaries. Taking advantage of the tremendous potential in the field of telecommuni-cations requires a high level of international cooperation. For example, steps must be taken to ensure that the equipment which sends signals from one country is compatible with the receivers located in other countries. Thus, one of the earliest as well as one of the continuing challenges for global policy makers in the field of communication has been to establish technical specifi-cations for equipment; for example, on the number of lines per picture and the number of pictures per second in television transmissions. Coordination has also been necessary in establishing international networks, such as in the laying of cables over land and across the oceans, which link national communication networks. Cooperation is also imperative in the handling of payments for transnational communications as well as in formulating operating and administrative procedures.
>
> (Soroos 1986: 324)

I shall return to issues of standardisation later, but first, to summarise the implications that flow from this, we can see that:

- the flow of information across borders has political implications
- there is a need for technical standardisation
- there is a danger of cultural standardisation

- the establishment of the infrastructure requires international cooperation
- management of the network itself requires global flows of capital and finance
- such management also requires a growth in service sectors to manage the process.

Taking these in sequence, the flow of information across borders has political implications. One aspect of sovereignty has always been the inviolability of a state's boundaries. It is what lies at the heart of the state system as it has existed since the rise of the modern state following the Treaty of Westphalia. The identity of a state rests with its ability to define interior as against exterior – internal order as against external anarchy. It is the boundary which divides those within the state, those who define themselves as 'us' (the domestic polity), over against those who are defined as 'them' (the 'outsiders'). The state is the idea of community to which those inside the care and protection of the state subscribe in order to form an aspect of their identity. It is the idea around which people can focus their protective instincts when their land or their ideals are threatened. It is also traditionally the largest spatial idea over which people will protect their and their neighbours' boundaries around a piece of geographic space. Even within groups of states that agree to work cooperatively, such as the EU, it is still nation-states that make foreign and defence policy decisions. Moreover, international telecommunications standards are themselves set by governments in the ITU based on choices made available by the existence of a range of technologies, not all of which are sufficiently compatible to enable seamless communication. In addition, the management of international networks requires global flows of capital and finance, and this is where some see a distinct blurring of the boundaries between states and non-state transnational actors. While many countries remain ill equipped to manage their telecommunications sectors, the management of the network and its connectivity issues requires a growth in the service sectors of the economies within these countries. This is evident in the rapid moves to privatise telecommunications networks in countries, for example like Vietnam, which has a poor service sector. In this instance government set the parameters of privatisation, including the provision of service agreements, while the private consortia involved provided the technical infrastructure. But this raises issues, too, of service provision to those areas that are not commercially viable for privately owned and operated service providers.

Who speaks and for whom?

There are, moreover, implications for developing countries in terms of the amount, kinds and direction of flow of information across their boundaries. There is also the issue of information about a country that bypasses its borders altogether. Briefly, these issues fall into three broad categories:

- those that carry potentially destabilising political messages
- those that carry culturally dominating information
- those that speak 'about' and speak 'for' the state by those outside the state.

These concerns have been echoed in statements made by representatives from some more developed of the developing countries, such as Malaysia, and form the basis for their concerns over developing national controls over Internet access and use. The political implications of cross-boundary information flows depend to a certain extent on the kind of information that is crossing the border, whose border is being crossed and in which direction the flow occurs. At some level all information is political, insofar as it entails choices and decisions about content in order to turn data into information. That is to say that in order to become information the data must be processed in some way. It has an 'angle', a customer focus which is directed towards some purpose. Thus information is never neutral. It is always already political. Thus international capital and financial flows are inherently political insofar as they represent encodings of value. Moreover, these flows are part of a zero-sum game. For there to be profit, there must be uneven distribution of wealth, in practice, if not always in theory. The idea of natural advantage or comparative advantage may work well in an ideal world, but in reality there are many factors in operation to work against the establishment of a truly level playing field. It is in the interests of the wealthier countries to ensure that poorer countries stay that way. Thus, when wealthy countries say that they will help poorer countries become wired, it would seem natural to ask why they are being so 'magnanimous'.

At one level it seems fairly straightforward to say that poorer countries benefit in terms of national pride at being able to participate in modernity, but in the end it is perhaps the shareholders in wealthy countries that stand to benefit most – in the subtle ways that some sub-Saharan countries are locked into a telecommunications system that ensures a flow of capital from the poorer South to the wealthier North. Other, cultural forms of information can serve more overtly political ends by providing a vision of the 'good life' to which poorer countries might aspire, if only they would take on certain western cultural trappings. Understandably, some countries on the receiving end of this information are concerned that humanity is becoming homogenised, and that they stand to lose their cultural identity in the rush to become Anglo-western. This is one of the main reasons cited by Singapore for enacting its draconian Internet censorship legislation in 1996. Malaysia, too, has noted this aspect of unfettered information flows, and has expressed concern that images and lifestyles presented on the Internet may offend, for example, Muslim sensibilities. Burma and Cambodia are not noted for their tolerance of opposition political groups. Their governments have both expressed concern at the consequences of open and unfettered access to the Internet, as all the while they come under increasing pressure to connect. Burma considers the Internet to be a threat to its national security insofar as the Internet enables dissident voices to promote anti-government messages. For this reason, Burma has made it illegal under pain of very severe penalties to own a device capable of connecting to the Internet unless it is licensed. This, however, is a privilege reserved for a few government and military officials and pro-government businesses. Another way that Burma censors the Net is through pricing access way beyond all but the very wealthiest. According to one report, the cost of international direct dialling (IDD) lines is around US$8 per minute (US$480 per hour) off peak and US$5 per minute (US$300 per hour) to Bangkok from outlying areas, making the cost of data communications through outbound calls prohibitively expensive. This xenophobia is not restricted to the Internet, however. For example, the most highly prohibited publications in Burma are not pornographic; they are the English-language newspapers from the 'Other Country' – Thailand. The *Bangkok Post* and *The Nation* newspapers offer extensive and critical coverage of Burma, particularly in the area of human rights abuses. At present, no newspapers other than the official *The New Light of Myanmar* are legally sold in Burma. The government fears (rightly) that the Internet would provide easy access by its citizens to dissident voices.

So, at this level at least, we are talking about developing world elites dealing with first world elites and large-scale transnational businesses. Balancing the multiplicity of interests within this inevitably leads to some interests being emphasised over others in asymmetrical ways. In addition, while the number of orbital positions for geosynchronous satellites is limited, so too are the number of countries that can take advantage in this way from their location.

Of the nearly 200 countries recognised by the UN, just over half, about 120 countries, have some form of Internet access. But this tells only part of the story. Of those that have some form of Internet access, by 1994, just 75 had basic Internet access, 52 were on BITNET, 129 had basic email services, and only 31 had full open system architecture. So there are degrees of being connected: this is important for proper consideration of who is, or perhaps more importantly who is not on the Internet.

Clearly, at a basic level, email access goes only so far. For information access via search engines or by structured searching of Internet sites, this is available to only 75 countries (as at 1994). Of those we need to examine the number of nodes within each country to determine the spread (and hence actual level of access) of the Internet.

In countries like India or South Africa, such access (even basic telephone access) is available only in the main cities, leaving large swathes of rural India and Africa without access or the prospect of access for the foreseeable future. Of the 52 countries in continental Africa, only three, South Africa, Zimbabwe and Egypt, have full Internet access (restricted to major cities), while the other countries have fewer than 5,000 users each. Out of a population of almost 900 million, only around 900,000 are online in some form (with the vast majority in South Africa). But, for the 25 million or so facing famine in sub-Saharan Africa, Internet access would seem to be a low priority.

The Internet access in South Africa is confined to the major urban areas. South Africa gained its first Internet link in 1989, and in 1994 the fibre-optic cable was established enabling high bandwidth telecommunications from Johannesburg to the rest of the world (see Goldstuck 1995). There are two major Internet service providers, Internet Africa and Internet Solution. In 1995 Johannesburg gained its first cybercafe. While this looks like an optimistic picture, it must be borne in mind that it is still only an elite few who have access. The arrival of the Internet to South

Africa was a top-down decision, which meant that South Africa's Internet architecture had no time for the grass-roots development that took place in other countries.

Access is a colonial issue

Access continues to be an issue. South Africa's then Deputy President Thabo Mbeki noted to the Group of Seven (G7) countries in February 1995 that there were more telephone lines in New York's Manhattan than there were in the whole of sub-Saharan Africa. There is the additional difficulty of incompatibilities between telephone systems within Africa. This is a legacy of British and other countries' colonial rule. For example a call placed from Dakar in Senegal to Lusaka in Zambia has to be routed from Dakar to Banjul in Gambia, from Banjul to London, then London to Lusaka (Panos 1995). This means that telecommunications revenues that might otherwise stay in sub-Saharan Africa flow to those in the developed North. Moreover, foreign telecommunications companies are increasingly being asked to invest in developing countries' telecommunications infrastructure. This has the same end result of profits being expatriated to the wealthy developed countries – even for local calls.

This colonial legacy has strong historical roots. Barry (1991) points out that in the mid-nineteenth century, communications networks (telegraph as well as shipping and rail) were regarded primarily as instruments of surveillance and direction. The colonies were seen as in need of centralised management from the 'home' countries, notably Britain, France and Belgium. He notes that in 1845 telegraph entrepreneur Richard Brett suggested to Sir Robert Peel the advantages of the telegraph, insofar as

> by its operation instructions might be conveyed instantaneously and the movements of forces so regulated that any available number of them might be brought together at a given point in the shortest possible time necessary for their convergence.
>
> (Brett 1845 in Barry 1991)

By 1900 telegraphic communications networks had come to be seen in a new light. As Barry notes, attention had moved away from the immediate problems of administering a dispersed military machine, and increasingly towards 'the global problems of ensuring the unity and strength of the national community against the threat of disintegration' (Barry 1991: 9). This included the dispersed community of British nationals throughout the empire. Moreover, an aspect of ensuring the integrity of the empire, it was important in nineteenth-century Britain to enable the margins to maintain contact with the centre to the exclusion of neighbouring countries which may have been part of someone else's empire. Hence a system was established which operated on a different technical standard from those which were used by other colonial powers. This variation in standards across countries meant that, to the present day, calls would have to be routed via London, rather than directly from colonial state to colonial state. Thus the legacy of a colonial telegraph system remains today in new forms of what may be termed 'legacy colonialism'. There is a need, then, for technological standards.

The cost of electronic information depends on delivery time of the message. Delivery time, in its turn, depends on three things:

* its complexity
* the quality of the line
* hardware speed.

The complexity is a function of how many packets are required to deliver a particular message. In the case of plain text, this can be very few, but in the case of images, graphs and so on – any graphical information – these can be very large indeed, requiring significant time to download, even in the most up-to-date fast systems.

The nature of the packet-switching technology is such that if a packet cannot get through by a specific node, it will keep trying until some way is found around the obstacle, or until such time as the obstruction is cleared. In the case of poor quality telephone lines, the obstruction may simply be 'noise' on the line which is extraneous to the message. Such noise may be 'read' by the node as data passing through, and hence block other data – the actual message traffic – until the line is clearer. This results in longer download times for those, particularly in rural areas, who have the oldest and least reliable telephone lines. In most rural areas, Internet connection entails a long-distance connection, and in some cases an international phone connection with very high call charges – this in countries where there is least wealth.

The third factor affecting data transfer speed is the hardware receiving the message. Here two factors are important. First, the speed at which the modem can receive the data, and second, the speed of the computer's central processing unit. Typically, the fastest equipment is the most modern. Such equipment may be readily available in highly developed countries, but is quite scarce in most countries on the African continent (Goldstuck 1995). This is for two reasons. First, South Africa, for example, still has high import tariffs on telecommunications and computing equipment – around 40 per cent. This means that companies tend to import only the less expensive – hence lower specification – equipment.

Second, Africa has also become a 'dumping' ground for legacy telecommunications and computing technologies (Castells 1996: 133ff). Western companies that have been left with unsold computer systems – systems rendered obsolete by newer technologies or otherwise those systems that have outlived their economic usefulness in the developed world – continue to find themselves in the dilemma of either throwing out the old systems as rubbish, or of selling them to countries for whom it would still represent an upgrade, often at prices comparable to those of current level technology. Indeed some less scrupulous companies attempt to market these systems as current technology. Part of that may be a legacy of the Cold War export control regime known as CoCom (Co-ordinating Committee on the Exports of Dual-Use Technologies). Either way, the end result is the same. Often developing countries are left with systems that the developed world considers too expensive to maintain, or that have been rendered obsolete by newer technologies. Thus in countries where online time is particularly expensive, this is compounded by unreliable low-bandwidth lines, slow modems and uneconomical legacy computing systems. This will only continue to retard the development of telecommunications infrastructure. Compliance, both with date-related and currency-related issues (such as the ability to handle multiple currencies in one country, e.g. Europe's Euro) may well show up how much of Africa's 'legacy' computer equipment was able to handle specific date-related software problems. We may well see developing countries considerably worse off where such systems have supplanted older paper modes of administration. Critical medical equipment could fail due to the inability of many countries to afford to upgrade their computer systems to date-compliant systems.

Even without the potential date/currency problems, the end result is still that such systems merely serve to maintain structural asymmetries between the wealthy North and the poorer South. These systems in the longer term are slower, less reliable, more expensive in terms of through-life cost, and cost more in terms of software support than do more modern systems.

For those African countries, such as South Africa, which have a telephone infrastructure, even local calls are charged in timed units, making lengthy online time expensive for those whose incomes are far less than those in more developed countries. In addition, these countries typically suffer from unreliable lines, which are slow to transmit data.

Large areas of rural Africa have yet to gain a telephone system of any kind. In rural Zambia, for example, there is no telecommunications infrastructure serving the Western Province. Mike Holderness, in his briefing to Panos, notes that Leonard Subulwa, Zambia's Minister for the Western Province, has to drive 250 km to communicate with officials in his constituency (Panos 1995).

Language and the Net

Language is another issue. The Internet, for all its rhetoric of globalisation, is primarily conducted in English. So for those who wish to access the Internet, a prerequisite is a good knowledge of English, which requires a western-influenced education. Such an education is clearly available only to the elites within developing countries, thus further marginalising those especially in rural areas. There are two reasons for this. First, there is the cultural reason that the Internet was designed for western and principally American use, and so little thought was given in the design as to how best to ensure greatest access by a range of different alphabetic or non-alphabetic scripts. This led to the second issue, which is a technical one. Email is very difficult to conduct in scripts other than Roman or Cyrillic character sets (Holderness in Panos 1995). Non-phonetic alphabets pose particular problems as they can be transmitted only as images, which raises the issue of bandwidth, as well as software compatibility. Languages such as Japanese, Hangul or Hindi are not universally readable by mail software.

In South Africa there are twelve official languages, but only English – a minority language – is available on the Internet (Jakobson 1996). Very few Afrikaans speakers are on the Internet, so access even by the elites in sub-Saharan Africa is restricted to those with a command of English. This means that even when information is available, it is available only to a few, and in a language that may not have terms necessary to express concepts of relevance to the receiving culture. There is, then the issue of a predominantly western voice speaking on behalf of developing world countries, either publicising a specific plight, or presenting them as a 'charming', 'traditional' tourist destination, without regard to any cultural sensitivities or political nuances affecting the people concerned.

In short, information about the South is primarily written from information and research produced in the North. This can lead to an erosion of cultural identity, national values and cultural integrity, through what Holderness describes as the homogenisation of humanity. There is what I mean in saying that there are dangers in standardising cultures.

Standardisation of cultures can lead to injustice, through what the French philosopher Jean-François Lyotard termed *différend*. *Différend* occurs when there is a conflict between two or more parties such that there is no common framework upon which to form a judgement. For example, a person may be wronged, but that wrong may not be recognised in the language in which the wrong is being tried (Lyotard 1988: xi). The same applies when aspects of a culture are being re-presented in a language that lacks the terms necessary to express important aspects of that culture.

In a sense this can work in both directions, creating more 'noise' in the communicative situation. For example, there may be important medical information made available by the Internet to a rural African doctor. English may be the doctor's third or fourth language, so aspects of the information may be garbled in the translation. This may be on top of cultural encodings that could in themselves alter important meanings. A simple cake recipe could go disastrously astray with the basic instruction to 'grease the pan', if an automotive lubricant were to be used instead of butter or margarine. While this raises a more general issue of translation, the point remains that time and again assumptions are overlooked when one country writes 'on behalf of' another country on the Internet.

Cultural 'pollution' is considered by some countries to be equivalent to pornography, and perhaps more dangerous to a totalitarian state, such as Burma. For this reason, many developing countries, particularly in South-East Asia, are concerned to establish controls on the information crossing their borders. This applies not merely to Internet, but to radio and television broadcast material and print material.

In Vietnam, limited Internet access is available, but account holders have to register for a licence from the General Directorate of Posts and Telecommunications. Strict regulations apply to Internet service providers. These include the injunction to 'prevent bad information from all outside sources from entering Vietnam'. In addition, users of Internet services and information are answerable to law for the content of the information they upload or download from the Internet. Other bans include any 'acts to seek, duplicate and upload onto the

Internet any information . . . which may affect national security and social order, or which do not conform to cultural and moral values' (Doan 1996: 7).

Singapore's regulations include references to political or religious material as being subject to state control. Singapore's three Internet service providers have had to take strong measures to block pornographic and other controversial content on the Internet, by routing all private traffic through proxy servers, which channel all Internet traffic into or out of Singapore through a few servers. This enables keyword filters to be applied. The systems would check a user request to enter a site against a list of banned sites before access is granted. This is overseen by the Singapore Broadcasting Authority. The rules ban pornography, depiction of violence, nudity and sex and 'propagation of sexual "perversions" such as homosexuality, lesbianism and paedophilia'. There seems an implied assumption that each of these could somehow be made equivalent to one another. In addition the regulations ban content which 'denigrates any race or religion, or which jeopardises public security or national defence, or undermines public confidence in the administration of justice or brings the government into hatred' (AFP (Agence France-Presse) 15 September 1996). The Philippines for its part has also enacted Internet legislation and has established a small police unit to monitor potential criminal use of the Internet.

What is interesting about these attempts to regulate the Internet is that it is done not merely in the name of protecting minors from unsuitable material, but to protect the state from political and religious dissidence and economic exploitation. At stake is not only cultural dilution from portrayals of the attractions of open and democratic societies, but also the attractions of modern consumerism, exemplified by multinational soft drink and fast food corporations.

Another issue is that the establishment of the infrastructure requires international cooperation. Developing countries on their own do not have the resources to build a modern telecommunications infrastructure from scratch. Indeed, in countries such as Cambodia or Mozambique, where the countryside is littered with hundreds of thousands of landmines as a legacy of decades of internal insurgency, the development of terrestrial systems becomes even less practicable. This was identified in a recent conference held in South Africa, the International Ministerial Conference on Information Society and Development (ISAD).

With a range of different systems, from analogue to digital, from terrestrial copper and fibre-optic cable to satellite, the telecommunications network needs to be managed on a global scale. This management is in the form of technical connection standards as well as in software protocols that deal with the handover from one system to the next without degradation of the information.

At issue for developing countries is that alone they have neither the expertise nor the resources to upgrade these connections to world's best practice. They must buy in the expertise, which increasingly means that outside companies contract to provide the services and the connections, and of course take the profits offshore. Such 'development' provides little real economic benefit to the countries concerned who remain largely without the expertise to maintain the systems, nor the income to properly take advantage of such counter-trade deals as may be offered.

In addition, such deals may leave the country more dependent than before on others to provide essential infrastructure services. With the increasing global-isation of information technologies, some developing countries see this as a means to 'leap-frog' the developed countries into establishing their own niche markets in high-technology areas. In theory this has much to offer, but many of these countries are newly independent and have little experience in managing and coming to grips with the structure of their own economies after long legacies of colonisation.

Simpson (1994) puts it this way:

> The twenty-five years between 1945 and 1970 saw the vast majority of colonial territories achieve independence. Abruptly new sovereign states came into existence; new governments were faced with the task, for the first time, of administering their countries . . . The populations of the developing countries looked to their new rulers, now their own kind and not foreign, for a promise of better things and for the means to obtain them . . . [Some] sought help from international agencies, such as the World Bank, from their former colonial power which had ruled them and from economic advisers both imported and home-grown. Their aim was to diminish rapidly the difference in the levels of economic attainment, standard of living, technical sophistication and economic independence between their country and that of the 'western' industrialised world. This was regarded as a goal which was not only attainable but as one which could be reached quickly.
>
> (Simpson 1994: 108)

Perhaps this is what lies behind the drive for developing countries to struggle onto the information 'super-highway' (always of course in inverted commas) at whatever cost, invoking the information society as an icon of modernisation and a mark of western industrial development.

Some countries, such as Singapore and more recently Malaysia, seem able to take advantage of these developments and profit from them in close and judicious joint-ventures. Despite the recent economic downturn, Malaysia's Multimedia Super Corridor (MSC) has attracted some heavyweight interest, lured by tax breaks and generous provision of land and profit repatriation rights, but Malaysian firms are not likely to benefit highly for some time to come. That said, Malaysia's Prime Minister Dr Mahathir is able to showcase this example of modernisation as a Malaysian initiative, even if the rest of the population will merely see greater divisions between the 'haves' and 'have-nots' within their own country.

Is this then a new form of colonisation? Perhaps we need an understanding of development that is based on the information aspects of development theory – the ability to learn to be in the 'main game' whatever that game may be at a particular time in economic history. As Reinert (1995) notes:

> Understanding the problems of *under*development is in a way a process of turning the many recent insights in the process of economic growth and

development upside down. This often implies looking at the same evidence, but from the side of the loser, not the winner.

(Reinert 1995: 168)

This brings me to a discussion of the final point of this section, which is that the management of the network also requires a growth in service sectors to manage the process. In most cases we are not seeing domestic service sectors of developing countries expand to anywhere near the extent of the developed world. This leads in practice to forms of mercantile colonisation through outsourcing the network management functions. This in turn leads to a number of consequences.

First, in order to develop a telecommunications infrastructure, developing countries, such as India, Vietnam, Thailand and Cambodia, are increasingly turning to private transnational corporations to set up and manage the network infrastructure. This leads to the rapid establishment of networks in the major urban centres, where such networks return a healthy profit, leaving rural infrastructure – where it exists at all – at a lesser stage of development. Thus in India, for example, there is a thriving software outsourcing industry, while the vast bulk of the Indian sub-continent has yet to get access to basic telephone facilities.

This can be summed up by the distinction to be drawn between those who are doing the developing and those who are being developed. At issue is who sets the agenda of development. While OECD (Organisation for Economic Cooperation and Development) countries and developing world elites stand to gain a great deal from globalisation, this can sometimes be at the expense of the wider domestic population's employment opportunities through a decrease in diversification of productive activity. This in turn can lead to cycles of debt and structural poverty, and increasing dependence on the World Bank and exposure to global economic patterns that are out of the control of developing countries.

In this chapter we have seen, then, that as telecommunications becomes increasingly globalised, bringing with it the promise of development and 'catch-up' for developing countries, that this is not without consequences. These are not always as positive as some development economists would have us believe.

Idealistic narratives of global access allowing for the Other to speak, or to provide counter-narratives to those of the developed world, stress the non-hierarchical structure of modern telecommunications. What is elided from these narratives is that, as networks are increasingly being run on behalf of developing states by global telecommunications firms, the profits are repatriated offshore and the country ends up no better off; indeed it can become worse off as it becomes hostage to monopolistic practices and increasingly dependent on the single telecommunications supplier. Some developing countries have sought to maxi-mise their short-term gains by auctioning off telecommunications contracts for different regions of the country. This can lead to incompatible systems being installed in neighbouring provinces within the same country, as has happened in Vietnam and India. In the absence of effective, informed domestic policy making and regulation, this risks the effective exclusion of 'less profitable' users from access as the infrastructures become ever more closely attuned to the needs and requirements of transnational, globally operating corporations.

The temptation in any such infrastructure development is to concentrate on those centres where there is a high return, with high data density through high-speed lines at the expense of those links to the network put in place for reasons of the social 'good'. Where the infrastructure is being developed, installed and maintained by private firms, it is difficult to see rural populations being supplied with network services. Where aid projects are becoming involved with online projects for rural communities, the funding is typically marginal and can be put in place only where the infrastructure exists already to support such projects. It is therefore an important political decision on the part of a developing country to turn to a private consortium of firms to supply telecommunications infrastructure. The parallel with rail networks is instructive here.

We have seen that the flow of information across borders has political implications, both for the ability of the nation-state to maintain control over its domestic development, and for its ability to shield the domestic economy from fluctuations in the global flows of supply and demand, resulting in perceptions that the nation-state is losing relevance.

In addition, the establishment of a global telecommunications infrastructure requires international cooperation. This is being managed at the international level through organisations such as the ITU. It is one arena in which national governments of developing countries are working in a situation of notional if not actual equality with developed countries to establish international technical standards.

Developing countries cannot establish their telecommunications infrastructure without international cooperation, which can lead to an erosion of national sovereignty. Developing countries need to call on developed countries to provide the technical expertise in both the construction and continuing maintenance of their telecommunications infrastructure.

There is, moreover, a need for technical standardisation. We have seen, for example, that Africa's colonial legacy has left it with deep problems of technical compatibility. These incompatibilities result in greater expenses for economies already stressed in providing essential services to their domestic population. These expenses result in greater movement offshore of funds normally kept within the domestic economy, in a continuing flow to their former colonisers.

As economies become increasingly globalised, so too do they experience erosion of cultural diversity, as they strive for symbols of modernity inextricably tied to western cultural value systems. What is particularly insidious about this is that the very striving for modernity is undertaken in order to show that they are now free of their former colonisers. From this, many developing countries fear cultural dilution through over-exposure to what is perceived as western moral decadence. These concerns have been voiced from Singapore to China as they embark on increased connectivity with the global economy.

In order to maintain the global network, the management of the network itself requires global flows of capital and finance. This results in increased inter-dependence, both economically and administratively between the developing world and a relatively few large transnational corporations. Such firms will typically focus on higher-return, high-density service industry-oriented urban networks, rather than on providing an effective country-wide infrastructure.

Management of a telecommunications infrastructure also requires a growth in service sectors of the domestic economy to manage the process. Some see this as colonialism by other means, as developing countries outsource technical and managerial skills to reap what benefits they can from being plugged into the global system. While some will find at least short-term niche markets, there are dangers that even such growth in service industries as some developing countries (those that are English-speaking and literate) may be short-lived, leaving greater debt and opportunity costs in its wake.

Some countries, such as Singapore and possibly Malaysia, will benefit greatly from globalisation, and some will 'leap-frog' their economies into burgeoning service-sector markets. Others will not. For many, the issue of identity will remain. It is in the politics of Self defined as against the Other that these issues will find their ultimate expression. At stake on the one hand is the developed world as Self, continuing to maintain structural relativity against the Other of the developing world. On the other hand lies the definitional struggle for developing countries to establish and maintain a sense of Self as against their former colonisers. At this level the nation-state will continue to play a pivotal role in mediating between the domestic polity and the international economy. Chapter 4 will expand further on the issue of the erosion of sovereignty engendered by and through the development process.

Summary

- As the global economy comes to depend increasingly on a global electronic communications system, then systemic exclusion from such a source and market for information will continue to see significant inequalities, not merely of economic competitive advantage, but of access to the means to acquire the life chances necessary to aspire to effective political and economic participation in the global system.

- If 80 per cent of the world's population have never made a telephone call, and more than half of the world's population live more than 100 miles from the nearest telephone line, then clearly the world is not yet living with a global information super-highway.

- The flow of information across borders has political implications, in terms of the role of political dissidence and the ability of a government to control such dissidence. There are dangers of cultural standardisation, and in the loss of linguistic diversity. Countries require international cooperation if there is to be a truly global information infrastructure, which raises issues of technical connectivity standards. Information flows will require a significant growth in service sectors of the economy in order to manage the process of information flows.

- Africa suffers from legacy systems and lack of modern telecommunications infrastructure. Many African nations seem set to remain marginalised in the information age.

- English, as the primary language of the Internet, itself serves to create barriers to access by those countries for whom English is not their main language.

- Some countries will benefit greatly from globalisation, and some will 'leap-frog' their economies into burgeoning service-sector markets. Others will not. There will remain large sections of humanity unconnected to the global economy, but whose lives will be affected by it.

4 Sovereignty, boundary making and the Net

Sovereignty

The state is here to stay, at least in some form, because it is tied to the constitution of identity and the traditional security role that it performs as the holder of the monopoly on the legitimate use of force. With a heavily skewed demographic profile, real opportunities to increase levels of democracy via the spread of the Internet are limited. Indeed, there is no universally agreed definition of 'democracy', and even less agreement on the modalities of its application. Moreover, while democracy serves well the processes and stability of strong developed nations, weaker states may consider that a precipitate move to democracy could prove destabilising. Such a view could find its expression in strictly controlled access to the Net. Issues of sovereignty are paramount here, and it is useful at this point to consider some of the theoretical issues underpinning the notion of sovereignty, and the question of levels, or orders of subjectivity, that are raised by the term. Are we dealing with the sovereignty of the individual, or the sovereignty of the state? To discuss this issue, it is worthwhile raising some theoretical issues that make it possible to think through such questions systematically. I want to argue here that what may be termed the 'cyborgisation' of the state raises fundamental issues of the sovereignty of the state as an object of knowledge. Moreover, I want to suggest that implications flow from this into the event-world of states, and the maintenance of state boundaries.

It is tempting to assert that the global spread of the Internet renders state boundaries malleable across a range of narratives of subjectivity. We have seen the Internet work as an instrument of economic and cultural change that does not always operate in the manner that those who construct emancipatory narratives would like us to believe. The Net, after all, 'has its own uses for things'.

I use the term 'cyborgisation', following Haraway (1991), in terms of the rise of a symbiotic relationship between the state and the global system into which it is inextricably enmeshed in a web of communications structures. Haraway uses the term to denote the interdependent relationship between people and the machines with which they work to gain an economic living. It is a relationship that conditions and controls the body as much as the body is the machine's operator. So too with states: the extent to which it is 'wired-in' to the international economy also constrains the range of possible independent action by that state.

With globalisation heavily driven by the developed world private sector, there is a shift in the focus of decision-making, both from the nation-state to transnational actors and from the public sector to the private sector. This is particularly the case in developing countries whose economic sovereignty is being increasingly eroded, with significant consequences for the ability of the government sector to play its necessary role in providing a secure basis for that section of the domestic polity which is unable to compete in the private sector market-place.

Held, among others, argues that there is a drive towards globalisation of the political realm that arises inherently from the breakdown of the state through economic globalisation. It is true that some functions that were formerly the sole province of the state are being taken up by transnational organisations, such as the UN, non-governmental organisations and other non-state actors.

I want to argue here, however, that states will continue to retain many of their functions as an aspect of their utility in the constitution of identity, and in the traditional security role of the state. I shall argue here that states will continue to be enacted as such, and that their boundary-making practices will, if anything, become ever more loudly invoked as more and more boundaries are called into question.

The Deleuzian state: going with the flow

I shall deal in this chapter with three sets of boundaries, whose narratives are increasingly being played out through the medium of the Internet. These are economic globalisation, human rights, and political activism. I want to examine these issue areas in relation to the bidirectional tension between the sovereignty of the Cartesian individual, and the sovereignty of the state. To do so, it is worth spending some time teasing out some of the theoretical underpinnings of states as Foucauldian 'speaking subjects', and to suggest that we are seeing a movement, through the cyborgisation of the state, from a Foucauldian author-state to a Deleuzian body-without-organs state.

In a sense the tension is between Deleuzian flows and Foucauldian subjects. Let me expand this a little further by referencing these names, which in this case stand in as shorthand tokens of the processes they can be said to represent. In order to do so, I want to make evident some of the theoretical material on subjectivity to which I have only alluded, up to this point.

Playing out the constitution of identity and hence subjectivity at the site of the margins requires that we speak to the notion of marginality itself. To speak in global economic terms is also to invoke terms such as 'core' and 'periphery'. These are themselves terms that territorialise. Boundaries are constructed in the binary opposition between core and periphery. This territorialisation is a manner of defining a subject that is thus marked out from other formations. The same is arguably true of the notion of subjectivity itself.

The Internet, as I have noted earlier, provides us with a powerful externalising metaphor for our own immersion in and constitution by the flows of social intercourse through our language or semiotic system. Deleuze and Guattari (1983) recognised this in the implicit cyborgisation of the body-without-organs. Subjectivities have always been networked or context-based. One could go so far as to say that the Deleuzian schizophrenia is the norm, the Oedipal the pathologically autistic exception.

Deleuze and Guattari (1983) saw the schizophrenic as the ultimate disaggregated individual. The body-without-organs was the body that was so plugged into the rest of the world that there were no longer definitive boundaries between Self and Other. The body-without-organs was a deterritorialised body. Deleuze and Guattari then argued that subjectivity required the individual to step across the boundaries – to transgress – in order to develop, or to become individual. That is to say that the subject emerged as a product of exception.

This position is close to the Sartrean existentialist position that one had to act in order to assert one's existence. Deleuze and Guattari contrasted this with the Freudian Oedipal subject, who was unitary and self-contained. The extreme end of this line of thought was, for Deleuze and Guattari, little short of autism – the ultimate self-containment. Deleuze developed this line of thought further in his consideration of the nation-state in *On the Line* (Deleuze and Guattari 1983). In this work he argued that for the nation-state to exist it was necessary to step beyond what had been articulated before – to deterritorialise – before it could establish a position for itself as a speaking subject. In all this, Deleuze and Guattari were not seeking to psychologise the state in the way that social scientists of the 1960s had sought to do so, through analysis of game theories and bureaucratic decision-making structures (see Schelling 1968; Allison 1976; Jervis 1970). Rather they were seeking to show that within their multiplicities (the schizophrenic) the state gained its identity from the manner in which it encountered the boundaries of other states, including in the diplomatic, or discursive arena.

By contrast, perhaps, Foucault's theory of subjectivity, best exemplified in his paper 'What is an Author?' (Foucault 1979), outlines a theory of the subject as *event*. He argues that authorship (a metaphor for subjectivity itself) is a product of the history of those texts that mark the boundaries between what has constituted the identity of the author and everything else. The 'author function' is thus the process by which a culture writes itself through the writer, who in turn becomes the site of writing. It also constitutes the site of an origin for commercial and cultural purposes insofar as the 'author' thus represents the site of intellectual property rights, and a site for valorisation of the author as heroic individual primarily in western discourse.

I want to argue that states are construed through essentially the same process. Indeed the case is far stronger for states-as-subjects than for individuals-as-subjects, since the state is so consciously and self-evidently a cultural artefact. Moreover, I want to suggest that in quite a literal way, the nature of power is itself intimately bound up with this identity making process. This is what Foucault means when, in his *History of Sexuality*, he speaks of power being the 'power of the negative' (Foucault 1984: 69). It is the power to mark off and maintain boundaries between Self and Other.

The Internet arguably complicates the picture for states insofar as it links the state more firmly into what may be termed a *distributed* subjectivity. Again perhaps we have always been distributed subjects – for as long as we have lived in communities with a shared sense of identity. Subjectivities have perhaps always been networked or context-based.

In this chapter I want to explore a theory of networked subjectivity which relates Deleuze's and Guattari's 'anti-Oedipal' subject with both the culturally immersed biological subject of the individual and the subject of territory as exemplified in sovereign states. In mapping this pathway I want to turn briefly to note that recent approaches to subjectivity offer a critique of the rational unitary subject of psychology – a critique of the 'Oedipal subject'. Such a view is predicated on the marination of the subject in discourse. Under this rubric the subject is not construed as unitary, but rather as a site upon which multiple subject positions may be enacted. States might readily be seen as such a site. This view would argue that, far from being a unitary and originary source, subjectivity is rather the effect of the processes of enacting (by differentiating/digitising) the subject. The subject may thus be seen as a symptom of its practices of boundary making. I also want to suggest that this process is multidimensional insofar as the subject, thus construed, is also an active participant in further practices of boundary making: that is to say that the subject, having been situated within a culture and within a set of practices, then makes use of this context to form the (provisional) basis for ethical action.

In addition, insofar as the subject is culturally construed by its entry into the symbolic order at a specific time and place, then the available subject positions are historically differentiated such that the foundations upon which action is predicated (including the ethical/moral order) are to a large extent historically contingent. That is not to say that states do not exist, nor is it to say that there is no ethical or moral aspect to the way states articulate their practices of state making, but rather, that the grounds on which states predicate their sites of action remain always already provisional.

This has implications for the sovereignty of states insofar as the progressive internetworking of states via the Internet and more broadly through electronic webs of communication and economic flows shift the ground on which are based many of the activities identified as constitutive of states. States, as I have mentioned earlier, do not operate in a completely unified way. Just as individuals articulate themselves differently in different contexts (for example when relating to other family members, children or as business people), so too do states articulate themselves in subtly different ways according to whether they are dealing with issues of military security, economic or cultural security.

In individual terms, in order to feel his or her way into a discourse community, the subject extends along the multiple and fragmentary planes of discourse, by way of irruptions/extrusions which test or transgress the social boundaries which circumscribe the subject. These practices form extensions of the subject into discourse. These forms of deterritorialisation are essential practices of risk taking to establish the boundary along which the subject travels in its becoming. The subject here is what Deleuze and Guattari describe as 'rhizomic'. They mean by this that the subject is immersed in continual flows of action, of discourse. Rhizomes are non-hierarchical flows from which the subject emerges by exception, or by extraction from the flow. States can be seen to operate this way such as, *inter alia*, in the process of exploring policy options.

For example, in establishing a policy on Internet censorship, western democratic states typically explore possible policy directions through position papers, which may go through a consultative process to a greater or lesser extent with the domestic polity, and, based partly on the public response and partly on perceived state interests, laws may be drafted to position the state in respect to this issue area. The state can then be seen to have marked itself out from, or in relation to, other states on this issue. The subject is rhizomic because in marking out the subject (as digital) from the matrix of discourse (which is analogic) the subject is precipitated into a fictive/figurative analogic subject position. The state in this case becomes the 'self who I tell myself I am' – a self-conscious self. This is accomplished through the narrative process derived from the deterritorialising practice of boundary making between state as Self (as digit) as against Other possible ways to be a state (the analogue) against which the state-as-Self is construed across time.

If we view the boundary-making practices of states as means of articulating the state, of inscribing its identity on the discursive (as well as geographical) landscape, then states can be said to practise, in Foucauldian terms, modes of authorship in the exercise of practices of authority. In an increasingly globalised world, then states as distributed subjects can be said to be concerned at the potential or actual loss of some of their *author*ity to, for example, a deterritorialised global economy.

From Deleuze and Guattari, subjects can be seen as organisational arrangements existing only in connection with other arrangements – in relation to other 'bodies-without-organs' – nodes within the matrix. This is particularly visible in the practices that constitute states. Indeed the notion of governance itself rests precisely on forms and modalities of organisation in relation to the international 'anarchy' played out between states. Deleuze and Guattari suggest that subjects are arranged according to lines of articulation, level of organisation, territorialities (not necessarily restricted to geographical territories); as well as being arranged – perhaps more significantly – along their lines of systematic dispersion, movements/moments of deterritorialisation and boundary violation. This brings Deleuze and Guattari close to the work of Foucault on the analysis of systemic dispersions by which the subject is characterised.

Analogically, these moments of deterritorialisation may be considered as lines of flow (Deleuze and Guattari 1983: 2); or digitally, they may be considered as ruptures. Such a view entails what Kristeva (1986: 94), following Plato, might term the *chora*-like 'zero' or space against which the One is defined and which forms part of the conditions under which the subject can be seen to emerge. The *chora*, from Plato, is the notional space of the potential to exist. It is the undifferentiated form from which meaningful forms emerge. For Kristeva, it is the possibility of the (illusory) binary which calls the subject into being. In this case, the state.

What is interesting about this is the drive or necessity by which we seek to bridge the gap between the One and the Zero (hole) with the idea of relationship. Such a relationship, or multiplicity of relationships, can be seen as lines of flow, which, in their ultimate dispersion, leads us inevitably to consider the conditions of emergence of the subject to be inherently 'schizophrenic' in Deleuze and Guattari's terms.

What is elided here, however, is that in the analysis of flows there is no dialectic. There is no being-towards something, for that something would entail a rupture/ rature (erasure) in terms of that which is not the 'something's' goal. So the schizophrenic subject is of necessity, anti-teleological. One might even call it 'autistic'. Under this rubric, the 'pathological' thereby exists in the artifice of culturally produced and militarily enforced boundaries dividing one subject off from the Other. In addition, I want to argue that this process happens at all levels from the biological individual to the community, ethnicity, belief system, corporation, state and geographic region. It is 'pathological' for Deleuze and Guattari because it represents a closing off of potential, a closing of boundaries which are always artificially produced and enacted.

In addition, the forms which articulate boundaries by demarcating inclusion and exclusion zones are linked closely with the nature of the flows and arrangements that constitute subjects, in this case, including states. Thus it is possible to argue that the forms and structures, not only of the modalities of the global economy, but also of the structures of the global telecommunications networks that serve to support it, themselves help to shape what the state means for any given society. Boundaries serve to define whether or not a state is core or periphery insofar as its boundaries are enacted within a global information economy.

In analysing the state in relation to the Internet, I have to this point considered those states best considered as Other to those that are internetworked in a major way, to portray them as systemically excluded from access to global markets, to global communications and to global community. I want here to discuss those who may to a greater or lesser extent be networked, but yet seem destined to remain Other to the developed west in terms of the relationship with the developed world through the issue of sovereignty as played out in some specific lines of articulation, or forms of organisation.

Specifically I want to examine the internetworked state with respect to

- sovereignty and globalisation
- democracy and human rights
- culture and identity.

In doing so, I want to suggest that there may be some systematic dispersions that provide challenges to specific aspects of states and their identity-making practices in the international realm.

Sovereign economies

Foucault suggests that in the analysis of the practices of boundary making at the level of the state:

> one has a triangle, sovereignty-discipline-government, which has as its primary target the population and as its essential mechanism the apparatuses of security.
>
> (Foucault in Burchell *et al.* 1991: 102)

These processes, for Foucault, have three locations of focus, government, population and political economy, which constitute

> from the eighteenth century onward a solid series, one which even today has assuredly not been dissolved.
>
> (Foucault in Burchell *et al.* 1991: 102)

Interestingly, the eighteenth century was precisely when the west was undergoing the process of internationalisation which even today is still expanding, though in different forms from those days of colonial expansion. It is interesting too to note that the eighteenth century saw the birth in modern times of rapid systems of communication and the emergence of systematic communications networks, such as the semaphore or 'optical telegraph' of Chappe in France and later in other parts of Europe.

The eighteenth century was a time of economic expansion for Europe and the opening of new colonies to feed the emerging industrial revolution. It called for new forms of administrative organisation as well as technologies of communication. It was a time that gave birth to administrative governance by which the population became data in ways they had not been before. Colonial government itself required the institutionalisation of systematic economic disparities that persist today in the former colonial developing world.

With the global spread of the Internet the new colonisers no longer need to leave their geographical territories to administer the new globalising economy. New forms of exploitation are emerging as the west outsources the menial tasks of the digital age. But the impacts for once will reach in both directions. As Castells (1996) notes:

> The architecture of the global economy features an asymmetrically interdependent world, organised around three major economic regions and increasingly polarised along an axis of opposition between productive, information-rich, affluent areas, and impoverished areas, economically devalued and socially excluded. Between the three dominant regions, Europe, North America, and the Asia-Pacific, the latter appears to be the most dynamic yet the most vulnerable because of its dependence upon the openness of the markets of the other regions. However the intertwining of economic processes between the three regions makes them practically inseparable in their fate.
>
> (Castells 1996: 145)

Africa, the Middle East and the former Soviet Union do not even rate a mention in this new economy. Indeed perhaps the greatest risk in the new economic order is not that of reduction of sovereignty, but structural irrelevance (Castells 1996: 135).

Tapscott in *The Digital Economy* (1996) uses the term 'disintermediation' to describe the new polarisations occurring in the knowledge economy. He suggests that the role of middle-persons is being undermined. He argues that broadband networks tend to polarise activity both toward the global and the local. The loser in all this is the role of the nation-state and the role of the middle (managerial) class:

> Gradually the comfortable reach of the nation-state as revenue raiser and infrastructure provider has collapsed into jobless growth, fiscal crisis, and investor relocation. Borders criss-crossed by road, rail, and fibre-optic cable became more permeable to goods, services, finance, and knowledge. Control over space, the geographic buffers of the nation, started to melt away with the decline of the so-called Golden Age of mass production. Compounding these changes in what, how and where we produce are the profound changes in East–West and North–South relationships as the binary balance of terror decentralises into a multiplicity of local conflicts. The combined impact of lifting many Cold War constraints and the proliferation of regional conflicts is giving rise to new trading patterns, investment flows and global migration.

> (Tapscott 1996: 310)

Machineries of state are responding to these developments in a number of ways. One is in the attempt to assert greater legislative control over the cross-border flows, through attempting to apply access and content controls on the Internet.

On the issue of global migration it is worth noting, too, that new forms of virtual labour migration are emerging with knowledge workers in one country being employed directly by knowledge clients in another, without physical relocation taking place. This also has implications for the client countries, as they develop interdependencies with other countries for such tasks as basic administration processing tasks for companies, to data input, to programming and systems analysis functions. This can lead to situations in which first world countries lose or significantly downsize their skilled workforce in favour of lower cost skilled workforces in countries further down the food chain. This can skew the demographics of first world companies in ways never before possible. It can also result in a deskilling of first world countries, as they begin to lose out on wage competitiveness. But I shall consider this in more detail in later chapters.

Democratisation and human rights

The rhetoric of democratisation through increased participation of the domestic polity in the political life of the state through the spread of Internet is problematic. At stake here is participation by whom? Demographically, those who have access, particularly in developing countries, are already part of the established elite who have an interest in maintaining the status quo. Increasingly, developing countries, particularly those with authoritarian governments, see themselves as having a great deal to lose and little to gain by allowing greater freedom of speech. While seen as a fundamental human right in the US, some developing countries see freedom of speech as a threat to their country's stability, and as an infringement of their sovereign right to govern. What is called into question here is the tyranny of developing world elites who question the extent to which freedom of speech can be viewed as a universal human right.

If we accept that under the US Constitution the right to bear arms is another term for the right of the sovereign individual subject to resist threat with force, and if we accept that under the UN Charter, states have a right to self-defence, and a right to enjoy their sovereign individuality, then the question is merely one of extension of these principles to the right of states to protect the sanctity of their borders – including their virtual borders. Freedom of speech is not going to be imposed from outside. It therefore becomes an issue of moral persuasion such that access to the global information economy must be seen to have tangible benefits to the country that outweigh the risks of allowing dissent.

States continue to act in their own self-interest. At issue is the extent to which sovereign identity is challenged by engagement with global flows. Burma, for example, an authoritarian and isolationist regime has responded to the Internet with draconian legislation which outlaws the possession of unlicensed modems, and that prices access so highly that it is unattainable for those outside of the powerful elite with close connections with the ruling State Law and Order Restoration Committee (SLORC). Nevertheless, even Burma's borders are permeable, and news of human rights abuses continues to leak out to the outside world. The Internet continues to play a role in this as news smuggled outside of Burma is quickly spread via the Internet by dissident expatriate groups working outside the country.

News continues to be spread by Aung San Suu Kyi through her own access to the Internet, by way of carefully worded messages and by her speeches. Her survival under the SLORC regime suggests that she is in a unique position within her country, and that there may be division, even within the SLORC, as to how best to handle her opposition. Her own connections and affection on the part of senior military leaders will doubtless contribute to her continued survival – that and her high profile plus the SLORC's desire to steer Burma closer into the ASEAN arena in order to reap economic benefits from the relationship.

The Internet also played a role in maintaining the flow of information from as early as the Tiananmen Square incident in China in 1989. That, along with fax and telephone messages, kept dissident groups informed on developments, and maintained a flow of information to the world that meant that China could not cover up the incident.

Among the processes of change being brought about by globalisation and the advent of digital communications is the change in the face of the political. When demonstrators in Russia and Albania hold up placards and banners written in English, it is clear that electronic media and the adoption of English as the lingua franca of the electronic media has rewritten the nature of political life at a global level.

States and the 'subject function'

It is this shift of power into the cultural sphere that perhaps most marks the shift into a globalised political milieu. Power has clearly moved beyond that of the state in ways that inscribe the local into the global in ways never before possible. There are implications in this for the shape of political life. Henceforth, political struggles will need to be able to be expressed in media terms which can be articulated within ever shorter sound-bites. Political struggles, however complex, will be condensed, however problematically, into sets of binary oppositions, and couched in heroic/epic forms. Not all political differences will translate into such neat packages, and such struggles risk being marginalised and kept from the world's gaze. Such struggles can become, in Lyotard's terms, *différend*. That is to say that they become unrecognisable within the language game by which struggles are articulated within the dominant discourses or modes of representation.

It is time to problematise what, until now, I have termed the 'developing world'. Within the economic sphere, the terms 'developed', 'less developed', 'developing', have shared meanings relating to a teleological mode of being. A being-towards something. Becoming developed. But these terms can tell only part of the story. The identity of the state is not a unitary subject, as I have pointed out earlier. Moreover, it would seem to be less of a subject than a confluence of flows. It is discontinuous. Such is the Deleuzian account of the anti-Oedipal subject. It is the networked subject. It is, perhaps, also the subject of the Foucauldian *event*. However defined, the identity of the state, whether developed or developing, is the outward sign, or symptom, of the practices by which it is defined. This is the case, whether the state is defined territorially, or ideationally, as in diaspora.

There can be problems in defining a state in terms of its status of 'development'. Australia, for example, has the hallmarks of a developed, first world state, but it has a rural Aboriginal population with inadequate access even to basic water supplies, and an Aboriginal infant mortality rate among the highest in the world. One state, two states of development. This is further complicated by the fragility of an economy dependent on the export of raw materials and primary produce. It is an economy that is subject to the vagaries of world mineral prices and to the continued availability of what is essentially a non-renewable resource. In the absence of a large value-adding and manufacturing sector, Australia's economy, while currently strong, may not always be so. That said, Australia's services sector is growing rapidly and quickly establishing for itself a position and reputation for world's best practice in many areas.

In the narrative that follows in the other two parts of this book, I want to suggest that global development processes may continue to proceed in opposite directions at an ever increasing pace. I want to suggest that the development of global digital telecommunications networks may well intensify the current discontinuities between the 'haves' and the 'have-nots'. This is not to say that the Internet is a good or a bad thing, merely that it is not neutral. The global spread of international networks looks set to act as a catalyst, adding speed to the present situation. Perhaps its very intensity is what will distinguish this time as a radical break with the past. But I suspect that what will distinguish this time is the radical break with discourses of continuity and development.

By that I want to suggest that the break is not a break with continuity, but with the *discourses* of continuity – the narratives, or mythos of continuity. The state is always already becoming. It is always in a state of flow and its identity emerges from the focus of narrative upon this or that confluence of flows, be it economic, military or cultural, or some combination or mixture of the three. One can therefore think of states in terms of what might be called, after Foucault, the 'subject function'.

What do we mean by this? By 'subject function' I mean simply the formations by which states are identified in terms of their articulation of boundaries between Self and Other, at whatever site that occurs. Thinking of states in these terms allows us to get away from notions of states as (relatively) unitary actors. And it allows us to do so in some quite useful ways. First, it allows us to disaggregate the state into the various narratives that serve to identify it. Second, it allows us to specify the *mise-en-scène* of the state, or to define the state in terms of the event or situation. In this way we can bring to bear specificities, such as the 'security state', or the 'economic state' or the 'cultural state' in terms of the state's relationship to its context. Finally, it allows us to speak of the state in relation to other levels of identity formation in ways that make sense across the levels. Thus we can refer to congruent processes constitutive of

- states
- multinational corporations
- non-governmental organisations
- ethnic groupings
- other

by providing a semiotic basis for analysis.

Into this dimension, we can add the catalytic force of the digital communications revolution adding speed to dimensionality. If we take together the communication space, the spread of English along with the media-isation of events, what emerges is a picture of the Other as the abject brought into the living rooms of the developed west. It is a picture that at once inoculates the Self against the Other, but at the same time as it collapses the distance between Self and Other, it also increases the awareness of the distance between the self-ness of the individual (the self of the body), and the self of that identity to which I subscribe (the state) the bodiless self (Deleuze's body-without-organs).

It is one thing to do this at the televisual level, but quite another (I would suggest) to do it at the level of the Internet, and more specifically at the level of email discussion lists. Here we have the mediation of the screen, but the knowledge that there is a direct connection between the body and the text, albeit an asynchronous one. It is a form that lends itself to the building of forms of community regardless of state borders.

Perhaps it is the mirror-imaging whereby I as a warm biological body type words onto a screen and recognise in the reply that a similar event is taking place, albeit across the world from .au or .za or .uk or any of the dozens of country-specific suffixes. It is all the more poignant to know that in order for the person from, say, .za (South Africa) to participate, the writing must be in English, which may be their second or third language, while in the full knowledge that of the twelve or so official languages in South Africa, none are represented (in many cases not representable, like Xhosa!) on the Internet.

All of this raises the question of sovereignty – for whom?

Summary

- With a heavily skewed demographic profile, real opportunities to increase levels of democracy via the spread of the Internet are limited.

- Globalisation is heavily driven by the developed world private sector. This leads to a shift in the focus of decision making, both from the nation-state to transnational actors and from the public sector to the private sector.

- This is particularly the case with the elites in developing countries, who may enjoy benefits from globalisation explicitly and structurally denied to the rest of the country's population.

- There remains a tension between individual and state sovereignty with respect to globalisation and communications networks. These may be played out at the level of human rights, issues of democracy and economic development.

- The progressive internetworking of states via the Internet and more broadly through electronic webs of communication and economic flows shift the ground on which are based many of the activities identified as constitutive of states.

- These shifts establish and alter the conditions of emergence of subjectivity at the level of the state and at the level of the individual. This may be described in terms of Deleuze and Guattari's notion of 'flow' or 'rhizome' and Foucault's idea of the 'subject'. This could be seen as the interplay between the analogue and the digital in philosophical terms.

- In addition, new polarisations are occurring in the information economy that could undermine the traditional ability of the state to undertake its 'duty of care'. This could result in creeping disenfranchisement and a rise in low-intensity conflict.

- The spread of the electronic media can give rise to new forms of injustice where conflicts may be marginalised from the lack of a media 'language' in which to couch the terms of the conflict. Such forms of injustice have been described by Lyotard as *différend*.

- If we take together the communication space, the spread of English along with the media-isation of events, what emerges is a picture of the Other as the abject brought into the living rooms of the developed west. What is needed is a reinscription of the body into the media process. This reinscription of forms of community is arguably possible through the interactivity of the Internet.

5   Culture and the Other on the Internet

This book argues that states exist by virtue of their practices of inclusion and exclusion. These practices are at their most visible when applied to what we identify as cultural products or symbolic life. Whoever has the means to control or disseminate cultural products controls how a state is viewed in the world, by other states, and by the domestic polity. How a state is viewed in the world constitutes – for all intents and purposes – its identity. Practices by other states that 'speak for' a state serve both to marginalise that state and to render it 'virtually' colonised. This chapter explores the issue of cultural production and colonisation with respect to the Internet.

Plato, in the *Republic*, recognised both the inherent contingency of the state, and the power of cultural production. The state, for Plato, arises from the traditional economic problem – that wants are unlimited, and that resources are limited, so there needs to be governance. The state arises, according to Plato, 'out of the needs of mankind; no one is self sufficing, but all of us have many wants. Can any other origin of a state be imagined?' (Plato 1992: 60).

So the state is a product of desire. In the same way language, too, is a product of desire. Words and other signifying practices stand in the place of that which is desired, both signifying the lack of something, and to signal the place where it would be if the desire could be satisfied. It is in the reaching out that we enter language, and in that same movement we enter the symbolic order in which we function as identities. So too with states. States, for Plato, are structures established where there are wants to be met and limited resources with which to meet them. The subscription to and maintenance of these structures are what constitutes the identity of the state. States are thus the by-product of cultural practices and are symbols that stand in the place of these processes to signify their continuing operation.

In both language and the state the key is the exchange of value. It is in the relationship between people, and in their interdependence, that collective identities, such as the state emerge. Plato argues (for Socrates) that such identities are the necessary outcome of fundamental economic and cultural exchange. It is, above all an economy of signs:

> as we have many wants, and many persons are needed to satisfy them, one takes a helper for one purpose and another for another; and when these

partners and helpers are gathered together in one habitation the body of the inhabitants is termed a state . . . and they exchange with one another, and one gives and another receives, under the idea that the exchange will be for their good . . . Then [Socrates said], let us begin and create in idea a state; and yet the true creator is necessity, which is the mother of our invention.

(Plato 1992: 60)

Cyberspace is another economy of signs. It is a notional space within which exchanges take place in a manner which is also constitutive of identity. There are both ethical and practical implications of this.

For all the rapid growth statistics for Asia, the Internet is still an American space. In fact between 1995 and 1996 the North American continent went from 75 per cent to around 83 per cent in actual node numbers, before declining, relatively, to around 65–70 per cent in 1998, depending on the survey (see World Internet population June, 1998, p. 26 of this book). Thus it is perhaps not too surprising that many countries see the Internet as too western dominated.

One aspect of identity making is in the naming process itself. To have a presence on the Internet one needs to have an Internet address which includes a domain name. This domain name provides a ground-level category by which one identifies oneself. Until 1997 there were just three: .edu (for educational institutions), .com (for commercial sites) and .gov (for government sites).

In addition to these, there were country-specific domain suffixes, such as .au for Australia, .za for South Africa, and so on. In 1997, under the pressure of rapid growth, the WWW domain name system was in serious danger of running out of available names. Moreover, certain company names applied to different companies in different countries. It was therefore easy for potential customers to mistake the company xxx.com for the company xxx.com.au for example (my apologies if there really are companies with these names).

The answer seemed to lie in an expansion of the international domain name system, so, in 1997, seven more domain names were proposed. These were firm (for a company), .store (for product sales), .web (with emphasis on the World-WideWeb), .arts (for cultural sites), .rec (for recreation), .info (for information) and .nom (for individuals who want an international domain name of their own). With .com addresses being largely taken up by US corporations, firms in other countries have found themselves either locked out from registering their company name, or stuck with country-specific suffixes. By using these new international domain names, companies in countries other than the US will have the opportunity to obtain an international Web address.

This does not, of course, mean that the country-specific suffixes will disappear. Some companies find a certain patriotism in retaining their country suffixes, such as the Australian mining firm BHP (bhp.com.au). But the problem of limited numbers of domains in a rapidly growing Internet will continue to arise periodically as Internet access becomes more widely available.

This vexed domain name problem has already become an issue for Europe. The EU has complained to the US government, contending that the new domain names are too vague and too US-centric (Wales and Hilvert 1997: 40). This is an interesting contention for the EU to make. That a group of western countries should see cultural difficulties in terms of US-centrism suggests strongly that there needs to be greater internationalisation of the standards-setting process on the Internet. If the EU has difficulties, how much more so must the countries of ASEAN feel?

Malaysia and the Multimedia Super Corridor

In 1995 the Malaysian Prime Minister, Dr Mahathir, noted that too much of the information on the Internet about Asia was sourced from the west, and particularly from the US. He called on ASEAN members to become more assertive about their presence on the Net, and to produce more content from an 'Asian' perspective. Malaysia has gone on to do much more than that, as the Internet has become a powerful symbol of modernisation. Mahathir's vision of a Multimedia Super Corridor, established about 30 km south of the capital, Kuala Lumpur, has already attracted some heavy-weight information technology players, including Microsoft, Sun Systems, NTT (Japanese telecom) and a host of other companies. Such is the power of a symbol. The MSC is being created to attract investment by the top multimedia, information technology and telecommunications companies. These companies have been offered extremely generous terms in order to establish a Silicon Valley-style enclave, or 'cyberjaya' as it is being called. These include substantial taxation breaks, relaxation of profit repatriation rules and easing of local employment rules. So what is in it for Malaysia? It seems that there are two things that flow from it. First, there is little doubt that there will be investment in the telecommunications infrastructure. Second, as breakthroughs are made, they can be attributed as Malaysian achievements, regardless of whether Malaysians are directly involved or not, and regardless of whether or not Malaysians stand to benefit directly from them. At issue is perception, bought at the price of certain sectors of sovereignty.

In further moves to identify the country as 'modern', other related cyber-projects are springing up throughout the country, even as far as Sarawak, and the infrastructure is slowly being put in place to be able to run a number of government functions electronically. This last seems a somewhat naive hope, as the western myths of the 'paperless office' of the 1980s have failed to materialise in the 1990s.

Other state government programmes include, in Alor Setar, the provision of multimedia facilities at public reading centres in five villages. In Johor Baharu it was intended that administrative business between the state government centre and district offices would be conducted electronically from mid-1997. Indeed the dream of the central government is to move all government business to electronic form by the year 2000. This will be run from a new government centre in the form of a satellite city to Kuala Lumpur to be known as 'Putrajaya'.

The MSC, launched in May 1997, will initially cover an area of 15 by 50 kilometres, from the Kuala Lumpur (KL) city centre in the north to the KL International Airport at Sepang in the south. The new development will include widespread education and awareness programmes throughout the country, and the establishment of a multimedia university which eventually is hoped to provide indigenous expertise for the cyberjaya. Much of the site is still palm oil plantations, but KL already has its first public access Internet booth, operated by a 'netcard' similar to the Malaysian phonecards. For 20 ringgit (about £5 sterling or US$7.50) anyone can have an hour on the Internet. It is still a novelty, however, as only wealthy foreigners have both the money and the interest. Anyone using the booth quickly attracts a crowd of interested onlookers. This says much about the extent to which the Internet is being advertised, and hence public curiosity about the Net, but also about the way the developed west is held up in the face of those still largely unable to afford the luxury.

Malaysia is developing rapidly; indeed Kuala Lumpur at times seems like one massive construction site, from the Petronas Towers (in order to have, however briefly, the record for the world's tallest building) and the Commonwealth Games venues, to massive office and hotel developments. It is a country whose growth is outstripping the development of the infrastructure needed to support it (and, perhaps, the economic strength needed to sustain it). There are regular power failures, almost daily. Increasingly there are also water supply failures – even in parts of Kuala Lumpur. Internet service providers are regularly put out of service for up to 48 hours at a time.

Interestingly, when Malaysia was examining the Internet censorship issue, the issue arose of Malaysia's competitive advantage over other South-East Asian nations, such as Singapore. While publicly expressing concern at the availability of pornography and dissident voices on the Internet, Dr Mahathir has announced that the MSC is to be exempt from such censorship. Then it was realised how difficult it would actually be to censor the rest of the country, while leaving an island of full access in the middle of the telecommunications infrastructure. The result was an announcement in 1996 by the Malaysian government that there would be no Internet censorship throughout the country. Whether it is a matter of policy, or of simply having too few people to police it, the Net thus far remains uncensored in Malaysia. Whether effective technologies of censorship emerge, once the MSC corridor is built, the specific outcome is actually less important than what these announcements mean for Malaysia. Dr Mahathir has realised that Singapore would not be able to offer the same levels of freedom to the same companies operating there, so there would be a competitive advantage in bidding for the investment of those companies.

That a non-censored Internet access should be set up for a restricted elite community raises a number of issues. First, the MSC is being established from the beginning as a 'hothouse' environment – a consciously elite space in which to foster the free interactions required to produce innovation. Second, the MSC is being deliberately set up as a space with privileges that are to be denied to other parts of the country. There are implications in this for those provincial centres intending to score electoral points from regional nodes of the cyberjaya, including plans for a cyber-village at Kuching in Sarawak.

In fact Sarawak continues to develop considerably faster than peninsular Malaysia, with unofficial figures claiming a growth rate of up to 20 per cent per annum, as opposed to between 7 and 8 per cent for the peninsula, although these figures will fall for the next couple of years in the wake of the current economic crisis. But then Sarawak is growing from a much lower economic base, so rapid percentage growth by comparison is perhaps not as significant as the kinds of development taking place. Financed by massive timber exports, along with oil, natural gas, and palm oil industries, Malaysia, and East Malaysia in particular, is trading its past for its future with exploitation of non-renewable energy and non-replaceable biodiversity. Despite new government regulations limiting the extent of logging, and a concerted replanting programme, the rivers run brown to the sea with soil erosion from continued logging. The replanting cannot replace the diversity of the rainforest that has been lost to clear-felling. What does this mean for the indigenous Iban people of Sarawak? What will be their future after the timber jobs run out, and their homelands no longer support their traditional way of life?

Certainly, Malaysia is a society in transition from 'developing' to 'modern' status, and looks set to make the transition successfully, providing the growth in the electronics industry does not falter. Kuching, the state capital of Sarawak, already has a cybercafe (in the Hilton Hotel) and plans for a new seat of local government. This new government district will be fully wired with high bandwidth fibre-optic cables linking the government buildings, and linking East Malaysia via a new T-3 cable with the Federal government in Kuala Lumpur. Again this area is still largely mangrove swamp, but the directions are being set for the first quarter of the twenty-first century. New industries are set to become established in the next few years as the economy moves to natural gas for power and petro-chemicals yield new industries in plastics and semi-conductor plants. New state-of-the-art silicon wafer manufacturing plants will be established, making full use of East Malaysia's abundance of fresh water.

Just down the road, indigenous Iban and Dayak people still live much as they have done for hundreds of years in their longhouses. They are no longer the head-hunters they were up to the 1960s and their longhouses are beginning to sprout TV aerials from the rooftops, but the ceilings are still adorned with the skulls of their ancestors. One wonders what these ancestors would make of the new technologies. The entrances are still guarded by carved icons, and the traditional *pua kumbu ikat* weavings are being sold in the local markets. Will these people too have access to the wired economy? Or will they just be another market, a cultural curiosity by which ethnologists might chart the steps to 'modernisation'?

Just as there are differential development strategies between the ethnic Malaysians and the indigenous people, so too is the population divided between the elite ethnic Malays, the ethnic Chinese who are the drivers of business, and the ethnic Indians, all separated in legislation by the Bumiputra laws that favour the ethnic Malays over all.

The problem with establishing a liminal space that is at once claiming national pride for innovation, while at the same time marking out Self–Other boundaries between those who are 'in' the MSC and those who are 'outside' but within the same country, is that there will always be problems of mediation between the 'haves' and the 'have-nots' within Malaysian society. So too there are issues for the mediation between the MSC and the rest of the world. There is a danger that those few Malaysians who get to work in the MSC will come in time to be seen as somehow 'less' Malaysian, even less 'Asian' than their compatriots in a strange form of inverse snobbery.

Essentially the MSC is designed to operate a form of 'privatised' sovereignty, where the major investors are the ones setting the parameters and legal framework for this state-within-a-state. New laws are being enacted to provide intellectual property rights protection for innovations developed within the MSC, while special economic zone status will be accorded to allow for the specific and unique sets of taxation, employment and freedom of communication regulations.

Such a situation is by no means unique – special economic zones have been established in a range of countries to provide local competitive advantages in order to attract trade and investment into otherwise poorer countries. Moreover, such economic zones have shown considerable promise in bringing economic wealth to such countries. But, as with the broader issue of urban population drift, there may need to be additional controls imposed on freedom of movement of the wider population in order to prevent the MSC, for example, growing faster than its capacity to absorb the population. So there are prices to be paid for the establishment of liminal spaces within a nation-state.

These prices are not necessarily to be seen in economic terms, but rather in social ones. Here is a case, perhaps, of *différend* such that regardless of the evident economic benefits, the costs in terms of limits to freedom (of speech, of movement) and in terms of cultural identity cannot be related in any meaningful way.

Another way to view this is that there are continuing processes of identity formation that need to be recognised in terms of a disaggregated society with multiple identity-formations. Seen in such a light, the MSC as a liminal space within Malaysia may be viewed as part of Malaysia's growing cultural diversity, rather than in terms of any sense of loss which harks back to an always mythical unified Malaysian identity. Indeed Malaysia, like Singapore, has always been a multi-ethnic society, with a balance of ethnicities between people of Malay, Chinese and Indian descent all working within a community that taken together comes to be viewed as Malaysian. Moreover, such diversity of ethnic backgrounds could build a greater sense of regional identity through regional groupings seen in terms of a common Asian heritage. That at least is the rhetoric that binds groupings, such as ASEAN, even as the latter expands with the entry of the Indo-Chinese countries of Vietnam, Cambodia, Laos and Burma. What remains debatable, however, is the extent to which such groupings will be able to function effectively as a region, and subsume certain functions, such as telecommuni-cations, to a broader regional identity. ASEAN is far from being a European Union, and rightly so. ASEAN countries' histories and cultural diversity are markedly different from the history of the kinds and levels of interaction that have characterised the peoples of Europe since the thirteenth century.

We must guard against the tendency to form grand unifying narratives that could make Asia seem in any sense a unitary identity. Moreover, as we shall observe in the next few chapters, there are significant problems even with conceiving of Europe itself as any kind of unitary identity.

Sovereignty is in any event a slippery and variable concept. Since the end of the Cold War the nature of national identity has changed. With the old, if problematic, certainties of superpower rivalry and global spheres of influence fading rapidly, new forms of identity are emerging. States are being rearticulated and people are aligning themselves with smaller, more local identity formations. In the west we have seen a resurgence in the rhetoric of 'family values' articulated loudly on behalf of the now largely mythical family unit of modernism – the so-called 'nuclear' family. Moreover, in Eastern Europe, the former Soviet Union countries have reasserted pre-Soviet national identities, and some have fragmented into forms of effective tribalism in Bosnia-Herzegovina.

With the spread of the Internet, there is scope for a newly international localism that is finding expression in 'virtual' communities, with some people going so far as to suggest that a new global cyberstate is forming. There are implications in this that will be explored later in this book, that have to do with the potential narrowness of single-interest communities. There are also signs that online communities will offer further dimensions to personal identity within an already complex world. But whether these will ultimately undermine the notion of state sovereignty is extremely doubtful. People still live within a physical location, and here the idea of cyber-sovereignty falters as it fails adequately to think through the place of the body in cyberspace.

There will remain liminal political and economic spaces, as there always have been. These have always been necessary to a greater or lesser extent in order for states to articulate their relations with other states in the world of diplomacy and international trade. There may be a number of cyberjayas that are called into being in the coming years, and many of these will be established as liminal spaces marking boundaries between developing states and the developed world, and between these economic islands and the states in which they reside. Sovereignty will be relaxed in careful and highly specified ways for these special economic zones to exist, but such relaxation of sovereignty will only extend so far as to allow them to operate effectively. They will, perhaps, be the most carefully controlled and managed spaces of all.

Laos

Laos (as at time of writing) is to all intents and purposes not (yet) on the Internet. There are suggestions that it has also one of the few remaining matrilineal societies, among the Lao Lum of rural Laos. This is changing, in part through the consequences of economic transformation which is set to accelerate with Laos' entry into ASEAN. Schenk-Sandbergen and Choulamany-Khamphoui (1995) notes, in a series of case studies on Mekong village irrigation projects, that where men may hold positions of authority, women's socio-economic power often counterbalances socially sanctioned male domination. But changes are coming that are endangering this position.

As Vientiane moves into a new phase of economic development, the state is transforming traditional ownership structures through land legislation that is transferring land ownership from women to men. Through land-tax reform, the state is conducting large-scale land surveys using private contractors from Vietnam. Land-titles are being registered as held by the 'head of the household', who is usually male. This effectively transfers the ownership of land traditionally passed down through the female line to the male side of the household, thereby creating a new system of individual land ownership. Processes of traditional and collective ownership are being undermined in Laos' new economic order. Up until now, women have been able to maintain their status through their economic power which their traditional rights of ownership, and traditional agricultural knowledge and skill base, have ensured. But a number of changes are conspiring to remove the basis of women's status within traditional Lao Lum society. These changes include:

* mechanisation and modernisation of agriculture
* land legislation and changes to land title
* increasing imports of factory-made cloth and other traditionally home-produced goods.

Women traditionally worked the land, including tilling by buffalo, and they were the traditional owners of the knowledge needed to secure continuing yields from their rice crops. By moving to an increased use of mechanised farming methods, with tractors taking the place of buffalo, the division of labour is shifting. Men, in Lao society, are considered to be the only ones capable of using a power tiller. Thus, as Schenk-Sandbergen and Choulamany-Khamphoui (1995) point out, the use of tractors automatically introduces a field of male decision making in modern inputs, such as the use of artificial chemical fertilisers and pesticides that had not been used in traditional farming methods. This process, they argue, reduces the traditional reliance on female skills and knowledge in the production of rice. As the buffalo are sold along the Mekong River, women are losing their position, their control and their access to the farming cycle, while being increasingly placed under a greater workload to pay for the mechanisation.

Once Laos joins the international community of networks, these networks will be taken up by men, on the basis of their traditional mastery of technology, thus ensuring that women are ever increasingly marginalised within Laotian society. The issue here is not that access to the Internet will change the traditional social structures, but rather that, as the process of modernisation and mechanisation takes hold in Laos, so women will be silenced and marginalised by the very technologies that some would hope would otherwise have provided a liberating voice.

Moreover, as the country itself becomes more exposed to western notions of fashionable dress, so too will this access increase the drive for more imported manufactured clothing, such as jeans, over and above the traditional woven fabrics of rural women, thus further reducing their capacity for income generation. As pressure grows on the diminishing capacity for income generation, so too does the time pressure on women who might otherwise have been able to secure a secondary education.

With the process of modernisation and globalisation shifting the economic and educational power base away from women, these same women will on both counts continue to be marginalised in any access to international technologies of networking at the global level. Thus their position will be spoken for by the male elites in Laos, in much the same way that ASEAN is arguing that their position is being spoken for by the west. Implicit in this is a potential reading of the 'developing world' as 'woman' in relation to the west.

Culture and identity in the knowledge economy

At issue here is the question of culture and identity in the knowledge economy. It includes issues of control and access that need to be raised in any consideration of the Internet as a force for democratisation.

The lead up to recent Indonesian elections and the subsequent overthrow of the Suharto regime saw the Internet become an active player as Indonesians sought alternative sources of information while the authorities tightened media controls. The left-wing People's Democratic Party went underground after they were blamed by Indonesian authorities for riots in Jakarta in July 1996. They continue to respond to accusations on Internet discussion lists. Activist groups are increasingly turning to the Internet and other electronic media to provide information on their activities, and on the activities of the Indonesian government. With only about 80,000 Indonesians online in 1998 (out of a population of almost 200 million), the Internet remains a small factor within Indonesia. However, it does allow international groups, such as Amnesty International, to remain informed in the event of human rights abuses and restrictions on civil liberties.

In March 1996, Indonesia's Information Minister indicated that they were no plans for Internet regulation. Clearly, with such a small number having access to the Internet within Indonesia, it is not yet seen to be a significant political force, particularly given that those with access would be those wealthy enough, or powerful enough to have benefited from the current regime, and would in any event therefore be likely to support the status quo. This view may change as the Internet gains a wider foothold, particularly among the politically aware student population.

Strange (1994), speaking of what she terms the 'knowledge economy', suggests that there are a number of issues for states, social groups and the international system in the current developments in communications technology and globalisation:

> Firstly, there are changes in the provision of and control over information and communication systems. Secondly, there are changes in the use of language and non-verbal channels of communication. And thirdly, there are changes in the fundamental perceptions of and beliefs about the human condition which influence value judgements and, through them, political and economic decisions and policies.
>
> (Strange 1994: 120)

All three of these are readily visible in discussions to date about the progressive globalisation of the Internet. Wired countries throughout the world are examining issues, not just of the control of information flows, but also of ownership of the means of dissemination, the extent of government versus privately operated infrastructure, and the impact of different technologies of dissemination. These are issues of sovereignty.

Second, and of particular concern to developing countries, is the use of language – whose language? The politics of English as the universal language of the Internet is still a hot topic of debate in South-East Asia, and will remain so for some time to come. As for non-verbal channels of communication, the Net, of course, is a multi-channel communications network. The use of visual and, increasingly, aural channels of communication through RealAudio and similar narrow-cast technologies is changing the way information is provided over the Net. This raises questions over the similarities/differences between netcasting and other broadcast modes of communication, such as radio and television. At stake here is the question of which legislation will be used as the model for censorship/suitability ratings. The debate still rages over whether the Internet is more like a personal letter or telephone conversation, or prime-time television. And where does 'push' technology fit in all this? Is it like direct mail marketing? Like television programming? Or like a wake-up call on the phone? Perhaps it is a combination of all these things. There are implications in this for the future of sovereignty. One thing is for certain, the Net and perceptions about the Net are shaping and influencing human culture across the globe. These perceptions, by weight of numbers, are overwhelmingly being generated in relation to western values, western culture and western economic agendas. These, too, are issues of sovereignty.

Third, none of these issues is new. Television has spread to almost all areas of the globe. Mobile phones are revolutionising communications in countries that do not have a land-line system in place. Since the beginning of colonial times, Australian Aboriginal painters have painted sailing ships, white-faced people and guns – icons of communication, cultural domination and power. *Iban ikat* weavers in Sarawak are weaving aircraft, helicopters, modern-day hunters and guns. Perhaps these are signs of a living culture, but these are also signs that signal loudly that wherever there is communication, cultural domination and the exercise of power, there is always an *Other* who is the recipient, the dominated, the disempowered.

In the chapters that follow I intend to show that what is true for the developing world is also true for the developed world. In all this, I am not saying the Net is inherently a 'bad thing' but that, like every form of communication, it brings with it responsibilities. Responsibilities that are not necessarily being taken on board by those with the power to act. The Net can empower, as well as disempower, but to read the hype over the advantages of the Net, there seems to be little space to render visible the Other of wired society.

Summary

- A state's identity is made visible through its cultural expression. Whoever controls the means to control or disseminate cultural products therefore has substantial control over a state's identity in the world.

- States are the by-product of discursive practices – they exist insofar as they are invoked *qua* states.

- States embody for their people an economy of values within a system of exchange. States embody a set of relations between people.

- Cyberspace, too, is an economy of signs. It is a notional space (a simulacrum) within which exchanges take place. It too, embodies a set of relations between people. Cyberspace cuts across state boundaries with ethical and practical implications for the sovereignty and integrity of the state.

- For all the rapid growth in Asia, the Internet remains a principally North American space. The recent expansion of domain names still left US companies with a substantial monopoly over .com names, leaving other domains for Other people – forever identified as 'Johnny-come-latelies'.

- Within the domain name system, there remains a place for country-specific domains, such as .au or .uk where companies or individuals wish to use such names for patriotic and brand recognition purposes. Country suffixes remain essential for the .gov domains.

- In response to the perception of western dominance of the Net, Malaysian Prime Minister Dr Mahathir called for greater content production from ASEAN countries. As the Internet becomes a symbol for modernisation and development, Malaysia has set about developing its own Silicon Valley in the form of the Multimedia Super Corridor.

- To appropriate the Internet as a sign of modernity, the MSC has had to be established as a separate, liminal space between Malaysia and the rest of the world, leaving it in a space that is also separate from the rest of Malaysia despite its (physical) location, both legally and culturally.

- As Laos develops, traditional matrilineal society is being undermined. Although not (yet) effectively on the Internet, the forces of globalisation are still impacting strongly on its culture, values and sovereignty.

- In Indonesia, the Internet is already being seen as a political force in the lead-up to recent elections. But other forms of political control are still wielded widely in Indonesian politics – especially against media critical of the government.

- Issues that need to be addressed in the knowledge economy include access and control, the politics of language and identity, and changes in fundamental perceptions and beliefs about the human condition that influence the conduct of a domestic polity's way of life.

- These issues have been with us since people first began trading and communicating with other cultures.

Part III
The developed world

6 Process: the key to the Cyborg

'Cyborg' is a useful metaphor for states. It combines in the one term:

* the sense of the interconnectedness of human beings within a society
* the sense of the artificiality of the states as structures
* the sense of idealism and forward vision that maintains states as sound identity structures.

In such a system, states can be viewed as the by-product of the interaction between human beings and the networks that connect them.

For Haraway (1991: 150), the term 'cyborg' contains within it the 'condensed image of both imagination and material reality, the two joined centres structuring any possibility of historical transformation'. The notion of cyborg is inherently about boundary making and identity, not merely between the human and the prosthetic machine, but between ideality and materiality. The enmeshing of these two realms marks an important departure for contemporary social and political life. As Haraway notes:

> The relation between organism and machine has been a border war. The stakes in the border war have been the territories of production, reproduction and imagination.
>
> (Haraway 1991: 150)

The linking within and between states by contemporary telecommunications systems at once ties people together within their 'wired' community, while posing new challenges as old hierarchical ways of doing business and relating to each other are potentially undermined by the interpenetration of states through these communicative networks.

Coupled with the continuing rapid growth of the Internet, and the seemingly near global spread of modern communication systems, is an explosion in the amount of information flowing within the information economy. Today the average office worker is dealing with and managing far more information than at any time in the past. Terms like 'paradigm shift' and 'the greatest revolution since the Renaissance' come easily to mind in describing the extent of change facing the contemporary developed world.

Multiple references to the present as though it were like the Renaissance are interesting. Why is this not like 'the greatest thing since Victorian times' or 'the greatest thing since the industrial revolution'? Why the Renaissance? A point of entry into this might lie with looking at what we think made the Renaissance so different from these other 'revolutionary' times. Of course to speak of the Renaissance as a discrete period is problematic, because any reading of the past will always be through the eyes of the present. Moreover, the factors that made the Renaissance stand out have themselves a lengthy genealogy which makes precise dating of this or any other period difficult. In twentieth-century rhetoric Renaissance was markedly different from previous times, more than anything because it marked the birth of humanism – the philosophical underpinning of modernism that was to characterise western urban life until the mid-twentieth century. So to look at what makes the current era so different, from that of the Renaissance, we need first to examine what distinguished the latter from the previous several hundred years.

In the 1420s a well-established architect, Filippo Brunelleschi, arrived in Florence. He was known as an innovator, and many of his mechanical inventions inspired Leonardo da Vinci when he saw them some twenty years later. Leonardo was one of a number of very talented engineers to be inspired by Brunelleschi's work. The town of Florence had a problem. With powerful patrons trying to out-do each other in the extravagances of their public buildings, the city fathers had finally over-reached themselves. In trying to build the world's largest church (shades of Dr Mahathir and the Petronas Towers) the designers had exceeded their construction ability. They called for tenders to find a person able to work out how to complete the half-finished structure.

The church, Santa Maria del Fiore, is perhaps better known as Florence Cathedral. Arnolfo di Cambio's initial plans for the church dated back to the mid-fourteenth century. Construction began, was abandoned, and began again. None of the succession of designers – including Giotto (who designed the bell tower), Andrea Pisano, Francesco Talenti and Bonaccorso Ghiberti – could solve the problem of how to span the space. Until this time, domes were begun by providing a timber span across the main vault, on which a framework would be erected. The base measured 55 metres across. No tree would be sufficiently tall or strong to support the necessary framework. But Brunelleschi's design was bold. He proposed a large dome that would be built without wooden centring. The authorities were in doubt. The structure would be massive, and there were concerns that it would not be self-supporting. But there was little choice.

Brunelleschi faced and addressed essentially three problems:

- to lighten the massive structure (40,000 tonnes and 90 metres high)
- to set up a worksite organisation that could efficiently handle each successive construction phase
- to ensure the stability of the brickwork courses by devising new ways to interlock the structure.

He solved the problems by developing technological force multipliers, by developing new workplace organisational structures and by using innovative techniques. In each of these respects we find resonances with life today, both online and in the workplace. What resulted was the largest unsupported masonry dome in Europe. Today we are dealing with new forms of business organisation that span across state boundaries, supporting massive organisational structures.

For Brunelleschi, technology was only part of the revolution. The rest was a philosophical outlook which, at one level, resulted in a set of management practices – a revolution no less important, albeit perhaps less immediately glamorous, or indeed obvious than his many ingenious inventions, including several types of cranes.

As workers in the information economy, we too are building a cathedral. We in the west are building a structure from within which is disseminated informational products which both reflect and shape the way we see the world.

The challenge of modern business is

- to lighten the massive structure
- to set up a worksite organisation that can efficiently handle each successive production phase
- to ensure its stability by finding new ways to interlock the structure with its surrounding architecture.

Brunelleschi needed to find new ways to build structures and organisation of work practices in response to a new way of looking at the world. This was the world of William of Ockham (*c.* 1300–1349), who provided the basis for the scientific and rational approach still in use today. It was a humanist world of new certainties that celebrated humanity based on Aristotelian principles. Aristotle's categories provided organisational structure to the disciplines we know today as those of language studies, mathematics, science, the arts and law. From that Renaissance world came clerical structures of organisation, vestiges of which appear today in our corporate and public sector structures.

The philosophical revolution we are undergoing today represents a fundamental dismantling of those old certainties. The boundaries between our disciplines – arbitrarily established so long ago, are now becoming less certain. Environmental and bio-resource issues have shaken our confidence that we are somehow above and apart from the world in which we live. We are, whether we like it or not, living in a post-humanist society. The former certainties of a bipolar political world have been overtaken by an erosion of the pre-eminent position of the nation-state in our structures of identity. We live in a world in which the economy of signs – of information – is rapidly overtaking our trade in physical things. We live in a world in which the state, for so long a seemingly stable entity, is so interpenetrated and internetworked by other forms of community, of business, of culture, that the power of the state over its own sovereignty is becoming eroded in key areas.

One of the characteristics of our emergent networked world is that we are dealing with a change in the way we conceive of change. In the world after the

Renaissance we could take heart in the idea that we were heading somewhere. We could take heart in the view that somewhere, if we could just figure out how to do it, we would reach an ideal point. The idea was that if we kept improving things, we would find the one best way to do something. We would reach an end-state. Processes were secondary. They were a means to an end. In the postmodern world, we have no such certainty. But then, in the Renaissance world the old certainty that somehow God would keep everything running smoothly was disappearing, and humankind found itself alone, and having to take responsibility for essentially human acts. Today the great individualising humanist philosophy of modernism is standing on less firm ground. Human kind no longer stands proudly apart from the rest of the world, but rather perceives an uncomfortable sense of interconnectedness. Chernobyl taught us the arrogance of state-based environmental regulations.

In the west, our view of the world has changed fundamentally. The world is no longer just a world of atoms. The way we understand the world is shaped by the concepts and processes by which we look at the world. It is shaped by our language and social structures. What we make of the world is a by-product of the processes by which we set about understanding the world.

Our sense of identity as a country, as a culture, as an organisation is a by-product of the processes by which we define a country, a culture, an organisation, a level of operations. There is nothing fundamentally stable about it. Each time we pin it down, we have already begun to change it. The world as we are coming to understand it is the outward sign of a bunch of continuous processes interacting with each other.

I want to suggest that *this* is the world we are living in today and are moving into tomorrow. The world into which we are moving is a world of change. Our challenge is to build a culture of positive change. A culture in which we see ourselves, our products, our customers as the by-products of processes, existing only insofar as we maintain the process. There are no natural customers, nor can they see us as natural producers. We are as valuable as our last product. There is room neither for complacency nor for inaction.

We no longer can afford to manage change as though it were a temporary state between fixed forms of organisation. We must manage change as an aspect of maintaining the organisation. It is a continuous process of identification, analysis and implementation of solutions to problems that arise within a continuous process.

It is not a comfortable way to live. But resistance, as they say in *Star Trek*, is futile. When Brunelleschi was building his cathedral, he found himself dealing with challenges that he was able to turn into opportunities:

- how to handle an unprecedented quantity of work
- how to organise the work in ways that made its fundamental instability contribute to the strength of the structure
- how to organise and design the work practices in ways that took the weight off the scaffolding and allowed the building itself take the weight of its own construction.

His revolution was as much in logistics and organisational practices as of technology. We are facing similar challenges. But this time we are in a digital age, and we are coping with far greater quantities of information than we have before. For Brunelleschi the challenge was to deal with the realities that there were limits to what one man could lift or carry. Today businesses and governments are limited by the amount of information one person can process.

Our force multipliers include computers and networked processes, matrix organisational structures, team-work and customer-in-the-loop management practices, just as Brunelleschi used pulleys, gears and pre-Fordist production line techniques. But in a very real sense we are building our own version of the cathedral.

In Part III I shall explore the current changes in terms of the way the developed world has begun to see itself in the context of 'globalisation' and the challenges posted by global networking for the state system and for the social structures within. What is important in all this is that what is changing in particular is not the use of this or that technology, but the *processes* by which life is enacted in society. It is the shift in ways of doing business, in forms of relationship, in articulations of society, that change is occurring. It is this rather than merely the means by which a message is communicated.

Indeed, arguably Brunelleschi's greatest contributions were not his inventions for lifting great weights, or his new forms of scaffolding, but rather in the work processes by which he organised the building site. New forms of logistic organisation so that material was being processed at the optimum site. Where stones needed transporting, he had them shaped in the quarries so that there would be less to transport. He also understood implicitly the principles behind shifting material – the physics behind the continuity of loads when organising machines for the loading and unloading of ships. Moreover he organised the structure in such a way that it would bear its own weight by distribution, thus relieving the scaffolding so that it could become a platform on which the masons and carpenters could work. From this Brunelleschi was able to lighten the entire structure, making possible a whole movement of architecture to large-scale buildings enclosing large spaces without the need for heavy internal walls to break up the interiors.

Today as the west seeks to handle more information at ever faster rates, there is a need for new and innovative management structures that lighten the load by sharing it with the customers of the information. If there are marked shifts arising from the so-called 'information revolution' it is in the social processes, the management structures, and forms of exchange as much as through technological innovation. Shifts in social practice made possible by technology will mark out this era as definably 'different' from previous times, as opposed to mere technological development by itself. As Castells (1996: 32) points out: 'New information technologies are not simply tools to be applied, but processes to be developed.'

I want to argue in this section that the crucial difference between the haves and have-nots in the information society will not necessarily be those with the networks alone, but those who can find innovative ways to use those networks. This has implications for the very structures of management upon which the prosperity of western capitalism depends. While technologies can be seen as the prostheses of the human form, extending our sight and hearing and sense of touch – even smell in the case of explosives sensors and new identification verification technologies – so too technologies of social organisation will shift to accommodate the new range of human interaction made possible by such 'cyborgisation'. Those who have benefited under older forms of social organisation will try to resist change. But these are the very people who will find themselves marginalised under new forms of social and economic organisation. Such forms of organisation might include flatter management structures and the elimination of steps in the older chains. Whole sectors of white-collar work can be compressed within matrix management structures more versatile and adaptable than hierarchical linear management structures.

The processes in place will affect the conduct of states in three broad arenas:

- war – the articulation of political space
- economy – the articulation of value and its exchange
- society – through the articulation of identity, the nature of community, gender issues and the nature of work.

These are the outcomes of the shift in societal processes made possible by new technologies of networking.

There is a cost to this. We have seen that the Internet is principally a North American structure, with 75 per cent of Net nodes being in the US alone. Like any revolutionary change there will be casualties. These will comprise those who are unable to make the transition to the new way of thinking and operating in civil society. We are already seeing large numbers of entrenched unemployed who are becoming surplus to the new economy. The human cost of this in the longer term may well come back to haunt the Hobbesian state being constructed by dry economic rationalism as one of the major outcomes of the death of modernism – the death of humanism itself. These features of late-twentieth-century capitalism have significant implications for the roles and responsibilities of those whose job it is to articulate states – those engaged in the processes of government. Indeed, as the entire rationale of the nation-state is called into question, the gap between the haves and the have-nots is widening at an ever increasing rate. What will be the social costs of all this as more and more people fail to catch the table morsels of trickle-down economics? As the economy of the wealthy and the privileged operates ever more efficiently, then ever fewer niches will exist within which the have-nots of society can function with any degree of security.

Under the pressures of globalisation and the open economy, unskilled work is disappearing or is moving to part-time, casual or contract work. This has implications for job security. It also has implications for gender, employment equity and conditions of service. As employment moves along these trends, we are seeing a short-term increase in the number of jobs for women, who are still typically paid less than men either through devaluation of level, loss of overtime, or shorter working hours, while being paid only for hours worked as part of a casual workforce. Within this trend, many men in this bracket are losing their jobs as basic manufacturing moves to increasing automation or relocates to countries with 'cheaper' workforces. So a new class of 'working poor' is entering the discourses of the wealthy west. In addition, even among developed world tele-outworkers there is stratification between high-demand contract programmers outsourced from major companies and unskilled data-entry teleworkers, principally women, many with child-care responsibilities. While the former can work hours to suit their lifestyle, and command high per hour rates, the latter tend to be less well paid and are subject to work fluctuation that suits their employer. The structure of outwork or telecommuting is such as to preclude effective unionisation and class-level employee/employer mediation and negotiation (Dawson and Turner 1989: 34–35 cited in Horner and Reeve 1991: 8).

Moreover this 'deskilling' of work is being accompanied by a devaluation of higher education as a human right in the west through the erosion of financial support mechanisms for students. Nor is the beneficiary of education being seen as society as a whole as it has in the past. By articulating the education debate as an individual enterprise, discourses of 'user-pays' paper over the fact that people – educated people – are a primary source of strength for society as a whole. Education renders a society adaptable and better equipped for a world in which change is becoming a way of life.

As we see a return to individualistic competitive society in the west, the role of women again becomes uncertain. In the competition for fewer and fewer full-time jobs, women are again being pushed aside as structures which sought to redress gender imbalances become starved of funding, as support for legal aid is removed as opportunities are again being denied women seeking to re-enter the workforce after parenthood no longer find or are no longer able to afford the high costs of retraining. So too does the quality of life for society as a whole decline.

If the features of a developing country include endemic lack of support systems, exploitation of the non-privileged (the out-workers, indigenous peoples, migrant people) and high levels of systemic stratification of society, then we are witnessing the decline of western society – the progressive third-world-isation of the west. But it is different. Whereas the developing world has hopes and aspirations, coupled with traditional extended family support systems, the non-privileged in the west have neither.

The rise of the west was built on individualising structures which progressively broke down the extended family. These structures systematically moved the primary focus and duty of care from the family to the state in the shift from feudalism to modernism over the four hundred years since the Renaissance.

With the coming of globalisation and the development of substantial networks, new processes of working and thinking are emerging, which leads to another form of stratification between the wired and the unwired in the developed west. The literature extolling the virtues of living online often fails to represent the ways in which the lives of the unwired Other within developed countries will be affected by the information revolution.

Issues of access in developed societies are different from those in developing economies. First, not everyone, even in the US, has a phone, let alone computer access. Yet already there are signs that ability to access the Internet is emerging as a criterion affecting employability in the US. If this is happening in one of the most wired countries in the world, then where does that leave the other developed countries?

Socio-economic and cultural factors, including race, gender and class affect not merely the financial aspects of getting online, but also the will to do so. Even in countries, like Australia, which have a system of university with deferrable fees, universities had a disproportionately high representation from middle and upper income families. These cultural aspects also have an impact on the extent to which people from low-income families perceive themselves as active participants in the global economy.

While those who work proactively to keep pace with the Net and its potential opportunities can thrive, those who come later will find increasing difficulty in keeping up with the growing sophistication of website development. As Web browsers become more capable, so too will individuals find it harder to produce websites that will have the impact of well-resourced and experienced companies. How many individuals today can pick up a primer on Java and produce interactive pages without first having some grounding in programming? What about VRML? Users can buy sophisticated software packages that can construct Web pages without any prior knowledge of HTML required, but such pages show their template heritage quickly, and have a stamp of 'sameness' about them.

All communities to a greater or lesser extent engage in cultural practices of inclusion and exclusion. Online communities are no exception. Forms of language mark out those who are experienced net users from those who are not. A so-called 'netiquette' has developed among experienced users in order to counteract the worst effects of low-bandwidth text-only forms of communication. Unwary new users, or 'newbies', break these conventions at their peril. They can find themselves 'flamed' (sent messages full of invective) or mail-bombed (sent very large volumes of material through their email account) for even fairly minor breaches, such as writing in all upper-case characters (equivalent to 'shouting'). I saw one new Bangladeshi user flamed for attempting to sell ethnic products via email groups. He probably did not have the bandwidth to set up a website, or the experience to know not to advertise via email. There is still a long way to go before the Net is truly global.

The indigents on the information super-highway will remain subject to the vagaries of global markets, left wondering why their governments no longer protect their jobs in the new open market. Moreover, as grievance mechanisms become further under-funded and job security becomes legislated away with the dissolution of 'unfair dismissal' laws, the democratic process itself becomes open to question.

Lewis Mumford pointed to the impact of technological change on economies and governance in the 1930s. While monastic clergy sought regularity in their lives as part of their devotion to duty within the ascetic life, the advent of clocks in the late twelfth century and the development of turret clocks for church steeples meant that gradually the regulation of life with productive activity could be done to the clock rather than to human time. In secular society, clocks were for a long time affordable only by the wealthy due to their complexity of manufacture. By the mid-sixteenth century domestic clocks became a sign of affluence, and punctuality became celebrated as a virtue. Again the first in this category were those with the means to afford the technology, and those who were the first to recognise that 'time is money' (Mumford 1934: 16). Time became an economy in itself. One could 'save' time. It could be spatialised, filled, wasted and tabled. Time became commodified. Moreover, people could be paid by the hour, rather than the day. Productivity could be measured in units per hour, and coordinated within production processes. These processes could then be broken down so that people themselves could be seen as metaphorical 'cogs in a machine' – like the parts of a clock.

Clocks too could be seen as archetypal of industrial accuracy and precision. People became submerged into the machinic. People became cyborgs in terms of being seen as extensions of mechanical processes. Mumford (1934: 227) pointed out that by the 1850s partial automation had been achieved by the textile plants in England 'without any great release of the human spirit'. He noted further that with complete automation, however, freedom of movement and initiative returned for 'that small part of the original working force now needed to operate the plant'. This concentration of freedom and initiative in the hands of the few leaders of industry was to become a characteristic of modernist industrial society.

Coupled with this was the introduction of printing to Europe. Printing introduced another form of standardisation, first in terms of spelling and style, then in terms of prescriptive rules of language, which constrained freedom of thought. Again these were taken up in industrial society as virtues for the individual worker. Books were seen as the ultimate in uniformity and repetition. Unlike the fallible monastic scribe, the typeset book made copy after copy, each identical with the last. Since that time, print has been seen to hold the power of *author*ity. 'It is written . . .' becomes reason enough to avoid question. Moreover the distance between the written word and its author effectively makes the source of power a kind of 'absent father' figure, in Freudian terms. Power is perhaps most effectively wielded when the source of the power is invisible and unquestionable. So the printed word, distributed throughout a territory, becomes an effective means of control and organisation for states and for large corporate structures such as railway companies. Print became the means with which to hold together an empire – even by teletype or telegraph. Those who were literate could hold positions of power and authority. Such people, educated into linear modes of thought, made model citizens who could become the bureaucrats and means by which modes of power could be reproduced. In contrast, those without such skills, or who did not conform to such 'standards' tended to be excluded from the workforce, or from any commanding role in the workforce.

As print served to standardise language and textual production values, and as clocks served to regulate individuals in time with corporate processes, so too is the Internet leading to specificities in modes of thought and expression. But these are different specificities from those of print and clock. The information economy today is more than merely literate. It is an economy that also demands graphicity as well as literacy. That is, it demands people who are semiotically literate as well as textually literate. It demands individuals who can make meaning with signs, including images, rather than individuals who are merely text-literate. This will become increasingly apparent with the generation that has grown up with the linear narratives of television and is now entering the informational workforce. Those who are merely literate will find themselves at a disadvantage on the Internet. People who have become accustomed to hypertext and the use of Internet search engines are already seeing the world through new eyes. They are seeing the world through non-linear ways of making meaning. As a result they can produce complex texts that make meaning as much through juxtaposition of textual and visual elements as through linear argument. These are the people who will be best able to take advantage of the postmodern world, when the linear, hierarchical modernist structures of the past have effectively collapsed. These are the people who are building new forms of business – virtual corporations – matrix organisations, and other structures able to get inside the decision cycle of their competitors in the information economy. As pressures build for smaller government sectors, governments too are facing the need to 'work smarter and faster' in an environment of decreasing revenue and dry monetarist policies.

As the economy increasingly threatens to bypass state structures, the nature of states as identity structures is itself under pressure. This has led to apocalyptic visions of states disappearing in a puff of irrelevance. States are under pressure, as is the very state system itself, but it is resilient from a number of perspectives. As the following chapters will show, the state will continue to have a role in the emerging world order (some would argue an emerging world chaos), both within the economy and within discourses of security. States continue to have and to exercise their duty of care within the bounds of their mandate. States will continue to prove useful as articulations of political space. Their role may even increase in places in order to provide for and to manage the care of those who find themselves in the place of the Other, those who are excluded from the economy of the information revolution. But they will do so, perhaps less as primary providers of the duty of care, but rather as the watchdogs who manage the processes of privatised care-giving services. We are seeing hints of this today, but care will need to be exercised in its practice so that it does not abdicate the duty of care entirely. We are dealing today with the early forms of a revolution of mind as much as of technology. That is the cyborg state.

Summary

- The term 'cyborg' can usefully be applied to states seen as the by-product of the interaction between human beings and the networks that connect them.

- The rise of humanism in the Renaissance displays many parallels with the world of today. The postmodern world is witnessing the conclusion of the humanist era.

- The challenge of modern business is to use networking as a source of strength rather than as a threat to be resisted.

- Today we need to view change in a new way, and embrace a culture of change management, rather than change resistance.

- There are social costs for the developed world in today's epistemic changes.

- Modernist technologies of printing and clocks shaped thought processes conducive to the industrial revolution. But networks are reshaping those thought processes. The unwired in the developed world will not have access to new cultures of thought.

- The role of states will continue in important ways to cushion the unwired from the worst excesses of globalisation. But it will have to do so in smarter ways due to reductions in the size of the government sector. Governments will move towards managing contractual arrangements with private suppliers of public goods, rather than supplying those services themselves.

7   economy@internet.com

It seems fashionable these days to speak of states in the past tense. States were what we had before the global economy. But now, with global communications networks, state boundaries seem about as effective as tissue paper being used to stop a cannon ball. Indeed, the 'guns versus butter' analogy has been with us a long time to describe the distinction between state power and political economy. The arguments are getting more sophisticated, but essentially they boil down to the question of tradeoff between the economic and military security roles of the state, and the extent to which large global corporations seem to be driving state policy, rather than the other way around. Another way to look at this might be to consider global corporations and states as passing like ships in the night – largely ignoring each other. I prefer to think of it more as ships and lighthouses.

There is an amusing and certainly completely apocryphal story traversing the Internet – one of the 'urban myths' of the Internet – concerning what is purported to be a conversation between two people via a maritime radio system (Mikkelson and Mikkelson 1997). The conversation runs like this:

FIRST SPEAKER Please divert your course 15 degrees to the north to avoid a collision, over.
SECOND SPEAKER Recommend you divert YOUR course 15 degrees, over.
FIRST SPEAKER This is the captain of a US Navy ship. I say again, divert your course, over.
SECOND SPEAKER No, I say again, divert YOUR course, over.
FIRST SPEAKER This is an aircraft carrier of the US Navy. We are a large warship. Divert your course now! Over.
SECOND SPEAKER This is a lighthouse, your call.

While a modern, well-equipped US warship would clearly be able to differentiate between a ship and a lighthouse, this improbable tale illustrates something of the relationship between states and economic flows. While the two are mutually dependent, the relationship between them often becomes confused in assertions that states are losing their power, or are declining into irrelevance.

The idea of the nation-state comes from the Greek city-state. It was the size that it was partly because the nature and speed of communications meant that this was the size of domestic polity that could be efficiently managed with the technologies of the day. This includes the technologies of organisation, as well as the physical technologies of communication. With advances in communication systems and structures of organisation, the state could become much larger. Some writers today think that the porosity of the state threatens its very existence due to state functions being privatised, and sources of state revenue becoming globalised. But if we go back into history we see that most of the traditional functions of the state have, at some time or another, been operated as privately owned outsourced functions. The Roman Army was largely a privately funded force. The economy has always to a greater or lesser extent operated as private, while state functions have interacted with the economy to varying degrees across time. We need therefore to consider what makes the state possible – what are the enabling technologies, and then we must pose the question: are these really disappearing or is it merely the fog of change? What are the functions of a nation-state? To what extent are these functions being undermined, or at the end of the day, are they merely changing form?

In this chapter, I want to suggest that nation-states are varied creatures. They exist in a wide range of forms, bearing, in Wittgenstein's (1983) terms, 'family resemblances'. For Giddens, the nation-state is a 'bordered power container' (Giddens 1987: 120) or more elaborately:

> a set of institutional forms of governance maintaining an administrative monopoly over a territory with demarcated boundaries (border), its rule being sanctioned by law and direct control of the means of internal and external violence.
>
> (Giddens 1987: 121)

This is essentially the Weberian concept of the state. If the state is first and foremost a structure for the provision of security, as Strange (1994) suggests, then the role of the economy becomes important only insofar as it has a bearing on the ability of the state to conduct its 'core business'.

Modern developed capitalist states have not only been concerned with military security – supplying services to prevent its people from dying in an untimely fashion from violence – although that remains one of the central functions of states to this day. The state has also been involved in the provision of secondary care services – social security in order to provide freedom from starvation in the event that the market fails to provide. States also provide an environment in which trade can take place, and in which the domestic economy can be shielded from some of the worst excesses of competitive business practice operating at a global level. Thus sunrise industries, for example, might gain a measure of protection until they have established themselves as survivors within the global economic system. Free market economists, such as Ohmae (1995), suggest that such businesses are inherently uncompetitive, and that it would be 'kinder' to let them fail at birth in a completely open market. While that might be free trading, there are tensions between this and fair trading, which need to be addressed as the global market system takes hold in a new way. States may well continue to play a significant role in this regard for the foreseeable future, within structures such as the World Trade Organisation (WTO). Such economists would like to see exchange rates based on purchasing power parity (PPP), arguing that this would benefit consumers and stimulate demand in the domestic economy, leading to employment growth without significant inflation. What this formulation elides is that while demand may be stimulated at the local level, this does not necessarily translate into jobs within that country. In the globalised system, the jobs may appear in the US or Korea or Malaysia, rather than Japan. In an internetworked world, economic security for the domestic polity may well rely increasingly on the structures of nation-states to even out class disparities and reduce as a result the potential growth in internal unrest that would inevitably flow from an increasingly extreme stratification of society.

Ohmae rightly suggests that economic borders have meaning more as 'contours of information flow' than as dividing lines between nation-states. This tension between flows and identities forms the basis for what follows.

Interestingly, states so far have proven remarkably resilient in the face of growing economic fluidity, and this suggests that the two are connected less by simplistic causal relations, than by more complex forms of interaction.

According to figures in *The Economist* (7 October 1995), the public spending ratio has increased on average in the OECD economies from 36 to 40 per cent of gross domestic product (GDP) since 1980. *The Economist* argues that despite increasing economic integration, national governments are tending to control more rather than less. If this were to have happened as a brief blip in a continuing trend away from government control, then one could argue, as Ohmae (1995) does, that increased government control is the last gasp of a dying nation-state.

It is true that governments now have, on the whole, less control over exchange rates, while retaining some control over interest rates. It is true, too, that if governments spend more than they raise in taxes, they ultimately have to borrow the difference, becoming perhaps somewhat more at the mercy of interest rates and, in extreme cases, having to make structural adjustments in the form of cuts to education and social programmes. While the trade in services has increased enormously, there is still a 'real' economy that will remain in place regardless of technological developments or the speed with which commodities are traded. Human beings still require food and manufactured items, and this provides a strong reason why nation-state borders will remain in place for a long time to come. The information economy is growing prodigiously, and is outstripping the 'real' economy in a number of key areas, such as financial services. But while such markets are fluid and treat national borders with disdain, not all capital investment is so fluid.

Manufacturing capital loses much of its mobility once it is turned into fixed assets. Such assets, including high value-adding labour, applies friction to cross-border flows. High-priced labour is not keen to travel once families are established and the children are at school. Such assets mean that companies lose elasticity of movement, and may therefore tolerate a certain level of government intrusion into the economy. There are few signs that this is decreasing. While such mobility may be more easily applied in developing countries, which have more to lose from capital outflow, the same economics does not apply in countries supplying highly skilled labour. Even highly successful countries do not develop evenly. There will always be some in a society who will do well, and others who will not do so well. The rise of the modern nation-state came about, in part, in response to the need to provide for those who need a safety net in order to avoid the adverse social outcomes of extreme poverty. In other words, states emerged in part in order to improve physical security for the domestic polity, by providing the means of survival for those otherwise unable to fend for themselves.

This form of security will continue to be provided for as long as states are able to maintain a sustainable taxation base. Indeed, in extreme cases, dry economists would like to see a rearticulation of political space such that regions of prosperity can grow like tall poppies among the arid wastes of the rest of humanity. Such arguments forget that economics is more than a balance sheet. Why, they argue, should the successful subsidise those who are not? Indeed, why should democracy give equal weight to votes regardless of social contribution? Such arguments assume that social contribution can be measured only in terms of one discourse formation – money. While money can be seen in some ways as a means of encoding value in ways that are translatable across national boundaries and across industrial sectors, it is not the only form of discourse. Nor is it the only form of value.

Where the 'ships passing in the night' metaphor becomes useful is in the distinction between two economies of flow: the business economy and the identity economy. I have noted earlier that states are the by-products of processes. These processes are only partially economic in the conventional sense. The other is a semiotic economy. An economy of signs to which individuals effectively subscribe, or to which they are subscribed at birth. This is the economy of nationalism, the economy of administration and the economy of military security. Taken together they add up in large measure to individual identity at the level of the state.

Offe (1996: 145) notes that individuals have a three-way relationship with the state:

- they are the creators of state authority
- they are potentially threatened by state force or coercion
- they are dependent on the services and provisions organised by the state.

Another way of looking at this is that individuals within the domestic polity articulate their nation-state identity through three discursive formations, comprising democratic 'voice', the rule of law and the operation of the welfare aspects of the state. All of these are forms of interaction between people organised 'in the name' of the state. People, then, are already operating within a networked society. In Deleuze and Guattari's (1983: 12 ff.) terms the state is 'rhizomic'. By that they mean that the state is more properly considered as an irruption from the flow of discourse. That it emerges as an identity structure is largely due to the boundaries that are enacted to call it into existence.

In the money economy, borders are seen as contours in the information flow, but information itself is that which is marked out from the flow. When we speak of moving into an information society, we are of course in many senses already there. The nature of identity itself is that some structure has been imposed – hence information.

Giddens (1987) sees nation-states primarily as organisational and administrative structures that rely upon procedures of surveillance for internal pacification and distribution of resources. Nation-states therefore function in terms of the ability to provide domestic order in the face of international anarchy. States, under Giddens' definition, follow the Weberian line that states are characterised by their monopoly over the legitimate use of force. That word 'legitimate' often gets left out when writers try to argue that states are disappearing because they no longer monopolise the use of force. States have never monopolised the use of force, but rather they monopolise the *legitimate* use of force.

But arguments over legitimacy aside, the main point here is that states are not merely an economic construct. Thus no matter how porous the state may become to flows of capital and investment, they also serve other functions that may not disappear so quickly in the face of borderless corporatism.

Confronted with borderless corporatism, however, states are adjusting to new ways of doing business, new ways of articulating their identity. As with any redefinition of identity, there will be a shift in who is included in the 'us' part of the equation, and who is left out, or excluded and defined as 'them' or as Other to the Self of the identity structure.

As government draws back from the direct provision of services, such as telecommunications, the users of such services become repositioned in the marketplace. The immediate result of deregulation and privatisation is that there is very strong competition among firms to provide high-return services to the urban corporate sector, while individual users – especially in rural areas who most need such services, find themselves positioned on the margins of the wired economy. As Mansell (1993 cited in Bannister *et al.* (1995: 45) points out, such people, without state intervention through effective regulatory legislation, could easily find themselves disadvantaged by low bandwidth and expensive connections. The idea of the telecommuter would quickly pall for those who may prefer to live in rural areas away from the city traffic jams.

Tapscott (1996: 316ff) suggests that governments, far from being irrelevant in the new internetworked economy, will in fact be central to the process of transition and management of change within nation-states. There is much to support this view. Governments for better or worse provide the conditions under which business can operate within states. Their policy leadership determines whether or not there will be large scale external investment. Tapscott (1996) suggests that governments can stimulate the new economy through example by being

- mission driven
- results oriented

- customer focused.

Taxpayers in many industrialised economies are calling for governments to change, become more efficient, and drive their tax dollar further. This challenge has been taken up in a number of countries, including the US, Canada, Australia and, more recently, the UK. These governments are each taking steps to introduce competition to service delivery, flatten their hierarchical structures and focus on prevention rather than cure. But it is early days yet.

In the education sector, governments throughout the developed world have overlooked that the 'user' is society as a whole, and not just the individual student. As a result, so-called 'user pays' policies are leaving out large numbers of capable students and laying waste to the very future to which these states aspire.

We are also seeing a market-place becoming far more complex than in the past. Rather than the dyad of producer/consumer we are already seeing other structures emerging between these two. Perhaps, after Tapscott (1996: 62 ff.), they could be termed 'conducers' and 'prosumers'. What do we mean by this? In a way it is a shorthand description of the changing nature of the relationship between consumer and producer in the new economy. Producers will increasingly operate in the services sector in order to facilitate a smoother market-place. They will render the environment conducive to business; this could be termed the 'smart push' approach. New facilitators will put increasingly disparate components of a system together, resulting in 'virtual corporations'. Such people would be broad generalists bringing together the specialisations needed to realise a product and bring it to the attention of the consumer. In the new economy their role will increasingly expand so that producers will increasingly become conducers.

Prosumers will fill the complementary position in the chain, that of 'smart pull' on behalf of the consumer. Increasingly, in the developed world, consumers will actively seek out the best deals, the products best tailored to meet their needs. These proactive consumers will perhaps be better described as 'prosumers'. Another aspect of this will be the growing power of consumer groups to act on behalf of consumers. These 'professional consumers' also fit this category of prosumer. Thus more of a continuum will emerge, as shown in the diagram.

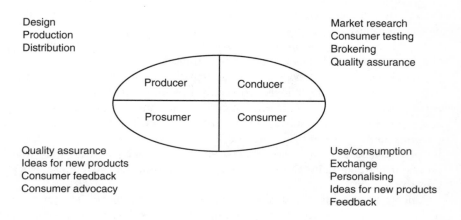

Design
Production
Distribution

Market research
Consumer testing
Brokering
Quality assurance

Producer   Conducer

Prosumer   Consumer

Quality assurance
Ideas for new products
Consumer feedback
Consumer advocacy

Use/consumption
Exchange
Personalising
Ideas for new products
Feedback

This will not necessarily mean more niche workers, merely that these roles or functions are becoming more integrated in the cycle, and that both individual consumers and firms will work more closely together to achieve outcomes.

First, at the government level, Tapscott (1996) sees governments using electronic networks to deliver services more efficiently, quickly and cost-effectively. This sounds optimistic, given that many consumers of government services are simply not in a position to afford to be linked into electronic networks themselves. Second, there is the question of cultural change that will require the rethinking of administrative processes to account for electronic flows of information. Most western governments are still operating out of nineteenth-century print paradigms that will be hard to overcome.

In the mean time, governments are responding to calls for downsizing, without necessarily thinking through the hidden costs of doing so. For example, governments throughout the OECD are reducing their support staff, who are typically at the lower end of government salary scales. Unless the work practices are redesigned, the same work then gets done by high salaried people, who are thus taking time out from what they were originally paid to do – develop policy options, manage processes and so on. The government of the day ends up losing on two counts, and costs – both financial and in declining levels of service – rise.

Such redesign is beginning to occur in selected areas of government. Tendering processes are increasingly being undertaken electronically, resulting in a significant decrease in replication and information handling. Some government departments are becoming more customer focused, and are aiming to provide more information, greater openness and faster service. Projects are being increasingly managed on networks that include the supplier in the process. Funds are dispersed using electronic funds transfer systems.

Services are being outsourced to specialist enterprises, rather than being handled internally where it is cost-effective to do so. Sometimes former government employees form their own enterprises and become specialist service providers to government. This has led cynics to define consultants as government employees who have been retrenched only to be rehired at triple their salary. At one level, this may not be an altogether bad thing, if such suppliers can provide the service more cost-effectively – with the emphasis on the effective – then outsourcing makes some sense.

The downside to this is that in a period of monumental transition, there is a very real danger that individuals will be left with truncated career paths, and lacking the very job security that made them want to participate as public servants in the first place. Government employees are typically paid considerably less than comparably skilled managers in private enterprise, and the tradeoff has tended to be acceptable if job security and satisfaction were supplied. The danger in operating government more like private enterprise is that good managers may well leave for private industry, while those of less ability remain. In short the transition process may well penalise those most able to make postmodern government work effectively.

Among the emerging positive signs, government departments are beginning to work more cooperatively as teams contributing to providing customer-oriented services, while sharing administrative burdens. While we are a long way from seeing virtual agencies coming together for short-term joint ventures involving project management, there are encouraging signs that government administrations are working closer together than ever before. Moreover, they are working more closely with industry and education sectors to provide centres of excellence on specific fields.

To say that because of international trade, the state is a spent force (Negroponte 1996; Ohmae 1995), is to ignore the history and operation of the international economic system. Government policies influence in a variety of ways the development of globalisation, and ameliorate the worst effects of global competition on the domestic economy. The challenges for national governments, according to a recent report to the OECD (1996a), are to

- facilitate globalisation
- ensure effective adjustment
- strengthen the capacity to deal with change
- strive for more open and contestable markets.

Clearly, then, governments will continue to have a strong role in mediating between the international and the domestic, by facilitating access to markets, while providing sufficient regulation to ensure a degree of security for the domestic economy. Globalisation in this sense refers to

> an evolving pattern of cross-border activities of firms involving international investment, trade and collaboration for the purposes of product development, production and sourcing, and marketing.
>
> (OECD 1996a: 9)

Underlying all this are three facets of globalisation:

- technological advances
- liberalisation of markets
- increased mobility of production factors.

Technological advances, perhaps more than globalisation itself, continues to have an impact on employment of non-skilled labour – as it has done since the industrial revolution. The pace of technological change, however, is now such that the effects on unemployment will continue to increase. Moreover, the pace of technological change is being increasingly driven by international competition, rather than domestic innovation.

As global financial and share markets go online the opportunities for investors to put their money into foreign equities are increasing dramatically, far outstripping national checks and balances currently in place. Aronson (1996: 328) suggests that this poses challenges for regulators to determine how they can protect investors from fraudulent practices in overseas markets without seeking extra-territorial powers that would almost certainly infringe on sovereignty. This is where

governments come in to their own in forming cooperative international agreements to exchange information on international crime.

Globalisation is bringing significant changes into the international economic
arena, favouring some areas over others. OECD investment has risen dramatically
in East Asia while other developing countries have seen their share fall. This
has been coupled with the growth in foreign ownership of firms in the OECD.
Moreover, investment has tended to concentrate in a few selected industries,
such as computers, chemicals, electronics and motor vehicles. The relative
importance of foreign owned firms is fairly high in Europe, Canada and Australia,
is of growing importance in the US and is of low importance in Japan, possibly
reflecting a higher degree of protectionism, or cultural bias in the latter case.

As such industries grow in the relative importance in each economy, these
economies become more fragile, despite strong growth in these sectors. With the
concentration on a few industries, sector fluctuations produce disproportionate
effects within the economy concerned. Moreover, with growing levels of foreign
ownership, the profits become increasingly repatriated to the country of ownership, rather than staying in-country to stimulate the local economy. As a result
where there may have been a trickle-down effect to other sectors of the economy,
the trickle increasingly leaks offshore.

As companies within these narrow sector bands seek to maximise their
competitive advantage, they become increasingly specialised in order to offer
country-specific advantages. As a result there is an intensification in local
specialisation to satisfy niches within a global trade system. Moreover the trade
becomes increasingly intra-firm rather than broad market-based firms. The
disadvantages of such effective 'monoculture' is that downturns in the sector
can hit some developed countries disproportionately hard. As large firms strive
for price advantage through 'outsourcing' the less profitable parts of their business, so more niches open for firms better able to compete on non-price factors,
such as quality and flexibility. Increasingly, however, such firms are competing
with other small specialised firms in other countries. Over-specialisation can have
its price.

Another aspect of this specialisation is the geographical clustering of high-
technology industries into 'technology parks'. Sometimes consciously developed
through favourable local conditions – special rates on power, land, taxation,
relaxed repatriation or labour legislation – these 'parks' can often exist in almost
complete isolation from the rest of the surrounding economy. The advantages of
such parks – perhaps so-named after one of the first technology parks, the Palo
Alto Research Centre (PARC) – include the collocation of innovative sunrise
industries, leading to research centres and universities well geared towards
supplying highly skilled graduates in 'relevant' disciplines.

A number of issues arise for governments in such a development scenario.
While attractive on the surface, with often rapid growth and the attraction of large
amounts of development capital into the country, the economy is left vulnerable to
fluctuations in the global market for these specialist items. By persuading
developed countries of the benefits of large numbers of small contracting firms

transnational parent companies are made freer of constraints to production price factors becoming increasingly mobile.

By outsourcing in a number of countries to small firms for the same production components, transnational companies build flexibility, while small localised firms lack the collective bargaining power of larger in-house components. Government policy therefore becomes torn between providing a favourable climate to attract foreign investment with the potential benefits of international markets for their exports, while also trying to retain some bargaining power on behalf of local industries. The almost inevitable outcome is greater presence and influence from foreign firms, coupled with increased opening of the economy. At the same time we are seeing greater interlinkages between economies at the regional level. Is this a form of third-world-isation of the developed world through high-technology industries? Certainly there are characteristics common to the developing world. Perhaps it is a form of homogenisation, or moving together of some formerly distinctive features of developed and developing worlds.

This regionalisation, far from sacrificing sovereignty, will likely strengthen the influence and role of governments along with a growing sense of national identity while at the same time establishing a new and regional identity. We are witnessing therefore a growing complexity in the system of governance. This is the natural result of growing instability and uncertainty in the postmodern world. For those that can move ever further up the food chain, the rewards are likely to be great, but there will be a lot of road-kill along the way.

The outcomes of this will be felt in security terms throughout the developed world, in terms of declining social well-being, increased sectoral poverty and endemic economic insecurity. In the extreme case, this is a recipe for cultural nihilism, the rise of mindless racism and the breeding ground for extremist ultra-nationalists. Examples of all of these have emerged in countries ranging from Germany and France to Australia and parts of the US.

Globalisation thus changes the context for policy across a wide range of social, economic and security issues, each requiring strong leadership to avoid extremist excesses.

On the social side, governments will have to move quickly and decisively in order to avoid localised but highly vocal minorities damaging international reputation, trade and foreign investment. Once damaged, the economic spiral can move downward into self-fulfilling prophecy if considerable effort is not expended to slow the outward tide of investment, and with it the remaining employment opportunities for the less skilled part of the workforce.

On the economic side, governments set the context for economic growth. As economies become increasingly linked and integrated through the global strategies of firms, so too does the competitive edge of industrially specialised firms become more volatile. Governments are therefore pressured to increase trade and invest-ment liberalisation, decreasing the differential between foreign and domestically produced goods and services. While minimising export friction, governments also come under increased pressure to provide the best possible climate for local business in ways that develops their competitiveness. This can include deregulation of industrial relations. But this almost always works to the detriment of those least able to bargain for their position, leading in extreme cases to the Hobbesian life – nasty, brutish and short.

Governments also have operated the lion's share of infrastructure development and support. Nowhere is this more evident than in each country's national information infrastructure. Continued development and expansion of bandwidth is required to carry the information superstructure including the mass of electronic funds transfers and data exchanges that make up a globalised developed world. This has required agreements at an international level to set standards and protocols for data transfer such as handshake protocols, transfer rates and so on. France's lack of government leadership in this area means that France has come to the Internet only very belatedly, despite moving early to a national-level information infrastructure with Minitel. Unfortunately, this system, which served national requirements very well, meant that France's connection to the 'global' Internet was not developed until 1996. This was an example where knowing one thing meant not knowing something else.

Increasingly, governments are selling off their infrastructure, starting with the most profitable – hence more easily sold. Historically, this has meant that infrastructure comes to be seen less as a public good or as an essential service, and more as a means for providing high returns to shareholders. Such a shift results in wholesale restructuring, in order to close down or significantly diminish costly, low-return services, while focusing on high-value, high-bandwidth services. The outcome, as the Australian Telecottages report (Horner and Reeve 1991) indicates, is that rural services tend to be reduced, or priced out of reach for non-wealthy rural customers.

The irony of this is that the actual cost of transmission per packet is very low – virtually unmeasurable (Economist 1996: 21–24), so if costs are charged on a distance rate, then current technologies render this largely unjustifiable. But people can see distance, and they can measure the cost of carrying physical objects across that distance, so it makes common sense that prices should be higher for greater distance travelled. The issue is actually one of infrastructure. As telephone service companies become privatised, they become increasingly reluctant to provided subsidised services for rural customers, whose infrastructure costs outweigh any likely profits from a low customer density.

All this should change, however, as more companies move to satellite-based systems, rather than wire-based systems. Once a constellation of between sixty and eighty satellites is in orbit to provide global service, it will soon cost the same to provide the service regardless of distance or traffic density. But it will take time for people to change their mind-set over physical distance. People will persist for some time in thinking of distance in common-sense terms as cost-per-unit of distance.

But common sense actually presents a false view when it comes to charging for Internet traffic. To begin with, network packets use telephone networks in a very miserly fashion. Where voice telephone calls tie up an entire line for the duration of the call, Internet packets do not need exclusive use of a line. They travel in the interstices of other traffic.

Moreover, as digital data, they can be compressed, unlike analogue telephones, and this goes some way to explain the widespread move in recent years to digital telephones. Internet packets share the entire bandwidth of the phone line with all kinds of other data, so it makes little sense to charge as though they were using the line in the same way as a phone call. All the fuss about Internet traffic supposedly swamping the phone system is misleading by several orders of magnitude. In Tasmania in April 1997, the phone system buckled under the weight of traffic. The reason? A pop group had come to town and bookings were coming into the local exchange at the rate of 100,000 in the first three hours after it opened. In fact almost every time the phone system has been in danger of buckling under bandwidth demands has been for reasons of voice phone traffic, rather than Internet use.

Recent moves in some countries to charge for data traffic separately over leased lines into Internet service providers – in some cases moving legislation to approve such charging – are primarily means of increasing profits for telephone company shareholders, rather than genuine issues of fair charges for fair use. The pressure to do so has come about in part in response to the development of Internet-based telephone technology that takes voice data, breaks it into data packets and 'streams' it to the receiving computer for conversion back into voice – all done in split-second intervals so that voice quality remains good, even though the users' messages are being packetised and compressed in real-time. Competition from Internet service providers can now, as a result of an Australian invention, provide telephone services via the Internet (Ozemail's Internet phone), even to users who do not have a computer. Such systems can result in international call charges being reduced to as little as one-third of the price of a standard international call. Increased competition could well see these prices drop even further.

In the developed world that has the technology and resources to launch hundreds of low earth orbit (LEO) satellites, physical boundaries are declining for the services sector of the global economy. The boundaries that remain are discursive ones. But discursive boundaries are not insignificant. We have seen in earlier chapters that states are identity structures that arise because they 'contain' the anarchy of the international political economy. They are disciplined spaces that in practical terms are about the largest identity structure available to human scale. In Weberian terms, states hold the monopoly over the legitimate use of force, and therein lies the rub. As we shall see, states offer the last line of defence for the individual; if only for that reason they will persist for a long time to come. For as long as people seek justice for those fellow human beings that can be identified as 'us' as opposed to 'them', states will continue to play a role.

As the outcome of continual processes, the role of states is changing. For Deleuze (1992), the shift is one from the 'discipline society' of the nineteenth century, to one of the 'society of control'. The former, he argues, is focused on the binary distinction between mass and individual, combining features of integration as well as resistance, as defining characteristics and modalities of operation. The latter deconstructs the boundary between mass and individual by focusing on the multiplicities of the individual, rendering them as 'dividuals'. As Deleuze (1992) notes:

The numerical language of control is made of codes that mark access to information, or reject it. We no longer find ourselves dealing with the mass/individual pair. Individuals have become 'dividuals', and masses, samples, data, markets, or 'banks'. Perhaps it is money that expresses the distinction between the two societies best, since discipline always referred back to minted money that locks gold as numerical standard, while control relates to rates of exchange, modulated according to a rate established by a set of standard currencies . . . the disciplinary man [*sic*] was a discontinuous producer of energy, but the man [*sic*] of control is undulatory, in orbit, in a continuous network.

(Deleuze 1992)

It is a matter of perception of course, for the binary distinction was always flawed. We have seen in earlier chapters that identity itself can best be considered as the outcome of an extractive industry, in which the individual is articulated as such for specific sets of essentially discursive practices. The same holds for states, or indeed the notion of a 'mass' be it mass society, mass culture or mass market. In all of these frameworks, modalities of disciplining space – whether real or virtual – are called into play. For this reason it is useful to examine these modalities, which are increasingly finding resonance with the term 'information warfare'.

Summary

- The distinction between state power and political economy has been around for a long time, yet in the discourses of globalisation states are said to be fading away. The linkage between the two may not be the simplistic causal relation that some contemporary writers suggest.

- Nation-states arose out of the Greek idea of the nation-state, which in turn grew from the city-state. Their size was limited because of technologies of communication and techniques of organisation. Advances in both areas allowed the nation-state to become much larger.

- If the nation-state is seen as a function of is boundary-making practices, then its primary function, in Weberian terms, is to provide security within that identity structure. If that is the case, then the economy becomes important only insofar as it affects the state's ability to conduct its 'core business'.

- Modern states provide not only military security but also the environment for other forms of security. This is partly through providing the framework in which economic activity takes place, and through supplying safety-net services to the domestic polity in the event that the market fails to provide.

- Free market economists suggest that the market should dictate which businesses survive and which do not in a purely Darwinian fashion. But there is a conflict of interest insofar as markets are not well geared for the provision of services on the basis of public good. This will continue for as long as businesses are aimed at generating maximum profits for shareholders, rather than providing maximum benefit to the consumer.

- For this reason, governments will still have an important role to play through providing an environment for business, while looking after the interests of the domestic polity.

- In the free-market economy, purchasing price parity mechanisms may reduce consumer prices substantially, thereby stimulating local demand, but this may translate into more jobs overseas, rather than domestically. National governments are therefore needed to mediate between domestic and international markets. There are no signs of this requirement diminishing, and the trends in public spending ratio are in fact in the reverse direction.

- For the postmodern state there are two principal economies of flow: the business economy and the identity economy. This is the distinction between the contour boundaries of the business economy, and Self/Other boundary of the identity economy.

- States are not merely an economic construct, so no matter how porous the state becomes to economic flows, other functions will not disappear. The face of the nation-state may change substantially, as governments learn from activities that businesses do well, and move to become more efficient in the provision of their core services, while managing the outsourcing of those activities more effectively handled by the market economy. The watchdog role of the state will be crucial in determining how effectively this change is managed.

- Globalisation brings about uneven development, even across sectors within the developed world. There will be substantial winners and substantial losers. There are dangers that the Darwinian business approach will lead to over-specialisation in local economies, producing market vulnerabilities and increased insecurity and uncertainty. The rise of regionalism is one way that states have moved to try to counter the worst excesses of the market economy through cooperative arrangements between states, both to open their markets, while providing competitive blocs to provide sufficient 'voice' to protect against uncompetitive practices such as 'dumping'.

- There will be many challenges faced by governments as they learn lessons from the market economy. Governments will make mistakes that will have adverse localised effects for the domestic polity. At the local level there will be an increase in polarisation of wealth, which will increase boundary-making activities within states where people find their livelihoods threatened by global forces. These activities will manifest as heightened nationalism, increased racism and political activism. This will increase the physical security role of the state.

8 The @ of war

'The way we make war reflects the way we make wealth.' This opening to Alvin and Heidi Toffler's *War and Anti-War* (1993: 3) shows something of the inter-relationship between economic identity and security identity – between the economic state and the security state. It is no accident that Sun Tzu's *The Art of War* (1994) is being marketed as a business planning tool, and terms like 'strategic management' are entering the discourse of business. Wherever there have been economic differentials, there have been conflicts. In the information age, the modalities of conflict are deconstructing the distinction between military and civilian in the face of widespread opening of trade boundaries.

This chapter raises the issue of shifting boundaries, showing how the conduct of war is developing a new environment in which military operations will take place. One of the chief distinctions is that we are likely to see the conduct of economic warfare in which the civil/military distinction will virtually disappear. This chapter looks at some characteristics of information warfare, examines the modalities of the conduct of information warfare and discusses some potential targets of information warfare. My aim here is not to rehash urban myths about banks being held to ransom by enterprising hackers, but rather to examine information warfare as a mode of identity warfare, and its attendant implications for states.

In the beginning

To do so, we need to look back at the emergence of the Internet itself. Paul Baran's (1962) RAND paper *On Distributed Communications* that outlined the concepts of packet-switching and non-hierarchical information distribution is predicated upon another shift in the warfare spectrum into the possibility of 'total war' through the use of nuclear weapons. Baran's paper opens with the words:

> Let us consider the synthesis of a communication network which will allow several hundred major communications stations to talk with one another after an enemy attack.
>
> (Baran 1962)

and later:

> We will soon be living in an era in which we cannot guarantee survivability
> of any single point.
>
> (Baran 1962)

He was right. But what he did not foresee in that paper was the impact of an
adversary gaining access to that network. Survivability through redundancy is
anathema to security and protection, as those who are trying to apply censorship
mechanisms to the Internet would avow.

However, in a later RAND paper (*Security, Secrecy and Tamper-free
Considerations*) Baran (1965) discusses precisely this issue, suggesting that
the existence of 'spies' within the supposedly secure system must be anticipated,
and suggests that protection is best obtained by raising the 'price' of obtaining
information beyond the desire to obtain that information. For Baran the issue is
one of risk management, in the recognition that risk avoidance is both unrealistic and
uneconomic.

Indeed this gets to the heart of the dilemma facing a developed world becoming
ever more dependent upon distributed information systems for the conduct
of military and economic affairs. It also gets to the heart of much of the debate
among the civilian population over privacy, censorship and encryption, which will
be covered in Chapters 9–11 in this book.

In this chapter, most of what follows can be reduced to the interplay and tensions
between open distributed networks such as the Internet, and its implications for
security, the economy and national defence.

I include the economy in the implications, because what applies at the level of the
state also applies in equal measure at the level of corporate business. In fact when
it comes to the will to act, the economy is more likely to become the focus of
information operations through the warring, not of states, but of rival businesses.
Moreover, it takes a great deal more to overcome the tendency to peace at the level
of the state than at the level of large businesses. But as we shall see, as boundaries
become ever more blurred, the distinction between peace and war in the
information age lies increasingly in the discourse formation in which it is carried out.

War as a communicative act

The nineteenth-century strategist Carl von Clausewitz (1987) noted that war is
'a continuation of policy by other means'. In other words, war is one aspect among
many of the ways in which nation-states conduct their 'inter-national' relations.
War is thus a form of communicative act, albeit with terrible consequences for
those involved, whether civilian or military.

Perhaps more than any other, the Cold War was first and foremost an
information warfare (IW). It was about the use of discursive tokens in the form
of nuclear weapons, in which actual use would have meant at least total loss for
whoever initiated the attack, and quite possibly the end of human habitation on the

planet. The Cold War was therefore about using the *threat* of nuclear weapons to influence the policies of the adversary. In this sense, the Cold War was possibly the first postmodern war. It was a war of signs. It was played out through force dispositions, through words and through significant looks, in the form of surveillance satellites, as well as through wars by proxy in developing countries far from the threat of nuclear force.

The Cold War meant a decisive inversion of the Clausewitzian formulation to one closer to the idea of policy being a continuation of conflict by other means. Although all wars are to a greater or lesser extent 'identity wars', the Cold War was the first really to enact itself consciously as an identity war – the west against what former US President Ronald Reagan termed the 'evil empire'.

The 1990 Gulf War perhaps decisively came to represent the identity war, through being seen as a televisual event first and foremost, and a military event only in a highly sanitised form through the mediation of the news media. It was a war that focused perhaps more than any other on gaining decisive control of the information space, or 'infosphere' as some have chosen to call it.

War as simulacra

Like Brunelleschi's cathedral, however, it was a lot more than that. It was a war of 'just-in-time' integrated logistics support. It was also a war of new networked technologies, and it was a war that taught a lot of people about the importance of information. So perhaps above all, it was a war of management practices. Taken together it came to mark the beginning of the so-called revolution in military affairs (RMA).

Information management so dominated western coverage of the Gulf War that French philosopher Jean Baudrillard was prompted to suggest that there were two separate wars taking place – the actual military conflict in which people died, were scarred, and lost homes, and the one the west saw on their TV screens. The latter he described as a 'simulation' of war in which the mediation was so complete as to have lost its connection with what was going on in the 'real' world. The title, *The Gulf War Did Not Take Place* (1995), under which Baudrillard's papers were collected, led many to miss his key point: that the west, outside of the immediate participants, did not 'experience' the Gulf War, rather they experienced something that emerged more like an interactive computer game.

Following the experience of the Vietnam War, the Gulf War was played out on two fronts: one as a military campaign in the Arabian Gulf, the other was played out at home, designed to disarm potential protest within the western states involved. Thus seen as a practice of boundary making between states, war can be seen to operate at the liminal space between states, constructing the boundary from both sides. Little wonder then, that those who saw active service found difficulty adjusting back to civilian life back home. Two realities had been enacted, the one bloody and real, the other sanitised and virtual.

The Gulf War was also a war between wired and unwired states. Despite the rhetoric of Saddam's army being the world's fourth largest, it was fighting with obsolete equipment and strongly hierarchical command structures that meant in a sense that it was waging a very different kind of warfare from that of the US and Coalition forces. So in terms of technology, the Gulf War was an asymmetric conflict.

As we shall see, IW lends itself particularly well to asymmetric conflict, but in future conflicts the asymmetries potentially could flow the other way. The developed world, and the US in particular, has become heavily dependent on its high technology systems. This in itself could lead to vulnerabilities at the hands of low-technology societies waging low-technology conflict, but perhaps also possessing niche weapons that could cause a disproportionate amount of damage to a technology-encumbered force.

Targeting civil information systems

That the US was vulnerable to pressure from home in the event that it faced heavy casualties would not be lost on anyone who observed the Gulf Conflict through CNN (Cable News Network). Consequently, in future conflicts, we may possibly see less robust civil systems being brought into the conflict, targeting the domestic polity, and perhaps even niche targeting through the dissemination of negative propaganda, and possibly through targeting of the economic system of the developed west.

Already, software glitches have resulted in cascade failures in telecommunications networks and power grids in the US. With routine diagnostic maintenance being increasingly conducted by remotely located engineers via the Internet, it is not beyond the bounds of possibility that the system could prove vulnerable to deliberate attempts to introduce hostile software. One example of such systems is the Supervisory Control and Data Acquisition (SCADA) system used world-wide on oil and gas pipelines, water treatment and other energy distribution infrastructure. These systems are designed to be remotely accessed to monitor and control flow rates, temperatures, pressures and critical components across large distributed systems along thousands of kilometres of pipeline (see Morgan 1997; Cobb 1997). According to the US General Accounting Office (1996), 'some operations would now be crippled if the supporting technology failed'.

An archaeology of information warfare

Rather than attempt to define information warfare – it is in many ways all things to all people – it is perhaps more realistic to take what Foucault calls an 'archaeological' approach. That is to say that rather than try to come up with a consensus definition, it is perhaps more useful to characterise the various phenomena of information warfare, or in a more localised way to speak of information operations, and to classify information operations in terms of the methods by which they hope to achieve their ends.

It is here that a semiotic approach might become fruitful. At the risk of sounding programmatic, there are a number of steps that become useful in this context. It is useful to ask ourselves what is it that distinguishes IW from other forms of warfare? What is the nature of the transformations that have led from a growing use of computers in systems to a revolution in military affairs. At some point there must have been sufficient changes brought about by these transformations to the extent that a new formation has emerged.

To examine a term such as information warfare, we must examine three criteria.

1 Criteria of formation: by this, I refer to criteria that bring together those aspects that define an event as IW – the rules by which we characterise something as information warfare, rather than as something else; the rules by which we define an operation as information warfare; the concepts of IW, and the rules governing the options of IW.
2 Criteria of transformation: these mark the limits to the definition of information warfare. They include all operations sufficient to take IW into a new level. At what point does IW become something else again? At what threshold can we say that a new kind of warfare has emerged?
3 Criteria of relation: what are the sets of relations within which IW sits? Is it purely military? How can we know? How does IW operate in relation to other kinds of military operations?

It is only by this means that we can separate out information warfare from other kinds of operations and establish an identity from the Deleuzian 'flow' of existence.

Assuming we can establish that IW is a new kind of warfare we need to examine what impact this decisive step will have on established forms of conflict, in order to determine the extent to which this new form of warfare requires a reworking of strategy and defence philosophy. These include

- the role and place of tradition
- habits of thought
- conventional means of warfare
- command structures.

By doing so, we must then establish the characteristics of the transformation that constitutes this change or shift into the 'revolution in military affairs'. These changes include changes in

- technology
- embeddedness of technology
- culture
- application of technology
- objectives
  — strategic
  — operational
  — tactical

- political objectives
- administrative structures
- command structures.

Any or all of which would serve to indicate those changes that will significantly affect the definition/characteristics of IW, its conceptual basis, or its theoretical options.

Next are those features at the strategic or supra-strategic level which would affect the nature of information warfare as a distinct form, and hence the nature and conduct of warfare at large. These include:

- displacement of boundaries: the traditional *milieux* of warfare
- the new position and role occupied by the participants: new roles emerging as a result of the deconstruction of hierarchical structures of national armed forces, the collapse of the military/civilian division and so on
- new modes of functioning: targeting the perceptions circulating within the decision environment of the commanders, rather than the commanders themselves
- new forms of localisation and circulation of what conflict means within particular communities: the so-called 'clash of civilisations' aspect.

Analysis done in this way will provide content to the otherwise empty term 'information warfare'. It will also provide the basis on which to construct a set of methodologies for analysing the changing nature of IW by locating the sites of practice and the modalities of its operation. It can potentially become a means for identifying the changing nature of the way we perceive change itself in this environment. By examining the field of possibilities and the types of transformation it becomes possible to at least understand something of the extent and reality of the changes that are occurring as I write.

Moreover, it is important to show that IW is not a static object; indeed the nature of warfare itself is not static, but with the rapidity of technological change it is important to focus on the realities of change, rather than being caught up in the mythology of 1980s hacker culture, as depicted in, for example, early issues of *Wired* magazine.

In addition it is important to analyse the play of dependencies between these various modalities of transformation. Broadly speaking, these can be broken down into:

- intra-institutional dependencies, such as the relation between dependent technologies – machine and software compatibilities – and operations and operational concepts of information warfare, and interoperability between the services within the armed forces
- inter-institutional dependencies, such as those between government, armed forces, business, and academic institutions
- extra-institutional dependencies, such as between warfare and transnational

economics, social movements, the nature of legitimacy (legal basis for the conduct of war), cultural formations – media, environment, and the capabilities of potential adversaries, and so on.

What we end up with in such an analysis, as Foucault suggests, is not a string of causalities but an 'interweaving of correlations'. History, as Foucault suggests, is the 'descriptive analysis and the theory of these transformations' (Foucault in Burchell *et al.* 1991: 58–59).

While it would be possible to write several books and still barely scratch the surface of this kind and detail of analysis, some broad themes are being touched on very lightly in the currently available open literature.

Aside from the all-but-useless definitions that hold IW to be anything to do with information, it is possible to characterise information warfare in terms of sites of operation. For this reason, 'information operations' is probably a more appropriate term.

Information operations in a more narrow definition refers to the targeting of computer-based distributed networks by a national-level adversary. That being the case, it is possible to exclude traditional electronic warfare (EW) except insofar as it targets the systems that distribute information from remote sensors to the decision makers. Of course, information systems need to be seen as part of the larger military system within which it is embedded.

As US Air Force Lt-Gen. Kenneth Minihan, director of the US National Security Agency (NSA), has pointed out: 'the traditional functions of operations, intelligence, and communications will be integrated into a seamless and simultaneous process' (Minihan 1997: 20).

In addition, information operations is much broader than traditional forms of command and control warfare (C^2W), insofar as information operations can target civilian infrastructure, becoming a national-level problem, rather than a purely military problem. Therein lies the rub, because just as globalisation has deconstructed much of the domestic/international distinction at the level of the economy, so too globalisation of information infrastructures is blurring a number of crucial boundaries that the traditional conduct of conflict was able to recognise.

So one of the first characteristics of IW is that many boundaries considered to hold for traditional forms of warfare no longer apply. These boundaries include those between state and non-state actors, because essentially, any system that is connected to the global network could potentially be targeted by any knowledgeable user with a computer and a modem.

This leads to another blurred boundary, and one that poses perhaps one of the greatest difficulties for nation-states, and that is the boundary between warfare, criminal activity and plain old-fashioned system failure. Many of the technologies being brought into use are expected to operate across a wide range of platforms – types of computer and types of network, to the extent that different operating systems sharing a network can sometimes have unintended consequences. These can range from system crashes to non-specific random errors. So there is an issue of threshold to be addressed in terms of protective security and military defence. The latter may be good at responding to definite signals, but the small inconsistencies that plague large systems make it difficult to tell when a decisive boundary has been crossed to be able to initiate a large-scale and well-resourced response.

While the lone hacker may cause some nuisance value to open military systems, there is considerable debate over the extent to which state actors are deliberately gearing up for offensive information operations using the techniques of hackers.

Information operations that include the integration of sensor-to-weapon chain can be viewed, as Admiral William Owens, vice-chairman of the US Joint Chiefs of Staff suggests, as a 'system of systems', providing 'information dominance' over the battle space (Nye and Owens 1996: 24). Such a system involves a multi-layered approach that more closely reflects the notion of a revolution in military affairs, than information warfare itself.

Nevertheless, as Libicki points out,

> a relatively low cost system of systems can be cobbled together using third-party satellite imagery, Unmanned Aerial Vehicles (UAVs), digital cameras, cellular communications and detailed terrain imagery on CD-ROMs. With it, less-than-rich countries can make US assets visible and hence put them at greater risk in, or even near, theatres of conflict.
>
> (Libicki 1996: 265)

Such clearing of the 'fog of war' can go a long way towards getting inside the adversary's decision cycle. But the point to be made here is that information operations can be relatively cheap, and hence available, if only by hire, to small countries fighting asymmetric warfare.

Space/time in warfare

The role of geography in warfare is changing with information operations. As Libicki (1996) notes, there is no front line, since targets can include support systems thousands of kilometres from the site of actual fire. Gray (1996: 274) rightly points out that geography will never be irrelevant in conflict, because sooner or later, conflict between states will be fought on actual territory with real guns killing real people. But information operations can provide a significant force multiplier.

In addition, traditional ideas of 'warning time' can be expected to be significantly eroded. Information operations can be conducted without warning, and without visible signs of preparation taking place. It could get to the point where a country has little inkling of attack until the power grid, the stock exchange, the banking system and air traffic control systems abruptly go off-line.

Such a scenario is currently far fetched, but has led some defence planners, including former US Secretary of State Warren Christopher, to speak of the potential for an electronic 'Pearl Harbor' (see Lever 1996). The difficulty with this scenario is that countries do not enter into conflict with each other without some reason, usually long-standing. So if a country were planning to enter live combat, there would be warning signs from other quarters in terms of stockpiling of war stocks, heightened military activity and other signs of conventional military build-up. This would be coupled with an escalation of diplomatic activity designed to seek a peaceful solution to the object of conflict.

So while information operations of themselves could be conducted without warning, the underlying reasons for the conflict would be visible for some time before the first hint of an attack.

Another characteristic of information operations is that they are designed to attack the decision support environment of the adversary. Hence they are first and foremost targeted at the adversary's perceptions. It is easy in the debate about information warfare and the revolution in military affairs to forget that conflicts are essentially about and between people.

On the initiating side information operations is about targeting the adversary's perception of the battle space in ways designed to slow down the adversary's decision-making processes, while at the same time trying to provide for itself the clearest most trusted picture of the adversary.

The analogy is frequently used of two people playing chess, where one sees the whole board, including the adversary's pieces, while the other can see only his or her own pieces. Moreover the adversary only sees when his or her own pieces are lost or captured, while the first sees exactly where all the pieces are on the board.

This is only part of the picture, because in addition to this, an adversary may find the national infrastructure targeted as well as their military forces. But the main characteristics are worth restating for clarity.

1   Information warfare can be cheap.
2   There may be zero warning time for any attack.
3   Information warfare blurs boundaries:
    — between war and peace
    — between state and non-state actors
    — between crime and day-to-day system failures
    — between domestic actors (criminals) and international actors (war fighters)
4   Information warfare has no clear front line:
    — the systems that are targeted can be anywhere in the country
    — the systems can be military systems, such as those involved in logistic support
    — the systems can be civilian systems, such as banking, telecommunications or the domestic power grid.
5   Information warfare targets perceptions, and hence the decision-making environment of a country's leaders.

At the network level, which can be at the strategic, operational or tactical levels of operations, computer networks may be vulnerable to a greater or lesser extent to broadly three types of weapons:

- physical weapons
- semantic weapons
- syntactic weapons.

By physical weapons, I am referring to a range of weapons designed to cause physical damage to critical nodes of a network. Such weapons include conventional high explosives, radio frequency weapons (jammers and the like), high-powered microwaves (conventional electro-magnetic pulse weapons) and directed energy weapons, such as lasers and so on.

Semantic weapons include all weapons that attack the quality of the information provided by the system. The aim is less to disable the system as to make it seem as though it were operating normally, but providing degraded or false information to the adversary. It can include various types of computer virus, exploitation of 'back doors' or trusted gateways into systems, the insertion of misinformation, including providing false images into televisual forms through techniques used in films like *Jurassic Park* or *Forrest Gump* in which new visual information is blended into existing data to provide a misleading image. It can also include providing information overload through burying the normally useful data in a sea of irrelevant information, or the provision of conflicting information through messages passed off as standard transmissions. The object here is to cloud the decision loop of the adversary to a point where the adversary loses trust in the system, abandoning what may have been a system that is otherwise perfectly functional.

Syntactic weapons are designed to attack the logical functioning of the adversary's systems. These can include a wide variety of computer viruses, the use of corrupt data or simply very large quantities of data resulting in denial of service from the system. Other forms of syntactic weapon can include selected data deletion, for example by using 'Web-crawler' technology such as is commonly used by Internet search engines, in order to target data files with specified key words, but deleting them, rather than merely cataloguing. Finally, there are switchable systems that on command may hand over control from the adversary to enable inputs from other sources. So there is quite a grab-bag of forms of information warfare.

I want to turn now to some of the bigger picture elements of the analytical methodology outlined earlier in this chapter. I stated earlier that in order to establish an identifiable discipline within the domain of warfare, we need to examine three criteria:

- criteria of formation
- criteria of transformation
- criteria of relation.

These can be broadly encompassed by the questions what constitutes it? What are its limits, and how is it related to other forms of warfare? Of course this is to a certain extent an oversimplification, as is any 'broad-brush' approach, but we are discussing dominant characteristics rather than close details at this point.

Criteria of formation

In the past, warfare has been characterised in terms of attrition versus manoeuvre warfare, depending on the manner in which it was conducted. Another form might be termed 'control warfare'. Arquilla (1994: 26) points out that attrition warfare aimed at exhausting opponents, wearing them down in the trenches. Wars from the Peloponnesian War to the First World War exemplify this form.

Manoeuvre warfare aimed at annihilation of opponents through greater mobility, through flanking manoeuvres, and concentration of firepower in what came to be known as *Blitzkrieg*, or literally 'lightning war'. This reached its zenith in the Second World War, and was dominated by combined arms manoeuvres, involving the coordination of different arms to provide multi-layered offensive strike capabilities. Examples of this kind can be found in Julius Caesar's campaigns, and in the mechanised campaigns of the Second World War. This form has since been reprised in the Korean War and the closing stages of the Gulf War. More recent examples include NATO's bombing of Kosovan television stations in April 1999 during the Balkans conflict and conversely the hacker attacks on NATO's website. While manoeuvre warfare often sought to sow confusion in the opponent by attacking communications, the object was simply denial of information.

Control warfare stems from dominance over the availability and use of information. While the Gulf War is often cited as the first information war, the techniques in conceptual terms can be said to hark back to the Mongol invasion of the Islamic empire of Khwarizm in the thirteenth century. As Arquilla and Ronfeldt note:

> The key to Mongol success was their absolute dominance of battlefield information . . . their 'arrow riders' kept field commanders, often separated by hundreds of miles, in daily communication. Even the Great Khan, sometimes thousands of miles away, was aware of developments in the field within days of their occurrence.
>
> (Arquilla and Ronfeldt 1993)

The technological advantage possessed by the Mongols consisted of their stocky but fast Mongolian horses. But it took an organisational leap to provide the shift in doctrine on Genghis Khan's behalf to turn the technology into a capability – a system of communication.

In the case of present-day information technology (IT), a number of separate technological developments, coupled with economic drivers, had to come together before electronic networking could became a strategic advantage. The so-called 'revolution in military affairs' (Nye and Owens 1996: 23) is the culmination of a wide range of technologies and, more importantly, of ways of using the technologies.

In many ways, the real RMA is a revolution in management affairs – how the battle space is managed. Here again, we see the military domain being influenced by the methodologies of wealth creation. Just as business and religious organisation gave rise to hierarchical command and control systems, so too are we seeing the military domain influenced by new internetworked matrix structures of organisation.

Information has always been important to the conduct of conflict, but today's information systems have compressed the informational time-frame, or decision loop to a point where information dominance can make a decisive difference at every level of operations. This is the crucial distinction that leads us to consider that a new discipline within the conduct of conflict has emerged. But at what point do we consider information operations to be treated as part of a separate discipline within warfare – what determines the threshold? For this we need to look at criteria of transformation.

Criteria of transformation

Information operations enter into a realm of their own when the information system itself is seen as decisive in the conduct of operations. In past conflicts, individual technologies may or may not have proved decisive. But the development of arms technologies, such as cross-bows, trebuchets, tanks, aircraft, capital ships, and ballistic and cruise missiles each contributed individually to combat dominance in one or another arena. But they did so principally as individual elements. So what has changed with the so-called revolution in military affairs? The answer lies with the systems approach that has come to pervade all aspects of contemporary advanced warfare. We have had structures, such as hierarchical command and control, and individual weapons, or combinations of weapons and platforms, and we have had functional role-driven approaches to warfare, such as combined arms divisions, or mechanised infantry, or maritime surface warfare. But a systems approach provides a means of bringing together both frameworks into a common understanding.

I have spoken of a revolution in management affairs, and it is this systemic total-picture approach that marks the decisive movement into information-based warfare. Perhaps the Gulf War gave us the pattern for a completely systems-oriented approach to warfare. Libicki (1995: 27) notes that Col. John A. Warden III, of the Air Staff Plans Directorate, developed a schema for describing an adversary in systemic terms. Warden's schema described an adversary as a 'system with five components'. These were rank ordered in importance as follows:

- leadership
- material essentials
- infrastructure
- the people
- the military.

Libicki (1995) notes that for Warden, 'the five components of state systems remain constant across particular types, and have a rank ordered importance.' In such a system, 'vertical and lateral links abound. Such a system affords a variety of nodes, allowing for cross-communication should major connections suffer disruption.' Thus warfare has moved decisively away from targeting just individual components within the system. Rather we can anticipate that information operations will focus on the linkages between them. That being the case, we can see that national information infrastructures quickly become a primary focus for such operations. As Libicki (1995: 29) elaborates: 'The ability to analyse opponents in systemic terms, identifying their key centres of gravity and vulnerabilities is a necessary condition for the successful achievement and exercise of information dominance.' This leads to the blurring of boundaries that I have mentioned earlier in this chapter, and will elaborate on when discussing the specific objectives of information warfare.

Criteria of relation

To expect that information operations alone will conclude the conflict is of course absurd. Wars are and will continue to be fought using people with guns in various forms and with the people closer to or further from their guns depending on the type of conflict involved. Because wars are in essence very noisy and bloody ways of communicating forcefully between states, such 'communication' will not be without loss of life. But to think of utopian ideas of information warfare cleanly and surgically targeting systems so that the adversary is defeated without blows being struck ignores the fact that people are an integral part of the systems involved. Gray (1996) rightly points out that

> human beings and their lethal instruments operate on land, at sea, in the air and in space. Cyberspace is a valuable, even invaluable overlay in each of those four geographical environments. But cyberspace does not transcend, transform, or neutralise the significance of those environments.
>
> (Gray 1996: 276)

At best then, information operations offers a 'force-multiplier' for otherwise conventional forms of warfare. It looks set to become an integral part of the overall war-fighting capability of a nation-state. Just as the means of waging conflict are integrally linked in with the civil and military support systems that make them possible, so information operations will become part and parcel of the conduct of military affairs.

I have alluded to the emergence of information operations as a decisively new form of warfare insofar as the conduct of warfare itself is in the process of undergoing a revolutionary degree of integration with the civil and other networks that support it. I want now to turn to the degree of impact this revolution in military affairs is having on the forms and structures of military organisation.

Tradition and change

The role and place of tradition is changing, and with it is changing the culture of military life. There are a couple of aspects to this. As with the civilian world, and especially within corporate culture, there is a move towards what Toffler (1981) describes as 'third wave' culture. New corporate formations are emerging. As the corporate world sees advantages in adaptability through concentrating its resources on maintaining a primary mission focus, and outsourcing all non-core business, so too, the military culture of the developed world is learning to focus its resources on the 'sharp end' of its core business – national defence – while at the same time enmeshing itself within the national civil infrastructure through defence/industry cooperation. Defence structures are changing to meet the challenges of cultural change by reducing their internal administrative support, and non-core areas of defence, such as catering and general services – building management, power supply, maintenance and other services.

In turn, the defence infrastructure is becoming more networked, not only within its own *milieux*, but also within the culture it defends. As a result, there are new synergies emerging between defence and civil infrastructure. With increased networked systems, command and control arrangements are being transformed, so that chain-of-command hierarchies are moving to more matrix-like structures. In times of conflict, the speed and quantity of information flow between war-fighter and strategic planner are being greatly increased, resulting in new kinds of team arrangement within otherwise 'second-wave' hierarchical structures. This allows for greater oversight at the highest levels leading to a greater understanding at command level of the battlefield picture, significantly enhancing the management of complex operations.

Old habits of thought are coming under increasing pressure, as linear print practices are transformed with electronic information distribution systems. Such transformations are critical to the postmodern armed forces. Arguably such changes are as critical as the shift away from cavalry structures in the First World War when horse cavalry was pitched against the new technology of tanks.

As Arquilla and Ronfeldt note:

> Advanced information and communications systems, properly applied can improve the efficiency of many kinds of activities. But improved efficiency is not the only, or even the best, possible effect. The new technology is also having a transforming effect, for it disrupts old ways of thinking and operating, provides capabilities to do things differently, and suggests how some things may be done better if done differently.
>
> (Arquilla and Ronfeldt 1993)

They go on to suggest that in addition to efficiencies, which may be considered first-order effects of new technology, there are also flow-on effects right through wider society. The outcome is that it is now 'possible to think of people, as well as databases and processors as resources on a network' (ibid.).

Organisationally, if the corporate world is any indication there will be a movement from hierarchical institutional structures to multi-organisational networks. This team approach, it is suggested, will result in often small organisations or parts of institutions linking together to act jointly, breaking down the single armed services cultures. Both the US 'Bottom-Up Review' and the Australian 'Defence Efficiency Review' seem set to institutionalise new forms of joint cooperation between the armed services, resulting potentially in single joint training, for example for basic training, or for academic courses, such as electrical engineering or catering trades, where these new organisations serve the armed services, but not in ways that significantly differentiate between these services. For this to work, it will require considerable cultural change within the services, who have built up long traditions of single-service operations.

Changing face of power

The characteristics of this revolution of military and of management affairs are wide ranging. On the technology side, there are moves towards a seamless sensor-to-weapon integration; logistics systems are becoming fully integrated along just-in-time principles (Hazlett 1995), radically reducing the economic costs of conducting operations through lack of wastage, or over-commitment of supplies, and intelligence systems are being integrated from the strategic to the tactical level. As Arquilla and Ronfeldt suggest:

> This form of warfare may involve diverse technologies, notably for C3I, for intelligence collection, processing and distribution, for tactical communications, positioning, identification-friend-or-foe (IFF), and for 'smart' weapons systems, to give but a few examples. It may also involve electronically blinding, jamming, deceiving, overloading, and intruding into an adversary's information and communication circuits.

(Arquilla and Ronfeldt 1993)

In essence, as societies become more networked, the nature of power itself is changing. We are moving from the culturally masculine power of penetration, to culturally feminine forms of relational power. These include the power of observation – the gaze – which quite literally finds its expression in the power of gossip to control. In all the discussion about sensor dominance, the power that is implied is the power of exposure.

Technologies of verification are about signalling the power of observation, and exposing violations of agreements in the international community in ways that undermine the sense of trust, or reputation, held by the errant state. It is a form of gazing over the back fence and making observations to the international community about the behaviour of this or that state. Such power has proved effective throughout the postmodern era since the beginning of the Cold War.

Transforming the boundary between civil and military

There are implications in all of this for the strategic and supra-strategic levels in which the nature of postmodern society, of which the RMA (in both senses) is merely one set of symptoms, is transforming the civil/military boundaries within nation-states.

The integration of civil and military systems is leading to a displacement of boundaries not only in terms of the *milieux* of warfare, but also in terms of kinds and scale of operations. With military bases increasingly dependent on civil power supply, civil banking and civil telecommunications. In the US alone, the Department of Defense (DoD) has a vast information infrastructure to protect, including over 2.1 million computers, 10,000 LANs, 100 long-distance networks, 200 command centres and 16 central computer processing facilities. In addition to the 2 million DoD computer users, there are estimated to be an addition 2 million non-DoD users that do regular business with the US Department of Defense (US General Accounting Office 1996). The boundaries between civil and military will continue to become increasingly blurred.

In addition, as new forms of networked organisation enter military structures and institutions, new roles will emerge for niche services, including consultancies, training, facilitating and organisation of strategic corporate planning, economic and financial services, strategic industries and so on. In short we can expect to see civil and military sectors becoming increasingly enmeshed or networked with each becoming stakeholders in the common future security of the nation-state. This will be coupled with information security being increasingly seen as a national problem, such that the corporate sector can benefit from niche advisory services provided by those best able to supply advice on information security.

In addition there are different definitions of conflict and security within different communities. Such definitions have expanded to include economic, environmental and social security. In this way states will continue to provide essential functions that are often ignored by proponents of economic globalisation. States are more than their economies. Because states contribute fundamental aspects of individual identity, they will always exist in some form of large-scale community to provide identity security for individual people.

RMA and simulation

At this point it is worth saying a few things about simulation. One aspect of the RMA is the development of new technologies of simulation, which are moving towards completely immersive interactive virtual reality environments. This has a number of applications, and a number of implications, both at the practical and philosophical levels.

At the practical level, simulation technologies can enable realistic training to take place in otherwise 'safe' environments. Such training can range from basic flight training to complete interactive combat simulations, in all three environments. Flight controllers can now be trained to guide aircraft in a range of situations in which a number of variables can be controlled to provide a full range of practice experiences. In addition submarine and mechanised land warfare can be conducted in virtual environments. Perhaps coming closer to breaking down the real/virtual division, combat operations can now be rehearsed, as happened in the Gulf War, using computer-generated three-dimensional terrain maps of actual geographical locations. To complete the cycle, increasingly, the sensor environment on modern fighter aircraft can present a virtual representation of sensor data, providing a 'look and shoot' capability in combat situations, where the target is not in physical line of sight, but exists as a representation of perhaps remotely located sensor data. Plans and research and development are well advanced towards fighter aircraft designed to be remotely piloted by a ground-based pilot who is supplied with a full simulation of the flight experience. Such aircraft could potentially manoeuvre far more quickly without fear of the pilot blacking out from high 'G'-forces during tight turns. Moreover, such aircraft could be used in areas where high-level air defence systems might make for a high-risk mission. Pilots cost millions of dollars to train, and it takes considerable time to train one – as it does to train a skilled tank crew or naval ship crew. So it makes increasingly good sense to keep such valuable human assets some distance from the immediate war zone.

Another use for simulation technologies is in the design of new equipment, such as aircraft, ships, submarines or tanks. Not only is it possible to see from drawings how everything will fit in the completed item, but also those who will get to use it can feel how much room there is, become familiar with the vessel or aircraft, train for operations, or practise maintenance skills – even before the first unit of type of the ship or aircraft is built. In a sense, then, we are seeing the potential for virtual crews to train on virtual ships or planes or tanks, in the defence of virtual states. Moreover they can do so thousands of miles away from where the actual item may be constructed or used.

Philosophical considerations

There are philosophical implications in this. States, as I have suggested earlier, are above all large-scale identity structures that exist as part of the identity of individuals – they are collective identities that are produced as by-products of their boundary-making practices. For as long as that remains the case then the use and means of waging conflict will remain a central part of a nation-state's constitutive activity, because conflict is central to defending or asserting boundaries (when boundaries mean far more than mere geographical boundaries). We must not forget, too, that in this complex world the use and means of boundary maintenance will also be carried out at the corporate level, through system security, encryption protocols, 'fire-walls' and so on.

Nation-states will remain an aspect of the knowledge economy for a long time to come. Their modalities of operation will adapt and change as people articulate their identities differently according to historically contingent factors. The complexities involved entail an examination of a range of boundary-making practices, from the fluidity of the boundary between the economic and the political sphere to gender and body/machine issues raised by theorists of the place of the body in broader structures identified by the term 'cyborg'.

Strange (1994) rightly alludes to the intimate relationship between the political and economic realms in noting that:

> markets for different sorts of things, being the creation of decisions and institutions that vary from sector to sector and from time to time, will not easily conform to an analysis that excludes political power and interest.
>
> (Strange 1994: 36)

Moreover, such political power and interest is, and largely remains within an essentially masculine discourse. Haraway (1991) suggests that this may be changing. As the security state joins the economic state in becoming less hierarchical and more of an integrated organism of networks, it seems appropriate to suggest that the terms of the debate have changed. As the state itself takes on more of the character of the cyborg it becomes fair to say that many of the old order, 'second-wave' discourses of power are giving way to systemic approaches that strategically integrate a range of historical Others.

Women and power

It is no accident that with the rise of the networked society, the role of women in power is also changing, albeit with a long way to go before anything resembling a demographic balance is achieved. As a community, the developed west is taking some early tentative steps in adapting to a broad cultural change that is emerging as a result of the widespread growth of both the technologies of and increasingly the culture of networks.

Haraway (1991) prefers:

> a network ideological image, suggesting the profusion of spaces and identities and the permeability of boundaries in the personal body and in the body politic. 'Networking' is both a feminist practice and a multinational corporate strategy – weaving is for oppositional cyborgs.
>
> (Haraway 1991: 170)

We are in fact seeing a deconstruction of the distinctions between the individual and the global, the domestic and the international, the strategic and the economic, the masculine and the feminine. But let us not fall into the easy trap of assuming that deconstruction means destruction. In postmodern philosophical writing, the word translates into something much closer to 'reconstrue'. Nothing in fact is taken away through deconstruction. Rather we should understand the term as rearticulation. This is where many writers fall for the notion that states are set to disappear. On the contrary, for all the reasons given earlier in this work, states will be around for a long time. But their modalities will change. New forms of social and political organisation will supplement the state – but not supplant it.

Local and global

We are seeing an increase in complexity, while at the same time we are developing the social and technical means to cope with that complexity, as expressed in terms like 'working smarter, not harder' developing flexible systems of networks that can adapt to change in new ways. Moreover we are seeing the rise in importance of local groups acting at a global level, coupled with the rise in the international community of transnational NGOs, such as the International Society of the Red Cross and Red Crescent becoming active participants in the international debate over the issue of the widespread use of anti-personnel landmines. Such organisations will not replace nation-states, but they will continue to contribute to the debate as active participants alongside nation-states in the international community. Similar voices are heard in the debates within the WTO over the issue of intellectual property rights, and in the ITU in setting the standards and protocols that enable global networks to develop and talk to each other.

But states will continue to articulate the political spaces of their constituent populations. Moreover there will continue to be conflicts between states, and in regional terms these conflicts may escalate into open warfare as new forms of Otherness are construed between the information haves and the information have-nots. In addition, the have/have-not divide will cut across the international plane in a number of complex ways through the whole range of social formations – class, gender, socio-economic status, race and religion.

When these conflicts come together at the national level, states will rely on gaining informational dominance of the battle space over the adversary, while seeking to protect their own information space. Small states engaged in asymmetric warfare could find relatively low-cost forms of information operations to be a useful and effective force multiplier. This is in an age when the developed west is becoming ever more dependent on its information infrastructure, and ever more vulnerable as it finds a need to spread its nodes or points of entry across a wide range of remote sites.

A developed nation engaged in open conflict with a small less-wired state could find its own economic system targeted, its banking system, its stock exchanges, its telecommunications and power grid systems, its logistic support networks being systematically targeted from almost any point on earth. Such activities could result in swaying the hearts and minds of the domestic polity of the developed west toward the conclusion that big states may find the cost of small wars far greater than they had bargained for.

The most difficult time ahead for developed states may well lie in the twilight zone of conflict short of war. Acts of economic terrorism may be hard to tell from random criminal activity or from simple system failure. How to respond both in time to meet these challenges before major damage is done, and determine who to target for a response will become increasingly difficult.

As the international system becomes more complex, new informational Others will emerge, making the issue of protective security for systems an increasingly important one both for nation-states and for any organisational structure that depends on grids and networks for its economic and physical security. Identity integrity is the prize at stake for any and all communities.

Part IV will discuss issues of boundary making between Self and Other at the level of individual, society and state, for the relationship between the individual and the state lies at the heart of the future of networked society.

Summary

- The growing interrelationship between economic and security identity means that the distinction between civil and military is becoming more blurred in the information age.

- The 1990 Gulf War, often seen as the epitome of information warfare, was as much a war of integrated logistics support as it was about information dominance.

- The multiplicity of definitions surrounding IW makes it more useful to examine the nature of operations that characterise information warfare.

- A framework for characterising IW should examine what sets it apart from other forms of warfare, what marks its limits, and how it relates to other forms of warfare. What emerges is thus an analysis of those practices that define IW, that mark out its conceptual basis and that provide the ground within which it can be said to operate.

- The next step is to identify where IW sits within the armed services and where it forms connections between the separate service arms. In addition, there are dependencies between government, armed forces and the domestic polity. Finally there are dependencies between the role of warfare and transnational economics, social institutions and cultural formations.

- What we observe is that a number of boundaries no longer apply, including between state and non-state actors; between warfare and criminal activity; and between criminal activity and random system failures.

- The role of geography is changing, but not becoming irrelevant.

- While some argue that IW will have no warning times, the same cannot be said for the conflicts within which IW will be embedded. Conflicts are essentially conflicts between people.

- Information warfare is one aspect of a broader 'revolution in military affairs', but it is not synonymous with it. The RMA is the culmination not only of a range of technologies, but also of ways of using technologies.

- Information has always been important to the conduct of conflict, but today's information systems have compressed the informational time-frame or decision loop to a point where information dominance can make a decisive difference at every level of operations.

- What sets IW apart is its focus on systems, rather than on individual elements or functions. It is characterised by a systemic, total-picture approach to information dominance, and as a result is as much about the management of information as about the technologies of distribution.

- Warfare has moved beyond targeting individual components in favour of targeting the links between them. It is prosecuted alongside other forms of conflict and as such will not be more than a force-multiplier, rather than a distinct mode of waging conflict.

- Developments in the corporate sphere have crossed over into all functions of state, bringing with it new synergies between defence and civil infrastructure. The integration of civil and military systems is also leading to a displacement of boundaries not only in terms of the *milieux* of warfare but also in terms of the kinds and scale of operations.

- As new forms of networked organisation enter military structures and institutions, new roles will emerge for niche services, further enmeshing civil and military sectors as stakeholders in the common future security of the nation-state.

- While states may change form, their linkage with fundamental aspects of individual identity will ensure that there will always be some form of large-scale community to provide identity security for individuals.

- Simulation technologies will allow faster design-to-operations cycles on new equipment as technicians and operators can begin training and procedures development before the initial equipment has been built.

- Such technologies can also present data from remote sensors to permit 'look-and-shoot' capabilities for the war-fighter, even where the target is not in physical line of sight. This immersion of the war-fighter in their data-stream will further integrate the human operator with the system.

- We are seeing a rearticulation of the relations between the individual and the global, the domestic and the international, the strategic and the economic and the masculine and the feminine. This is what is meant by the deconstruction of the state. But states will continue to articulate the political spaces of their constituent populations, as new forms of Otherness emerge between the information haves and have-nots.

Part IV
Internet and society

9   Virtually real/really virtual

Authenticity is arguably the central question of the 1990s. It is a curious question, and one that reveals much about the anxieties being felt within and across societies around the developed world. Authentication has become a catch-cry for any form of business transaction on the Internet, and this is extended to any form of exchange across the Net – including social conversation and other forms of relationship.

How do we know that the person who wrote this or that piece of writing was really that person and not an impostor? If Elvis Aron Presley were to turn up on a chat room (Internet relay chat or IRC) somewhere, how many would believe that it was the famous musician from Tennessee? Surely all our other media (electronic and paper) have combined to assert that Elvis died in 1977. And what about his death certificate – a piece of paper signed by a doctor to affirm the date and time of his death.

Such a certificate can be issued only by one who is *author*-ised to do so. Someone who, by virtue of participation in certain discourses of legitimation, has the legal sanction to have their word trusted, even (or perhaps especially) when written on a standard form, on behalf of the 'appropriate' authorities. Such an event is referred to by the linguistic philosopher J. L. Austin (1975: 6) as a performative speech act. This is what is invoked when people in a marriage ceremony declare 'I will' before the celebrant declares that a marriage has taken place. The same explains why laws under the Westminster system are referred to as 'Acts' of Parliament.

So not only is it the fact of something being written down, but also there are discourses of legitimation to be invoked in the 'proper' way in order to have a description or narrative established as authentic. In paper formats those procedures have been around for a long time in the west. But it was not always so. Long before electronic computers mediated communication, other virtual realities were similarly distrusted.

Sometime between 411 and 404 BC, Plato wrote a dialogue in the *Phaedrus* outlining what is presented as Socrates' deep distrust of another information technology – writing. It is perhaps ironic that we know of Socrates' distrust of writing only through Plato's writings. Are we then to distrust the distrust by virtue of their being mediated through the pen of Plato?

Plato writing as Socrates would have us think so. He considers information technology (in his case writing) to lead to several consequences:

- Those who acquire it will not exercise their memories and become forgetful.
- It is a resource for cataloguing, not for understanding.
- People will be falsely led to believe they are knowledgable when they are actually ignorant, and this will make them a burden to society.
- Education by this means will be shallow – a student asked the meaning of something will be unable to do more than repeat the same thing over and over again.
- Information will be distributed equally to those that need it and to those who have no business with it.
- There will not be the capability to distinguish between suitable and unsuitable readers.
- There will be no way to verify the accuracy of what has been written or the truth of its authorship.
- At best its value will lie as a diversion for use by people in a holiday mood.
- It will be only a faint shadow of real speech with real people and so it should not be allowed to take the place of real interactions.

According to this argument, people will become shallow, have short attention spans, be unable to create anything original and will wind up as a burden to society. Unauthorised people, even children, will have access to the wrong information, perhaps pornography, and those who spend their lives immersed in it will not have real interactions with real people. Versions of this argument have been brought out with the introduction of every new information technology, from printing presses to radio, telephone and television, and now the Internet. The arguments are not new. Nor are they any more sophisticated than when they were raised over two thousand years ago.

Essentially, Plato raises five concerns:

- Education will suffer because it presents information rather than promoting thought.
- Information security will be compromised.
- Authorship will be difficult to authenticate.
- It will be nothing more than a shallow distraction, devoid of serious purpose.
- People will stop interacting with real people.

Indeed much of what has been written, both for and against the Internet, has done little more than address a range of these concerns. And it is over these issues that boundaries have been drawn between Internet advocates and those who see the Net as a danger to society and western civilisation as we know it.

Much of the debate hinges on the final point of those listed above: it should not be allowed to take the place of real interactions. Real as opposed to what? When we pick up a telephone, are we not talking to another person? Aside, that is, from voice-mail or recorded information systems; but even in these systems, we are at some point dealing with another human being. Even voice-mail was put together so that people can find the right person to speak to – at least when the system works properly. But when we speak to our friends on the phone, despite the technological mediation that turns our voice into bits of data, transmits them through a range of wired and wireless devices, and finally reconverts our data bits into sound in ways that approximate the human voice that initiated the sound – despite all of that mediation, we consider ourselves to be speaking to the other person.

If I have a job interview over the telephone, it is no more a virtual interview than a 'real' interview. Despite clear differences in modes of presentation – I might wear jeans to a telephone interview and a suit to a 'real' one – the performative speech act is the same. I may or may not get the job, but I am engaged in the right speech act.

So what about the reality of virtual communities? We have seen throughout much of this book so far arguments pointing to the virtuality of real communities, such as states. What we are dealing with here is a philosophical question concerning the nature/culture divide, with implications for the reality of virtual communities, and for the social construction of identity.

In response to those who assert that nature is becoming over technologised, Allucquere Rosanne Stone (in Benedikt 1991: 101) notes that this is a false dichotomy, which assumes that two separate categories exist: '"nature" which is "over here" and a category "technology" . . . which is "over there"'. She points out that François Dagonet argues that the category 'nature' has not existed 'since the first humans deliberately planted gardens'. Moreover, Stone argues:

> nature . . . has become nothing more (or less) than an ordering factor . . . a *strategy* for maintaining boundaries for political and economic ends, and thus a way of making meaning.
>
> (Stone in Benedikt 1991: 102, original emphasis)

This boundary extends significantly into the academic divide between the humanities and the 'masculine', 'hard' sciences (Lykke and Braidotti 1996: 13ff). Scientific discourses thrive on binary dichotomies and have problems with transgressive artefacts that refuse easy categorisation as one or Other of culture versus nature. Perhaps this goes some way to explain the difficulties some people have with the idea of the Internet being without centralised authority – anarchic in the classical sense. Moreover, some, such as Hélène Cixous (see Moi 1985: 104; see also 'La Jeune Née' [The Newly Born Woman] in Sellers 1994: 37–38), suggest that such a mode of binary thought is inherently patriarchal wherein each pair of a binary can be analysed as a hierarchy, such that those characteristics identified as culturally 'feminine' can be read as the negative, or powerless characteristics.

Indeed the Internet has been seen and is widely regarded still as a 'boys' playground'. This seems ironic given the essentially non-hierarchical structure of the Internet itself. Moreover, Internet communities based on email discussion lists are structurally inclusive in terms of conversational turn-taking. Where such discussion lists can act as exclusively masculine domains is in language use and content. The lack of bandwidth means that statements intended to be read ironically, often present as simply cruel or aggressive, or both. It is for this reason that experienced Internet users take some care, engaging in the use of 'netiquette' – politeness forms that either moderate the abruptness of statements, or that provide diacritics in the form of 'emoticons' or 'smileys' constructed from ASCII punctuation, such as colons, hyphens and parentheses : -). Moreover, computers, from the early days of military use and masculine-dominated big business, have come from a masculine culture. But that is changing as computers become more graphically based and user-friendly, and as more women gain more access to online networks.

The list of forms of Internet-based online communities described with the epithet 'virtual' is getting longer by the day – 'virtual communities', 'virtual banks', 'virtual sex', 'virtual shopping malls', and so on can easily blind us to the reality of these communities.

While the 'space' within which such communication occurs is 'virtual', the communities that operate within them are nonetheless real. The 'space' is the space within which telephone conversations take place – the notional space between one telephone receiver and another, separated by wires and all the other technological mediations that make such conversations transparent to the participants. What differs, perhaps, is the addition of a visual component in the form of what is presented on each participant's computer screen.

The visual metaphor, developed out of text-based file transfer protocols and into the hypertext-based WWW, arrived in 1993 with the work of Tim Berners-Lee of CERN (the European Council for Nuclear Research), who designed the hyperlinks, and Marc Andreesen, who designed Mosaic and later Netscape software. The result was graphical representation of information on screen giving a presence to what novelist William Gibson (1984) termed 'cyberspace'.

Within this space, many kinds of 'virtual' community have arisen. The word 'virtual' is in inverted commas to indicate that the communities are real, but the space in which they take place is virtual.

Among the more widely discussed forms of online community are MUDs and MOOs. These are online 'spaces' where people are represented by textual descriptions; the latter include textual descriptions of objects that can be manipulated by the online participants or avatars.

Turkle (1996: 178ff) notes that these avatars are able to express in concrete terms an important aspect of individual identity formation. Drawing on Lacanian psychoanalytic theory, Turkle sees these multiple avatars as external represen-tations of the multiple identities which collectively form the individual.

I want to suggest that this is where the relationship between individuals and states as identity structures intersect in important ways, each as multiplicities of discursive elements. In this sense I want to extend Turkle's work on individual identity on the Net to encompass a range of identity structures from individuals to nation-states. To do so, I seek to combine elements of Lacan's theory of individual identity with elements of Foucault's 'author function' to arrive at a theory of networked identity that can be seen to operate at all levels of discourse, from individuals to states. Such a theory is crucial to an understanding of the fluid nature of identity. In addition it provides a means of understanding the complexity of interactions between what is taking place on the Internet at the level of the individual and what this means for the nation-state.

Two processes combine to allow/cause the individual to enter the social world. The first is via what Lacan (1982: 1–7 esp. p. 4) terms the 'mirror stage'. In the mirror stage individual children see themselves as Other, exterior to the child who does the seeing. This necessitates a division between the 'I' that is seen and the 'I' that does the seeing. The outcome is that children note a gap between themselves and the world around them. It is in the desire to overcome or bridge this gap that the child enters the symbolic order through language.

The second process is through language which necessitates a division between the 'I' of discourse (that is the socially construed idea of what the term 'I' means) and the 'I' who speaks.

So individuals enter the social world through language. In the process individuals establish and maintain their identity. At the same time, the individual is positioned by the social contexts in which language is used. The society in which the individual is embedded produces the forms in which social relations can be enacted. The individual thus represents a social formation within the symbolic order.

Individuals speak their identity across a range of discursive situations. Among these are situations that require the individual to speak for or in the place of other individuals. Examples of this include the family as a site of intervention for a range of practices concerned with health, economic viability, social conformity, within legal discourses and so on, extending up to larger formations such as organisations, firms or nation-states. Moreover as individuals we articulate a range of personae or identity structures such as spouse, parent, lecturer, lover, shopper, Internet wizard, author and so on.

Thus insofar as the individual represents and is represented by and within a range of discourses, the individual cannot be said to be unitary, continuous or cohesive. It follows then, that the individual may be construed as such only insofar as he or she enacts a specific regime of boundaries, establishing and maintaining the identity of self in opposition to the anarchic exterior.

For Turkle (1996) the use of multiple identities in cyberspace merely extends the range of selves available, thus making the individual in a sense more complete, and more comfortable insofar as it is possible to 'try out' or model a range of points of view. In short, the notion of individuals being unitary is itself an illusion. The self of language and of the symbolic order at large is always 'virtual' – a simulation. Thus moves into other modes of mediation are metonymic rather than metaphoric – an extension, rather than a different order of existence. This is why postmodernists prefer the term 'alterity' rather than difference, that is, an interplay among a matrix of alternatives, rather than the more hierarchical binary dichotomies that characterised modernist thought.

For me the reality of cyber-community was brought home in my participation in what began as an academic forum and turned into a community. Cybermind, a forum for discussion of the philosophy and psychology of cyberspace, began with a series of exchanges of a more or less formal academic nature. Like all email lists, this one spent some time on pedantic aspects, such as spelling, and, from the nature of the topic, some time discussing whether or not it was possible to have online communities.

Then, about three weeks after the list began, one of the co-moderators, Michael Current, died from diabetes complications. The list was notified by a short message. There was a flurry of messages asking if this was some kind of hoax in poor taste, then a message from the other co-moderator, Alan Sondheim, stating flatly that Michael Current's parents had been telephoned and they had confirmed the news. Quite abruptly the list went quiet, from around a hundred messages per day to about two or three.

Then one by one, the participants began asking about the sense of grief they were feeling for someone they had never 'met'. Was the grief merely 'virtual'? Clearly there were shared emotions throughout the participants, each reacting in their own way. I felt the same sense of loss and sadness. Others would receive messages from Michael Current after his death due to their being held up on a server somewhere, which caused some to feel disoriented. As the list discussed their reactions, the tone of the messages changed, and it became apparent that with the sharing of feelings there was also a growing sense of shared community. It is a sense that continues today, and that makes Cybermind one of the longer lasting email lists, having now survived for around four years (at time of writing). The list has found a dynamic balance between 'academic' discussion and off-topic expressions of feelings, including poetry, the changing seasons, relationships and births.

I suspect that Cybermind is a relatively rare case, with its own historical reasons for developing in the way that it has, but it is by no means unique. What is interesting is that, having met in physical life some of the participants in and from various countries including the US, the UK, India, Kazakhstan and Australia, I have found the meetings to be remarkable more for the sense of meeting an old friend than for meeting a stranger.

It seems that despite the low bandwidth of text there is a sense of shared authenticity which runs counter to reports of more casual encounters on Internet relay chat or in MOO spaces. Perhaps that is more of a characteristic of longer-term associations than of brief encounters. But then the same holds for physical life too.

Sherry Turkle provides perhaps one of the best descriptions of the reality of virtual life, regardless of the medium in which it is played out:

> the idea that you are constituted by and through language is not an abstract idea if you're confronted with the necessity of creating a character in a MUD. You just do it. Your words are your deeds, your words are your body. And you feel these word-deeds quite viscerally.

(Turkle in Brockman 1997: 307)

The implications for nation-states are important. Now more than ever before people can form online communities based on common interests, and be closer to each other across a number of countries (in Cybermind's case some forty countries) than to people living in the same city or the same street. Should we consider this to be a threat to states or should it be celebrated as a life-affirming enhancement to the diversity and sense of community within nation-states? As we shall see, different states have different views on how to respond to this. Some respond to calls for censorship and restrictions on use, while others take a more *laissez-faire* approach.

Another of Plato's concerns is that education will suffer as a result of overdependence on information technology. For him it was a question of memory. People will lose their memory because they come to depend on being able to look up something. So information technology will provide databases – 'receipts' for information. These concerns are still being raised by sceptics of the information super-highway.

David Gelertner has concerns that computers make it too easy for us to do certain things:

> Schools have been lousy for two decades, teachers have been unwilling to teach what students don't like to learn, and basic skills have been suffering. With computers you can say 'don't worry about the basic stuff, because a spellchecker can check your spelling and a grammar checker can check your grammar, a drawing program can make your pictures come out right, and a smart database program can do your research.' We wind up with uneducated morons.
>
> (Gelertner in Brockman 1997: 110)

This is almost word for word what Plato said that writing would do to us. He is not a lone voice in the wilderness. Howard Rheingold notes:

> Just as we can suggest that glasses or contact lenses might one day become the integrated prosthesis of a species whose gaze has gone, so can we fear that artificial intelligence and its technical aids will become the prosthesis of a species whose thought will have disappeared.
>
> (Rheingold in Brockman 1997: 238)

This fear was brought home to many when IBM's Deep Blue computer played a grand master, Anatoly Kasparov, at a chess competition in 1995. Kasparov won convincingly, but in 1996 a more powerful version called Deeper Blue forced him to an overall draw, having won some and lost a couple. The media went into a frenzy over a contest that was portrayed, not as a mere chess match, but as a fundamental contest between human and machine. What was left out of the debate was that the contest was actually between a team of very human programmers and engineers, and a chess grand master, mediated by a machine. But Frankenstein myths of cyborg monsters make for powerful images in the popular media.

Clifford Stoll sees the Internet as largely content-less, noting the distinction between information and data:

> Unlike information, data has no content, it has no context, it has little utility, it lacks accuracy, it lacks pedigree [!], and it lacks timeliness. Most of all it lacks usefulness.
>
> (Stoll in Brockman 1997: 280)

I imagine Plato would agree if he were to see schools using books today, but I wonder if the Internet might actually provide the interactivity he craved from the spoken word? When my daughter began dialling out to the Internet rather than reaching for an encyclopedia, I became particularly interested in how she would make use of what she found. It was an assignment on 'Space', and she had decided to look at the Apollo 13 mission, having then recently seen the movie.

After using a search engine to narrow the field, she dialled into NASA, and with some clicking around, soon had the diaries written by the astronauts during the mission, following the day-to-day trials of a mission that went wrong. As an early high-school student she was doing primary research using archival material that would not have been available by other means, much less thought of. This is research normally done at university level. She wrote, as I recall, about people under stress in truly extraordinary surroundings. A human tale. What would she have obtained from an encyclopedia? At best a table listing the Apollo missions, perhaps the names of the astronauts. The Internet is shallow? Perhaps that remains an open question.

Yes, there are home pages for Barbie dolls and the Simpsons – it is a question of how we use the tool, rather than blaming the tool for the quantity of shallow content. The Internet is clearly not an end in itself, so the issue of education is one of how to produce more sophisticated readers of multimedia, rather than blind criticism that there are images as well as text. The business and government communities are going to need people able to work comfortably in intranet environments – indeed facility with the Internet is rapidly becoming a factor in employability in the US.

The Internet provides depth in two ways. First, it provides images as well as text, and is generally speaking within a more richly visual environment; and second, it provides the facility for hypertext linking. Critics want to liken hyperlinking to channel surfing on TV, but there is a difference. Hyperlinking allows readers to construct their own narrative sequence to the information they want to retrieve. Readers are engaged in an active process, constantly making choices about whether to go down this or that pathway.

Textual documents can be enriched with links to their source material or explanatory notes, or related material. Moreover, and perhaps of greatest importance, is the way hypertext breaks down the linearity and hierarchical structure of linear writing. The web is closer to what Cixous called *écriture féminine* (feminine inscription) than segregated and bound volumes of print.

There are important implications for this in the way people develop their very thought processes. We are long past the time when mythical 'renaissance persons' could hold all the world's knowledge in their mind – it was probably a myth long before the Renaissance. Perhaps today learning needs to focus on how to access the data one needs in life, and how to read it with a critical eye. These are the human aspects of education, and are perhaps the most neglected by those who want to focus solely on spelling and grammar. The world today is a complex world of change. Information is being put out of date before it reaches print, let alone before it has languished in a school library for twenty years. So even in schools there will be a significant social and educational division between those who receive an active education using online tools in a critical and multifaceted environment, and those who receive a narrow, linear and hierarchical education – who will be best equipped for a changing world? Clearly then, there will be information haves and have-nots within the developed world, in ways that matter critically to the continued development of those countries.

Plato was concerned that information technology would be a shallow experience. This is an interesting, if somewhat curious thing to say. It presumes first and foremost that there is a thing called 'depth' and that such 'depth' is important. Depth as opposed to what?

Clifford Stoll, author of *Silicon Snake Oil* (1996), suggests that the Net is like channel surfing on a TV set. Everything is presented in bite-sized chunks, and people can click aimlessly from page to page passing time while waiting for the next page to download. For David Gelertner, the Internet is a 'fad' (Brockman 1997: 106). He sees the Net to be in its prehistory phase, before people find out what to do with it. Like most articulate people, they are both right. To a point. But they have both missed the main point, which is that we no longer live in a hierarchical world of levels. We live in a world of surfaces. Moreover we live in a world of surfaces that produce identities at the intersection points between one surface and another. The Net is an excellent metaphor for this process, which was identified in the 1960s by the likes of Roland Barthes, Hélène Cixous, Michel Foucault, Julia Kristeva and Jacques Lacan (see Rice and Waugh 1991: 109–281).

What is becoming important is the interplay between the surfaces of our culture. We speak of identity as multifaceted, lending strength to novelist Neal Stephenson's (1995) metaphor of the 'diamond age'. An age in which identity is constantly shifting, playing one form of light off against another, and existing in that interplay. If that is the case, the nostalgia for core values, for a core identity or an Aristotelian universal on which we could hang our identity and preach one way of life over others on the assumption that it somehow had access to the real reality, is nothing more than an exercise in self-delusion, a facade of depth. But this is something quite different from the so-called nihilism of the postmodern condition. It does not indicate an absence of ethics, far from it. For if individuals are identified by and through their signifying practices – their language, their actions – and if these actions are meaningful only insofar as they identify boundaries between Self and Other, then individuals, as a philosophical imperative, must take responsibility for their own actions. Indeed individuals must take responsibility for their own being, their very identity as a member of this or that community.

So ethics re-enters the debate insofar as each social community negotiates its own way of dealing with the world, its means of constructing Self as against the Other. Thus ethics can be seen as historically contingent. Moreover, since each social community comes up against all other communities with which it has to deal, then these ethics can be considered permanently under siege – essentially contested. Such ethics are perhaps even stronger than those produced in an historical era when ethics were considered to be 'god-given', because such an ethical system allowed the individuals to evade or sidestep responsibility for their own actions.

From this, it is possible to see governance in cyberspace coming to resemble the governance that takes place within international law, rather than that of a national model. In the international sphere there is no overarching policing mechanism. The International Court of Justice operates only when both parties agree to be bound by its jurisdiction. For this reason, the international community is seen as essentially anarchic. It is anarchic to the extent to which potential disputes or disagreements have to be negotiated towards a solution, rather than settled by blind appeal to a higher authority, for in the international community, all nations are considered equal for the purposes of law. The same holds for the Internet, since what can be said or done may be legal in one country but illegal in another.

This causes considerable angst for those who wish to see the Internet controlled or regulated in terms of the content that can be posted to the Internet for the world to see and download. There are also questions of how governance might be conducted between members of an online community. This can be illustrated by what has come to be known as the 'rape in cyberspace' episode. It has been written about at some length by Julian Dibbell in Dery (1994: 236–261). The scenario took place in a multi-user domain known as Lambda MOO (an object-oriented MUD). At the risk of repeating widely circulating versions of this tale, I shall outline the events briefly to illustrate the point.

Essentially, the person operating one character, or avatar, managed to gain sufficient programming access on the system to be able to take control over other avatars operated by other people. What he then did was to make these other avatars engage in unwanted sexual activity with other avatars. This was taken to be a form of cyber-rape which caused a great deal of real emotional pain and sense of violation on the part of the owners of these avatars. The US legal system (in which jurisdiction the event took place) was not structured in ways that would enable recognition of the crime in the discourse of physical life. At best some recompense might be sought through libel laws or perhaps violation of intellectual property rights. Instead, the matter was discussed widely on Lambda MOO, and a resolution was sought within the online community. The community, after considerable discussion, voted to delete the character – a sort of virtual death sentence in the form of banishment. Despite his later reappearance, having obtained a new Internet account and a new character description, the new character was considerably more subdued than the virtual rapist and, perhaps more importantly, the online community had developed a system of consensual governance. They had developed, to a more sophisticated level, their boundaries between Self and Other through defining what would or would not constitute acceptable behaviour within that community.

Moreover, they developed technological tools for personal self-defence through an '@boot' command which would summarily remove a character that was causing offence. But despite this, cyberspace is not an egalitarian place, for all its myth-making pretensions to the contrary. MOO-spaces are hierarchical; many of them are run and operated by committees who wield considerably more power than they could in 'real' life. As 'wizards' they hold programming power to amend or delete any character or object created in the virtual space. Moreover, there are levels of technical access ranging from 'look and talk' access of guests, through to the ability to build objects in the virtual domain, and finally to full programming access reserved for the all-powerful wizards.

The level of interactivity suggests that something more profound than channel-flicking is going on. Clearly the participants are not 'passive consumers', but rather active participants within a two-way communicative process.

Plato was concerned about information security in much the same way as the developed world has become concerned about securing young users of the Internet from exposure to adult material – generally regarded as material with an explicitly sexual content. Plato's concerns were that people would have access to information that should not be distributed to them, or that material would be read by unsuitable readers. He was concerned that the information technology (of writing) could not distinguish between suitable and unsuitable readers. Although I shall go into this in more detail in Chapter 10, it is worth touching on a couple of points.

The Internet reflects wider society. Just as there is pornographic material available from news-stands, there is pornographic material available via the Internet. Unlike news-stands, you have to look for pornographic material on the Internet. It has to be a deliberate act – I have been surfing the Internet since just before the introduction of graphical browsers, and have never accidentally stumbled across pornography from clicking around sites of interest. The material that is online consists at best of low-resolution images – worse than newsprint – and the extreme material, by which I mean that which depicts violent or bestial sex or sex with minors, seems to be well locked behind paid subscription services. How many minors these days have a credit card account? The adult sites I have seen all have 'front doors' warning accidental tourists of adult content. So the chances of children accidentally blundering into such sites seems in fact smaller than a child accidentally wandering into an adults-only night-club or sex shop. But I do not hear the same calls for minors to be restricted in their access to city streets in physical life. In the vast majority of cases, minors accessing the Internet do so through their parents' accounts, and it seems to me that this is where responsibility needs to be directed. There is software, such as 'Netnanny', 'Cybernanny' and others, freely available and readily downloaded from the Internet which will actively block access to the more extreme sites, and in most countries, there are existing laws to cover the production and distribution of adult-rated material.

Plato is also concerned that there will be no way to verify the accuracy of what has been written or the truth of its authorship. This has implications, both in terms of the quality of information available online, and for commerce via the Internet. Business works on trust, but as former US President Ronald Reagan famously put it, we should 'trust but verify'.

Technologies are being developed to safeguard commerce on the Internet, but nothing is absolutely assured. Encryption standards are being developed to enable the secure transfer of funds and of credit card information via the Internet. But it is not yet to a point where it is entirely secure. But as noted earlier, what is important perhaps is risk management. The practical goal in secure commerce is perhaps better viewed in terms of raising the cost of cracking the system above the benefits to be reaped by the cracker. As we move above 150-character encryption keys we enter the realm of very expensive computing power if the system is to be cracked – especially if it is to be done so in sufficient time to make use of the information. If it takes a criminal three months to crack an encryption key, but the key itself is changed every week, the system can be reasonably considered to be secure.

Indeed the bulk of information security is based on human procedural security – this is in fact where most systems fall down if they do at all. Hackers do have access to so-called sniffer programs to try to pick up passwords or unencrypted credit card numbers, but even standard email used properly can offer a measure of protection. Email is sent in streams of packets of information. The system routes each packet according to millisecond variations in network traffic, so the chances of two sequential emails being sent to the same place by the same route are in fact fairly remote. One bookshop in the UK makes use of this by getting people to send half of their number in one email message, the other half in a subsequent message. Even with a sniffer program, a hacker would – if very lucky – get half of one credit card number. The chances of getting both halves would be considerably less than those of winning the lottery.

But encryption is serious business, and not just for the relatively small amounts of Internet commerce being conducted at present. The world's banking system sends vast sums of money daily around the world. Billions of US dollars worth of exchange value are transmitted electronically. Encryption at this level becomes a national-level issue, and many countries have a government authority, often vested in defence or prime ministerial portfolios, whose job is to set encryption standards and safeguards for the national information infrastructure.

Concerns over the widespread dissemination of information technology are by no means new. Indeed there are perennial issues that are raised with each new development, from writing, to the telegraph, to the telephone, to radio and television, and to the Internet. Many Renaissance engineers wrote down descriptions of their inventions in some form of code or cipher. Today we are still grappling with the same problems articulated through new technologies. Perhaps these are the issues that need to be raised in any form of communication from one human being to another.

Perhaps it is broader than that. Perhaps these fears are the fears we hold for our own sense of identity. Are we authentic to ourselves? How can we be sure? The enduring nature of these debates suggests that the fears expressed by Plato reflect real concerns within society for the stability and security of personal and social identity. These are concerns that strike at what it means to be human, what it means to be a part of society. The way these fears are addressed reflects the structure and underlying philosophical make-up of the communities concerned. As the developed world moves into a post-humanist, post-industrial age, society is forced to adjust to new ways of thinking about the Self and the nature of community. Perhaps more than any other visible sign system in the developed world, the Internet stands as a mirror to ourselves.

Summary

- In popular discourse, the Internet is often presented as a dangerous and anarchic space. At the heart of the arguments against the Internet lies the issue of authenticity.

- Plato listed a number of criticisms of a then emergent and politically important information technology – writing.

- Plato was concerned that education standards would suffer, that there would be insufficient information security, that authorship could not be verified, that it would be shallow, and that people would stop interacting with real people. These thoughts echo much of the current concerns expressed over the Internet.

- This chapter argues that virtual communities are real communities that exist in a virtual space. People are still talking to people, albeit mediated by computers. It is no different from people talking on the telephone, except that the technology interface is different.

- In addition, the real/virtual distinction breaks down because human discourse is already mediated through language and social conventions – we can no longer harken back nostalgically to a 'state of nature'.

- Turkle suggests that online communities reflect in concrete terms recent psychoanalytic approaches to subjectivity insofar as they concretise the notion of the subject as constituted by and through language.

- People can form a closer sense of community identification online than they often can with people across the street. Communities of interest formed in this way can present challenges to nation-states.

- The Internet can be used effectively in education, so long as the focus remains on educating the child to become a more effective reader of complex multimedia texts.

- Hypertext linking within Internet documents places the onus of responsibility on readers to produce the best narrative sequence for themselves.

- The surface/depth metaphor is no longer appropriate in a world where meaning is made in the interplay of surfaces.

- From this emerges an ethics of responsibility, which has political and personal consequences. In a postmodern world it has become crucial for each person to take responsibility for their own actions. In a world of surfaces, responsibility can no longer be abrogated to a 'universal' value system. This is not a nihilist denial, rather a recognition of each individual as an active participant in society, with responsibilities to all other members of that society.

- While the Internet continues to reflect wider society there will be distasteful elements. There is pornography on the Internet, as there is in cities. Consequently any controls applied in cyberspace must reflect those currently in force within wider society.

- Information security and authentication protocols are important issues for the Internet. Much information security depends on human procedural security. Encryption is about raising the cost of gaining unauthorised access to information above the benefits to be gained by such access. It is therefore about risk management.

- Concerns about the Internet reflect deeper concerns within society for the stability and security of personal and social identity.

10 Internet censorship
US, Europe and Australia

Plato, as we saw in Chapter 9, expressed concerns about writing. One of the fears he expressed concerned access by people who were not 'suitable' for the material presented:

> once a thing is committed to writing it circulates equally among those who understand the subject and those who have no business with it; a writing cannot distinguish between suitable and unsuitable readers. And if it is ill-treated or unfairly abused it always needs its parent to come to its rescue.
>
> (Plato 1973: 97)

It seems that we have always had concerns about who reads what, and whether or not they are 'suitable'. Interestingly, the same paternalistic remedies are proposed in the form of what everyone hopes will be benevolent censorship. What is left out in this formulation is the question of who authorises what is suitable or not suitable in terms of a readership. Who is best qualified to interpret or to speak for a community, and what happens when writing from a community in which a form of writing is deemed acceptable is transferred to a community space where it is not deemed acceptable. This, it seems to me, is the dilemma of the Internet.

We have on the one hand the legacy of Plato, who argued against the dangers of information technology in the form of writing, while on the other hand we have Bakhtin's (1981) *Carnival* of Internet culture, as expressed in *Mondo 2000* (Rucker *et al*. 1993), which proposes that:

- Information wants to be free
- Access should always be unlimited and total
- Always yield to the hands-on imperative
- Mistrust authority
- Do it yourself
- Fight the power
- Feed the noise back into the system
- Surf the edges

(Gareth Branwyn, in Rucker *et al*. 1993: 66)

Clearly there is a divergence of interests portrayed in these two philosophical positions.

In the course of this chapter I want to pull out some of the rhetorical strategies used in the Internet censorship debate, both by government, which carries the role of enshrining in legislation the mores of society, and by those who would find difficulty with overly simplistic and heavy-handed interpretations of what comprises that society. We can read a lot about a culture from what it tries to regulate. Here again, in the pornography debate we see an example of a culture building boundaries between what is 'acceptable' and what is not. A useful place to begin this exploration is with the US and its ill-fated attempts to introduce the Communications Decency Act (CDA). Its definitions and concerns speak volumes about a specific community's assumptions of how children develop. Moreover, there are significant aspects of the issue that are revealed in what is not said – the significant absences within the legislation.

In what follows, I shall explore the US experience, the European deliberations over Internet regulation, and the Australian experience in trying to enact regulatory legislation at state and federal levels.

The US experience

The debate in the US hinged on the question of regulating the Internet's ability to make pornographic material available to minors. Those opposed to regulation focused on arguments emphasising the US constitutional right to freedom of speech. At issue was how the Internet itself was to be defined – would it be in the broadcast media paradigm or in the telephone paradigm? That it had to be one or the other is itself interesting, for a new medium that had characteristics of both: it was in fact neither – but for the purposes of legislation it had to be defined in one or the other terms.

The CDA, approved in the US District Court in 1995, would have held Internet service providers responsible for material of a sexually explicit nature, including 'representations of sexual and excretory acts and organs' being 'made available' to people under 18 years of age – the age of majority in most states of the US. The controls extended to the use of 'any telecommunications facility' to 'transmit' verbal, visual or textual representations of such acts. This would make any person who used an expletive while talking on a mobile phone in a public place potentially open to prosecution, and also AIDS information lines, sexual counselling services, breast cancer support groups and so on. Arguments such as these helped to sway members of the Supreme Court when the Act was successfully appealed in the District Court in 1996, and again in the Supreme Court in 1997.

In the Supreme Court appeal against the overthrow of the CDA it was asserted that the District Court had created

> a previously nonexistent license to knowingly send indecent pornography directly to known children and to knowingly display it to minor children on computer networks . . . this ruling would force this nation's federal and state

legislatures to surrender their compelling interests in protecting children from pornography, in favour of the economic interests and ideological interests of computer pornography providers.

The appeal went on to assert the dangers of the Internet being in increasing numbers of family homes and especially outside of family homes where children would be beyond parental supervision – such as in schools and public libraries. The argument was fed with claims in the media about freely available pornographic material being available at the click of an electronic mouse. The normally respectable *Time Magazine* (Elmer-DeWitt 1994) made similar assertions at the time the CDA was being debated in the District Court, in an article on cyberporn that was later shown to be based on false information. While *Time Magazine* was duped by a purportedly serious study on pornography on the Internet, it nonetheless served to repeat and hence reinforce widespread myths about the Internet and sexually explicit content.

Certainly there is sexually explicit material on the Internet. But almost all of it is sequestered behind pages giving warning that material on succeeding pages may offend, and that admittance is only for those over 18 years of age. Then, barring some fairly tame magazine-style images at newsprint resolution, further access requires payment by credit card. So, even assuming that almost all minors accessing the Internet do so via their parents' accounts, and hence subject to parental supervision, or parental installation of gate-keeping software, it is an even more remote probability that those children will have their own credit cards against which to charge their further viewing. Equivalent material of considerably higher print quality can be found at most local news-stands.

That there is a market for such material among adolescent minors, and that legislators wish to restrict that information from their gaze probably says more about the legislators than about the minors or the 'pornographers'. Children are renowned for their curiosity. As adolescents become aware that their bodies are changing they become curious about sex and sexuality. But what of the legislators? Perhaps what is at stake is a popular Disney-like mythology of childhood innocence, and that maturity, articulated as sexuality, is a sign that these children will soon enough be leaving home and starting their own families. Is it after all about parental control – keeping children as children through ignorance? Laura Miller suggests:

> What's really at stake in the scare over kids and cyberporn isn't the forcible corruption of presexual minds with insidious electronic filth. It's the spectre of childhood sexual curiosity unfettered by parental controls ... rather than as a drive rising up in children themselves, the pull of impending maturity.
>
> (Miller 1995: 43)

Do legislators really think that these same children will not find other physical outlets for their investigations of their new-grown bodies?

Indeed ethical debates rage over the extent to which states should become involved in regulating the bodies of their citizens. Much of the debate, moreover, revolves around what Gatens (1996: 134) refers to as 'sexual imaginaries'. That is, viewing a group of people (notably women and children) through principally masculine patriarchal frameworks in ways that have political consequences. As Gatens notes:

> While each sex entertains its own 'imaginings' about the other sex, such imaginings have asymmetrical implications given the historical predominance of men as producers of public culture and theory.
>
> (Gatens 1996: 135)

Gatens, drawing on Spinoza's view that modes of knowing are also modes of being, suggests that

> if knowledge is a mode of being rather than having, then the failure of voluntarist politics . . . is inevitable. If our beliefs, opinions and imaginings are not 'possessions' of which we can take an inventory, then it is not surprising that we cannot discard them by an act of will.
>
> (Gatens 1996: 135)

Indeed these 'imaginings' about the nature of children, the nature of sexuality and about the 'nature' of the Internet, conspire to position legislatures throughout the masculine developed world in favour of regulation over domestic responsibility. Perhaps this is not too surprising considering that women have been similarly positioned under law throughout the history of the developed west. It is interesting, therefore, that in the end the argument for overthrowing the Communications Decency Act revolved, not around the affirmation of childhood sexuality, but rather around arguments over 'freedom of speech'. In other words the site of the discussion was moved to that of a more empowered masculine political discourse – that of constitutional law.

The CDA was declared unconstitutional under the US Constitution's First Amendment (1791), thereby 'rising above' all other arguments about the state's duty of care, or about the definition of 'decency'. There might have been an argument about the right of parents to exercise control over what their child sees on a computer, and the right of a child to experience the Internet in much the same way as a child would experience a city. But these were excluded from the framework of discussion. What was also excluded was the extent to which laws covering the dissemination of pornography already apply to print, broadcast and telephonic communications, and thus further regulation would in fact have been unnecessary. This begs the question of why a nation-state should therefore be interested in being technically able to restrict the dissemination of certain kinds of information, should it be deemed in the national interest to do so. I shall take up this question later in the chapter.

The European experience

In Europe, not only have individual countries sought to address the issue of Internet regulation, but also they have sought to address the issue at a multilateral level in a rage of forums, such as the OECD, the Council of Europe and the European Commission. At the February 1997 Ministerial Council Meeting of the OECD, Belgium put forward a proposal for multilateral cooperation against child pornography on the Internet, to be discussed in the Committee on Information, Computers and Communication Policy (ICCP). The proposal arose from a high profile case of an Internet-based paedophile ring brought to court in Belgium in 1996. The OECD echoed the importance of cooperative work between national law-enforcement officials in this area, as part of continuing efforts to improve multilateral cooperation on broader transnational law enforcement issues.

This is one of the first attempts to recognise the legal aspects of the transnational nature of the Internet. What is interesting is that, as with other multilateral efforts, these are based on increased cooperation between states, using their national law-enforcement mechanisms, rather than an attempt to set up a multilateral organisation. Again we see the continuing role of nation-states, rather than their erosion.

In recognition of the transnational nature of the Internet, the Belgian government called for the negotiation of a legally binding international convention on Internet content regulation. A number of issues emerge from this that have implications for policy makers around the world.

- Over-hasty regulation could have adverse consequences on emerging Internet industries. For example, if Internet service providers are made responsible for content, then they will have to monitor the content that passes through their servers. Not only would this be expensive and technically all but impossible, but it could in turn could reduce the security of commercial transactions conducted via the Internet, resulting in loss of confidence and loss of business.
- As with other areas, such as cryptography, intellectual property rights and international connection protocols, industry participants need to be involved in the process, to avoid the worst excesses of further problems being caused by proposed solutions.
- The Internet is not a legal vacuum. In the case of pornography, many countries already have existing legislation concerning the production, distribution and dissemination of pornographic material.
- Finally, the international community itself does not operate in a vacuum, so efforts conducted in one forum, such as the OECD will need to be coordinated with other multilateral efforts to ensure that contradictory agreements do not emerge.

There are a number of reasons for and against proposals for international conventions. On the positive side are issues such as coordinated regulatory mechanisms, perhaps accompanied by complementary domestic legislation. But against that are questions concerning the number of signatories to such a convention, the bureaucratic mechanisms that need to be established, both at national and international levels to administer the provisions of such a convention, and the costs associated with such mechanisms. If not all countries sign up to the convention, then the potential remains for regulation to be rendered ineffective by pornographers operating in countries that are not signatories. This is already the case with content providers outside of the US supplying material that the US is technically powerless to prevent. In addition, many countries lack sufficient Internet expertise in legislative circles to be able to construct viable legislation. For this reason, Australia, for example, only recently established national level legislation for Internet regulation, although some legislation has appeared at State level. As we shall see in the next section, it requires considerable coordination between state and federal legislatures to ensure fair, equitable and viable legislation.

One consequence of a country lacking sufficient Internet expertise in legislative circles has been shown in Germany over the CompuServe case. In this case the US Internet service provider CompuServe was prosecuted for 'allowing' pornographic material to pass through its servers – this despite the fact that, with the existing technology, CompuServe managers were unable to be selective in the passage of data on their network. Potentially, it is possible to use software filters to screen out documents containing particular key words, or Internet sites known to contain offensive material, but there are problems with that technique. In late 1995 Germany lodged a complaint against CompuServe. According to a German prosecutor, about 200 of the Internet's sex-related 'newsgroups' violated German law. Lacking the means to screen by country, CompuServe promptly blocked access worldwide to sites containing words such as 'breast', 'sex', 'intercourse' and so on – the usual suspects. The immediate effect was to deny worldwide access to breast cancer support groups, sexually transmitted diseases information services, family planning advice services, and gay and lesbian information services. It was two months before CompuServe could isolate Germany and reopen these sites to the rest of the world. CompuServe has subsequently refined its keyword filters so that these other, non-proscribed services have returned even in Germany.

Nonetheless a legal precedent was set with the conviction in May 1998 of former head of the German division of CompuServe, Felix Somm. In the process, the Munich District Court ignored a change of heart by the State Prosecutor, handing down a two-year suspended sentence. This was despite the prosecutors noting that under Germany's new multimedia law, Somm should not be liable for banned materials on the Internet. The district court at Bavaria, in which the case was heard, is the most conservative of Germany's state courts. The issue here is one where an Internet service provider is being held responsible for, in this case, pornographic material being passed through its servers. While key-word blocks went part of the way to solving the problem, pornographic sites merely developed codenames that were not picked up by the filters and continued business as usual.

As John Gilmore (1997), co-founder of the Electronic Frontier Foundation, put it in March 1994, 'The Internet treats censorship as damage and [finds] routes around it.'

As at January 1998, the European Commission plans to promote regional and global cooperation on the legal and technical problems caused by the Internet. The initiative, which was instigated by German Commissioner Martin Bangemann, argues that, with information increasingly circulating across borders, a new framework is needed to help governments and industry coordinate their approach to issues, such as technical standards, data privacy, licences, encryption and illegal material.

The European Commission (the EU's executive body based in Brussels) is developing policy advice for the EU telecommunications ministers. While industry is wary of proposals aimed at adding an extra layer of global regulation over the top of national legislation, there is a recognition that anything affecting telecommunications requires looking at global developments. To this end, the Global Internet Project, a consortium of companies representing about a dozen European, US and Japanese software and telecommunications companies has called on the Commission to call an international conference with strong industry involvement to discuss these issues through an industry-led, market-driven approach. The US, while not opposed to international 'understandings', would not like to see new formal regulatory or intergovernmental bodies formed, in addition to the OECD, the WTO and the ITU.

The Australian experience

In the Australian context I want to focus on two quite similar approaches, undertaken by State governments to the issue of Internet censorship – one successful, the other unsuccessful. These are the Western Australia (WA) Censorship Act 1996 and the draft New South Wales (NSW) Censorship Bill (rejected 1996). Rather than focusing on obscure legal arguments, I want rather to focus on how these two pieces of legislation construct the Internet user, and some assumptions made about the nature of the technologies involved. In the process, I want to tease out something of the way governments perceive themselves and their role in the community.

In Australia, the Internet censorship debate concerns issues of pornographic material being 'made available' to minors. For the purposes of the NSW draft Bill this would include:

- material that would be refused classification (RC)
- material that would be unsuitable for minors of any age, such as a film classified (X) or (R)
- a publication that would be classified 1 or 2 (i.e. including explicit sexual or sexually related material)
- material unsuitable for minors under 15, classified (MA+).

NSW State Attorney General, Mr Jeff Shaw QC, MLC, stated that the measures in the proposed legislation were designed to 'protect children and others from intentionally or accidentally accessing abhorrent and objectionable material'. 'Children and others': the children are defined in terms of those under 15, while the 'others' are not. Under the draft Bill these Others would be 'protected' from intentionally accessing material deemed abhorrent and objectionable, presumably by some form of board of censors. In addition, the draft Bill:

- covered material carried on all online services, such as the Internet, bulletin boards and email
- specifically targeted content providers, Internet service providers and users.

I shall return to these last two aspects later, but first let us consider who is being protected from what, and by whom.

Under Australian law, the protected users are construed as at least under 15 years of age. These are minors. Interestingly, however, the number of minors with their own Internet accounts is statistically minute. So these minors are presumably those accessing this material via their parents' or school's accounts. Indeed the number of schools in Australia with Internet accounts, let alone those which allow unfettered student access to such accounts, is equally minute at the present time. So it is safe to say that most under-15 year olds are accessing the Internet from parents' accounts in their own homes.

The censorship is therefore principally directed at adult accounts. Moreover, it could be interpreted to suggest that adults are not capable of taking responsibility for their children's actions – unlike the way parents have since time began. I am not passing judgement here over whether or not parents should be responsible for their children's activities, merely saying that the draft Bill assumes that they will not continue to act as responsible parents.

If legislators wished to target the end-user in terms of material downloaded onto the user's hard disk, there are problems too, insofar as the act of clicking on a link is sufficient to initiate the process of downloading the Web page, for example, for viewing. Without going into the difficulties of FTP files which need to be downloaded in their entirety to be read with an off-line program, there would remain the issue of so-called *cache* files. These are files created so that if a person browsing the Web wanted to return to a previously accessed page, it can be retrieved from a cache on the user's own hard disk. Let me clarify this. If someone had inadvertently downloaded some pornographic material in the course of browsing, that material would reside for some time on the user's hard disk in the Web browser's cache. The reason for this is that to conserve bandwidth – the amount of data actually sloshing through the telephone lines – many Web browsers, such as Netscape or Internet Explorer, actually save the pages you have visited in a work-space called a cache. These are accessed when you press the 'back' button so you do not have to wait for the whole page to download again. The browser keeps a catalogue of the pages in the cache by creating what is called a 'cache log' file.

Perhaps one way around the issue of users having illegal/objectionable material on their hard disk would be to eliminate the function of a Web browser which creates the cache files.

This would lead to a considerable increase in traffic load on an already stressed telecommunications system, because each return would result in a completely new download of the page. This can also be time consuming where pages use large graphics.

Then there is the vexed issue of so-called 'cookie' files. These are small text files created when users visit some Internet pages on the Web. They enable the manager of those pages to record how a user navigated the site. It also tells which sites the user went to, following a search using one of the popular search engines. The information can be passed to advertisers who can then build up a customer profile, in order to target advertising to individual Web users. The information contained in cookie files can benefit the user in providing, for example, tailored news feeds, or automatic identification, or maintain information on online shopping baskets while the user is browsing, for example, an online bookshop. The downside is that a certain amount of information is then publicly available, and can be passed on to sites which advertise on the pages the user has visited. Cookie files can contain information about the server the visitor came from, the type of machine and browser software used to view the site, and in some cases the user's email address. Privacy advocates have tried to introduce legislation to limit the passage of cookie traffic, but to date it is still up to users to decide whether or not to disallow cookies through their browser software.

Let me turn now to the material being censored. Under the proposed NSW draft Bill the material being censored would be that which attracts or would attract certain classifications by the Australian Office of the Board of Censors. There is a problem here, insofar as very few people actually know the criteria by which material is judged pornographic – indeed that is precisely why the board exists. The whole process of exchanging email, however, would slow down considerably if each packet of data, each piece of email, each net page (wherever produced in the world) and each online discussion group had to pass through the Board of Censors before being forwarded to the Internet users with the appropriate classification attached. This would be the online equivalent to the notorious 'Red Flag Act' 1904 which required car users in the UK to drive behind a person walking with a red flag in order to warn horse-drawn traffic that an automobile was approaching. Needless to say the Act did not last long, and the famous London to Brighton car rally each year commemorates the repeal of the Act in 1906.

The NSW draft Bill covered material carried on all online services – Internet, bulletin boards and email. Such a Bill would make it possible to repeat the German experience and potentially result in the conviction of Internet service providers over material the ISPs can not legally access. I shall return to this later, but the issue hinges on the definition applied to data – is it like a telephone conversation or is it like a television broadcast? The NSW draft Bill would treat private email in the same category as prime-time broadcast television. It would be the equivalent of having to provide an Office of the Board of Censors rating for every personal telephone conversation, or every conversation held in a cafe or on a street corner. Clearly in these 'physical life' examples there is a good deal of self-censorship, otherwise known as 'tact' that comes in to play, out of knowledge of the speech situation, and of one's 'reading' of the likely response from those immediately involved.

The Internet does reflect the broader community in almost every way. It can be useful to consider what would happen if a city were described in the same terms that are commonly used by the print and electronic media to describe the Internet. After all, if the proposed legislation reflects community values, then perhaps it should stand the test of being applied to 'real life'.

In March 1996, a NSW Member of Parliament (MP) renewed calls for controls on Internet access after a young boy mangled his hand on a home-made bomb assembled from information downloaded from the Net. The device was constructed from a soda siphon and a firework. The MP said that a home-made bomb guide called the *Terrorist's Handbook* was accessible to young children who could switch on to the Internet. There are two aspects to this that warrant further discussion. First, it is interesting that there were no calls to control the sale of soda siphons or fireworks. Second, the *Terrorist's Handbook* contains nothing that is not also available elsewhere in print. Moreover, for the really big bangs, you would need at least an upper high school understanding of chemistry and physics to be able to concoct an explosive from the recipes. Similar concerns were raised after the Tokyo sarin nerve gas incident in 1995 and in April 1999, when the two teenagers who carried out the Columbine High School shootings and bomb attacks in Denver, Colorado, had apparently constructed their 'pipe' bombs following instructions obtained on the Internet; their gang, the 'Trenchcoat Mafia', has its own Web page. Fifteen people died, including the two gunmen. But the information on sarin nerve gas is already in the public domain and can be found in most local public libraries in almost any first-year university textbook on biochemistry. If knowledge were the issue, then by logical extension perhaps a set of warnings should be issued to parents of any children likely to study, say, physics and chemistry, to the effect that by learning these subjects they too will be able to make bombs.

Clearly, there is some absurdity creeping into the legislative process, for if we really believed some of the more sensational media stories about the Internet, and then applied them to the wider society in which the Internet is situated both culturally and physically, then we could be forgiven for concluding that cities contain nothing but shops selling pornography, graffiti using obscene language, and libraries full of pornographic and bomb recipe books.

The NSW draft Bill also sought to fine or jail for twelve months people caught advertising pornographic material in the Internet. But hardly an evening goes by on radio or television without several advertisements for adult video and book shops in each Australian State capital city, or classified ads in the daily newspapers, which advertise pornographic material. So there is perhaps an issue of consistency to be raised in this context.

I would like to turn now to the issue of content providers and Internet service providers as targets of Internet censorship legislation within Australia.

Application of the proposed and actual laws to content providers can be done at best only on a national basis; indeed since we are basically discussing State legislation, the laws would actually be applicable only to content providers in whose State the legislation applies. But even if the Australian Commonwealth government should enact similar legislation there would be problems. With at least 95 per cent of Internet content providers being outside Australia, actual policing of the Internet in terms of content providers would present considerable difficulties in terms of jurisdiction. To a large extent this is the heart of the problem facing anyone trying to apply censorship to this part of the cycle.

The other aspect of this is that content providers are already subject to laws currently applicable in relation to publications, or, indeed, in relation to the use of telecommunications equipment, which is perhaps more to the point. The Internet is, after all, physically carried by telecommunications systems, rather than broadcast systems.

Finally I want to turn to the issue of censorship at the point of distribution – the Internet service provider.

Under the WA Censorship Act 1996 a computer service includes, *inter alia*, 'the transmission of computer data from one computer to another, and the transmission of computer data . . . from a computer to a terminal device'. Under the Act, a person can be charged with using a computer service to 'make restricted material available to a minor'. Thus ISPs could be held accountable on the basis of having made such material available. While the ISP may have recourse to the defence that such 'transmission' (to use the legal term) was done unknowingly, the onus would rest with the service providers to prove that they were unknowing in their distribution of such material, or that they had complied with a code of practice. With the Act in force since 1 November 1996, no such code of practice had been devised at the time of writing.

In Western Australia, the Censorship Act provides that police are not required to have a warrant to search the premises of Internet service providers, including all records, logs, private email and anything else on the service provider's system. This would seem inconsistent with the Commonwealth Telecommunications (Interception) Act 1979, which provides that only officers of State or Federal police forces with a warrant from the Attorney General, or officers of the Australian Security Intelligence Organisation (ASIO) holding a warrant issued by the Director General of Security under the provisions of the ASIO Act 1979, may intercept a communication carried by a telecommunications system. Such interception is defined in terms of listening to or recording by any means a communication passing over the telecommunications system without the knowledge of the person making that communication. And to be perfectly clear on this point, the Telecommunications (Interception) Act 1979 defines a communication as:

any conversation or message whether:

(a) in the form of:
    (i) speech, music or other sounds;

   (ii) data;
   (iii) text;
   (iv) visual images, whether or not animated; or
   (v) signals; or

(b)   in any other form or in any combination of forms.

Clearly e-mail falls into this category, as would anything carried by an Internet service provider.

Thus the WA Censorship Act 1996 would seem to be directly inconsistent with the Commonwealth Telecommunications (Interception) Act 1979. I have little doubt that such inconsistencies would lead to difficulties in enforcing any action arising from the WA Act. This Act is incompatible with the Commonwealth Act, and so would seem on the face of it unenforceable. The same cannot be said for the NSW draft Bill.

I have dwelt here for some little time on the provisions of the Commonwealth Telecommunications (Interception) Act, because it has particular bearing on the NSW draft Bill. It is worth keeping in mind that this legislation was put forward as a model designed so that legislation throughout Australia might follow this pattern. Under the provisions of the NSW draft Bill, ISPs could be held accountable for any material of an 'objectionable' nature that passes through their system. The relevant provision states:

> An online service provider must not permit objectionable material to be available for access or retrieval by users of the service.

One of the defences allowed to ISPs is that they have taken steps to assure themselves that objectionable material is not being passed through their system. This includes specifically:

> procedures (such as random checks of material available through the online service) conducted by the on-line service provider to monitor material being transmitted or that may be accessed on the on-line system.

This goes beyond the WA legislation insofar as it specifically requires online service providers to break a Commonwealth law in order to comply with the State law – or that would have been its effect if the Bill had been passed in NSW.

So, what are we saying in all this?

- First, the legislation, both as it stands now, and as has been proposed, is unworkable in its present form.
- Second, it targets content providers, service providers and users in ways that show ignorance of the technology.
- Third, the legislation that has been proposed is at best inconsistent and at worst is in complete conflict with existing Commonwealth and international laws. In the extreme case it requires people to break a Commonwealth law to comply with a State law.

By way of a footnote to all this, an interdepartmental committee was set up between State and Federal authorities to resolve these inconsistencies between legislation at all levels of government within Australia.

Let me turn now to some broader issues to provide a context for all this. At a philosophical level, Internet censorship in Australia – indeed worldwide – is about boundary making and subjectivity. It is about construing the sovereign state as Subject, as against the Other of the international community of states. It commits the fallacy of the 'domestic analogy' – domestic order as against international anarchy and chaos. It also operates at the domestic level by construing the State as Self – the *subject*, and the domestic individual as *abject* (to use Kristeva's term). There are specific ways in which the legislation seeks to do so. The legislation invokes myths of childhood innocence and suggests that the whole Internet should be like a child's playground.

The reality of the Internet is, however, that it reflects greater society – in all its aspects. I want to suggest here that what is needed above all is education, rather than contradictory, and in many ways redundant legislation. What is illegal in physical life is still illegal in cyberspace, and still subject to current legislation. Clearly some form of education is needed, not merely to tell parents to restrict their children's access to the Internet, but rather to educate the children about 'stranger danger' in cyberspace. We already do that as a society, in discussions about the seemingly nice guy with the lollies and the large car – those same guys are out there on the Net, sometimes masquerading as other kids. If they want to meet in real life – we may let them or not as we feel. But there is nothing stopping a parent accompanying them as if they were meeting a pen pal for the first time. Of course the police are there in cyberspace too, also masquerading as kids – paedophilia is a crime in most advanced countries, including Australia. Police the world over are learning the tricks used by criminals, and beating them at their own game. Most times Internet messages leave trails and can be traced back to their origin. Even anonymiser services have been known to cooperate with police in criminal investigations.

There is pornography on the Net, but not a great deal in comparison with all the other information that is there, and there is good reason for that. Pornography uses graphic images, which use a lot of bandwidth – hundreds of times more than text. Most people have relatively slow modems in their homes, so images take a long time to download. Images also take up a lot of storage space, so large pornographic databases are few and far between. Moreover, at best the images, when downloaded and viewed on the screen, are displayed, depending on the particular make and model, at approximately 75 dots per inch – about the same resolution as a newspaper or a dot-matrix printer. The local news-stand has glossy magazines full of images printed at 600–1,200 dots per inch or higher.

There is software freely available for adults to restrict access to at least the main pornographic sites; the others take a lot of searching for, and even then access is via credit card. If we are really so concerned about soft porn images we perhaps first need to tackle billboard advertising and magazine stands, as these are more readily available and at considerably higher resolution than anything one can find on the Net.

When it comes down to it, the Internet is about communication. As a result of the Internet and the technical difficulties of censorship, it is increasingly difficult for countries to get away with systematic human rights abuses. Burma, Peru, Chile, Argentina, China, Vietnam and even Australia have all had human rights abuses publicised as a result of the Internet. There are counselling services on the Internet – including breast cancer support groups, grief counselling groups and medical information groups. New anti-AIDS drugs are being documented and discussed on the Internet. Medical advice is being provided at a distance. Recent examples of this include advice to those helping to deliver babies in outback farms and children's illnesses diagnosed via CUseeme, which is desktop video tele-conferencing via the Internet. Both sender and receiver need to have a digital video camera (some are specially made to sit on a computer), a microphone (some computers have these built in) and some software (freely available on the Net). One dials up a central server and using CUseeme software you can talk to the other person and see them in rather jerky frame-by-frame fashion on your monitor, while they can see you, hence the name CUseeme (see you, see me). (I used this as early as 1996 from a house in Perth, Western Australia, using a standard Macintosh PowerPC equipped with a small golf-ball-sized camera, and spoke to people in the US via this system.) Internet technologies have allowed doctors to listen to heartbeats, and to exchange charts with other doctors to get advice on specialist areas. In Africa, medical and agricultural information is being provided via the Internet to remote communities as part of UN aid projects. Isolated people around the world are finding common interest communities.

There are issues of civil liberties which remain to be addressed, and different countries have varying views on what constitutes fair intrusiveness. At the end of the day, I suspect that most advanced countries are fairly sensible when it comes to issues of censorship. The Australian government, for example, seems to be less concerned about whether or not you say something rude in your email than with the issue of when something on the Internet constitutes a danger to the broader community, or to national security.

When does the Internet threaten the existence of the state? When does it threaten what it means to be a free person in Australian society? Thinking this through, it becomes plain that for Australia, the attempts at legislation, however flawed, have at least been aimed at providing the state with an ability to act if the need should occur – for example to be able to charge someone with an offence if they incite racial vilification, or if they want to solicit children for sex. In that sense, it matters less that the technology cannot be effectively censored, than that the means exist to be able to act in the event of criminal activity. In this it is important to place media portrayals of the Internet in perspective. There is a small percentage of criminals on the Internet. So too, there is a small percentage of criminals in Canberra, or Sydney or anywhere else in Australia. It does not stop us allowing our children to play in parks, or go shopping – even in newsagents. But as responsible parents it would seem just as important to learn about the Internet, about the traps and pitfalls as well as the benefits, and to educate our children about how to deal with them. This does not require state censorship, although a good 'stranger danger' campaign in the schools could go a long way to reducing what dangers there are.

In this chapter I have not sought to answer the rights or wrongs of censorship. Rather my intention has been to explore some of the issues arising out of the way different states have tackled the Internet censorship issue.

The legislation enacted in WA and in NSW seems flawed. The NSW proposed Internet censorship Bill was thrown out as completely unworkable. But the result has been that Internet censorship has been placed on the agenda for Australia. People are out there discussing the issue, even if in often misinformed ways. In my view, before we enact national legislation on Internet censorship, we need to be clear about what it is we want out of the legislation. We need to think in terms of what does it set out to achieve? To be fair, a national-level committee has recently been established between Federal and State legislatures in order to ensure that State legislation will not conflict with Federal legislation, and it is to be hoped that the resulting legislation will reflect a realistic view of what can and cannot be achieved given the current state of technology. A good place to start would be to have the process informed by three things:

- a realistic assessment of the threats
- a thorough understanding of the nature of the technology
- a realistic assessment of what is achievable.

From this it seems reasonable to hope that realistic legislation can be developed for use where a clear crime has been committed.

Summary

- Since Plato there have been concerns with 'unsuitable' people having access to information. Questions remain over who decides what is unsuitable for whom.

- There is a tension between those who want to see more regulation on the Internet and those who wish to maintain the 'frontier' mentality of freedom of information. These stem from philosophical differences.

- We can read a lot from what a culture tries to regulate, because it is the site at which identity structures are being maintained.

- The US tried to enact the Communications Decency Act raising questions over whether the Internet would be defined in broadcast television terms or in telephonic terms. As a hybrid of both the Internet cannot easily be fitted into either paradigm.

- The debate's focus on regulating children's access to sexually explicit material showed the US preoccupation with a mythology of childhood innocence.

- The CDA was overthrown in the US Supreme Court on the basis of the constitutional right to freedom of speech under the First Amendment, rather than in the arena of the politics of sexuality. This reveals an underlying aspect of gendered political debate in US society.

- The European experience has taken the regulation debate beyond national boundaries into multilateral forums. But these are still based on improving cooperation between national law-enforcement agencies. This shows that, despite the Internet being a transnational issue, those issues arising from regulation are still carried out at the nation-state level. A number of policy issues arise from this.

- Australia has enacted some State and national legislation, based on the broadcast media model. Proposed model national legislation follows the broadcast media format, but encounters contradictions in relation to currently existing legislation concerning telecommunications. These contradictions will need to be resolved before Australia can enact viable national-level legislation.

- Regardless of how the individual debates are carried out, there remains the issue of national security. By developing mechanisms for controlling information on the Internet, these mechanisms can be called into play in other arenas should national security warrant such action. The pornography debate is thus a useful device for mobilising consent to develop such mechanisms.

11 alt.cyberspace.binaries. philosophy

The Internet is more than a messaging system. It is also a cultural artefact. As a technology it embodies a way of thinking. Like a piece of sculpture the Internet is a physical thing that encodes meaning within its structure. By embodying a way of thinking it can change the way of thinking of those who use it on a regular basis. New habits of thought emerge from an awareness of the way the Internet structures information. Some would suggest that the whole problem with the Internet is that it does not structure information. But that view highlights the distinction between anarchy and chaos. The two terms are not interchangeable.

States, too, are cultural artefacts that embody ways of thinking. States encode meaning within their structure. Indeed states embody a particular world-view based on connecting identity with landscape, and articulating boundaries in terms of space and time. I want to argue in this chapter that the Internet challenges certain aspects of the connection between identity and landscape by the manner in which it can be said to collapse spatial and temporal boundaries.

Hedley Bull (1977) proposes that states usefully mark the boundary between domestic order and international anarchy. The distinction, he argues, is that individuals within a sovereign state are subject to a common government – unlike the international community of states that have no such government. The international community is therefore by definition anarchic. He stresses, however, that this does not necessarily mean that the international system is chaotic. There can be international order, even in anarchy. But in this chapter, I want to move away from the more explicit discussion about states, to talk about the broader issues of boundary making and the implications of the spatialisation of information away from linear narratives that have until now bounded the individual within relatively narrow modernist discursive confines. The Internet arguably allows individuals to expand on identities based on geographical territories, towards identities based more on the cultural terrain of cyberspace. Can there be a state purely based in cyberspace?

Traditionalists might want to deny the possibility on the grounds that people live in geographical space, and Internet servers are based within sovereign territories – subject already to the vagaries of state-based legislation. The people within such a notional cyberspatial state are also already subject to state-based legislation, and so cannot secede into cyberspace. But another way to look at this, which is equally problematic for those wishing to explore new forms of governance, is that we are already living in virtual states. That is to say that the state is nothing more or less than a legal fiction – an important one, but a fiction nonetheless. The state is Hobbes' 'Leviathan' insofar as it is constituted as a legal individual entity, but constantly shifting map boundaries remind us that the state is historically contingent and essentially contested. The state, as I said at the outset, is like an email discussion list – an identity to which we subscribe, and thereby derive the benefits and responsibilities of a cooperative society. The problem then is not whether a fictive (culturally produced) state can exist in cyberspace as opposed to 'real' states, but rather whether there can be a fiction within a fiction. It is analogous to the problem that Heidegger (1969) faced in coming to grips with the notion of metaphor – if language is the first order of metaphor, can metaphors exist without the pre-supposition that language provides some form of unmediated access to the 'real'. In other words, can there be a metaphor of metaphor? Clearly there is a distinction to be drawn between states in the real world and state-like entities in cyberspace, but it is not the obvious one. The distinction is a philosophical one and is based on the reinsertion of history into culture, as well as the place of the body in cyberspace.

Like states, the Internet, too, is structurally and functionally anarchic, but it is not chaotic. At least not in the simple dictionary understanding of the term. Anarchy is fundamentally about self-government. People choose what to put on the Net – it does not happen randomly. People choose what they view on the Internet – they have to make a positive move to click their way from site to site. This is reflected in the Greek and Latin derivations of the word 'cyberspace' and other terms used in relation to Internet, such as 'hypertext'.

It is not insignificant that the emergence of the Internet has brought with it a whole new range of linguistic expressions that reflect or describe in some way the deeper philosophical traits embedded in the technology. It is also worth noting that the Internet is a western development, and one that has embedded within itself language drawn from Greek and Roman language – the language of western civilisation. The word 'Cyber' comes from the Greek 'κυβερ', which means to steer, to discipline or to govern. So there is a sense of governance embodied within the term 'cyberspace'. The Internet is metaphorically spatialised, so it is worth taking a moment to look at the Latin derivation of 'space' in the context of cyberspace.

Space in both the English and Latin forms (space, spatium) contains three senses. The first, significantly, has to do with time or duration, including:

- lapse or extent between two definite points
- delay or deferment
- leisure or opportunity
- amount or extent of time
- period or interval of time.

Clearly the Internet collapses space through time, making access to large amounts of information available very quickly to users around the world. Collaborative projects can now be accomplished online with participants in different countries, as I did in 1989 writing a paper with a colleague in the UK, while I was based in Australia, saving months that would otherwise have been spent exchanging 'snail mail' and awaiting each other's response. The telephone and related systems (such as fax) provide a sense of immediacy that has at least partly carried over into the Internet. But the Internet has its frustrations. In many ways it is still an information goat-track rather than a super-highway, and will remain so for as long as modems remain slow, phone services traverse copper wires, and computer processing time restricts speed of display. Hence one could be forgiven for thinking that the Internet is best described by the term 'delay', or 'deferment'. The Internet provides both leisure and opportunity, depending on which side of the prosumer/conducer divide you sit. Increasingly this will be both sides, and at the same time. Moreover the Internet can be said to bring home both the notion of time as in the time zone in which one lives, and time compression between people who are geographically separated. This is especially the case in real-time exchanges, such as occur in chat rooms, MUDs or MOOs.

The second element of 'space' encompasses aspects of area or extent. These can include:

- linear distance
- superficial extent or area
- continuous unbounded extension in every direction
- stellar depths
- a more or less limited area or extent
- an interval, a length, a distance
- an interval or blank between words in written matter.

Taken in concert with the prefix 'cyber' we can see the Internet as governing or controlling (the effects of) distance to the extent that it allow people to interact with each other and with each other's work at great distance.

Some see the Internet as an interplay of surfaces, and some consider the Internet's content to be little more than superficial. Philosophically the surface/depth argument has yet to be resolved, but there is a breadth of information already available, and as marketing gurus are finding, sites need to have real content in order to hold the attention of an info-surfer.

The question remains, however, over whether or not brevity can necessarily be construed as superficiality. Some might see it as the very soul of wit. The challenge for Internet authors is to be able to make every word count. Moreover, Internet authors will face the challenge of so arranging their words that their key point can be made in fewer than 300 words. This is more than a sound-bite, but not much more. It does not tolerate the verbosity born of the print paradigm. The irony is that the Internet is also extremely extensive. Indeed the work is no longer bounded by its covers in the same way as a book. The main point of the work may be made briefly, but each key word within the text can be hyperlinked to other texts, other documents on a completely different site across the globe, available at the click of a mouse button.

The text can find itself built outwards with almost limitless extension in every direction. The challenge for Internet authors is to be able to think past the linear paradigm of print.

Insofar as the web is in part connected via telecommunications satellites, it could perhaps be considered to have depths beyond the planet. Indeed the Mars Pathfinder mission saw images loaded onto the Internet almost as soon as they were being received on earth by Mission Control. Interestingly, too, the Mars Pathfinder base craft maintained its contact with the roving Sojourner vehicle using Transfer Control Protocols and Internet Protocols. Although not yet inter-stellar, Internet technologies have already found their uses in space. In addition, US Space Shuttle astronauts are kept in regular email contact with amateur enthusiasts around the world via the NASA website.

Cyberspace is large, and will soon have global coverage, if not global penetration. That is, in time, those with the means will be able to access the Internet from any point in the world, although that is quite different from suggesting that everyone will have access to the Internet. Indeed this will only make the disparities, between the information haves and have-nots, loom larger and more visibly. In this sense the Internet can also be said to occupy a more or less limited area or extent. Not so much in terms of coverage, but in terms of percentage of people online. Internet users will make up only a relatively small percentage of the world's population – still an elite group. The Internet also encompasses intervals, lengths and distances – time lags, time zone lags, lengths both in spatial and temporal terms and distances, through communities operating beyond the constraints of the local. As a result new identity formations (through common interest, but geographically dispersed) are coming into being. Moreover, new ways of thinking about the space between people are being articulated through relationship rather than through collocation.

This brings me to the final point on spatial definition. Spaces are opening up between words through hypertext links. Textual production on the Internet is more akin to what Lévi-Strauss (1966: 17, quoted in Deleuze and Guattari 1983: 7) termed *bricolage*, that is to say the building up of something, not through its essential unities, but through its dispersions, its collisions and collusions with other material – audio, video, textual or graphic. This will set new challenges for intellectual property rights as more texts are produced by 'sampling' directly from other texts. Authorship will be a function of the person who brings material together rather than the person who 'creates' the material. Works will be done in more collaborative team efforts in which the author becomes the team rather then the originary 'author' in the traditional sense.

We can expect to see new forms of literacy emerge requiring people to become far more sophisticated in their ability to 'read'/decode images as well as text. In the transition, as traditional values become de-emphasised, such as spelling and prescriptive grammar, in favour of typography, layout and design, new forms of reading will encompass semiotics and systemic and functional descriptive grammars. Deep structures will be abandoned in favour of better understanding of the interplay of multiple surfaces of textuality. This in turn will have consequences for the way in which education is structured. As search engines take us past hierarchical file structures, so too will meaningful education require us to move beyond hierarchical 'discipline' structures more deeply into interdisciplinary forms. Aspects traditionally taught under the rubric of 'English', for example, will be expanded to incorporate non-linear forms of literacy through multimedia and hypertext works.

The idea of interlinking documents or pieces of information together in ways navigable by a user was first put forward by Vannevar Bush (1945) in his article 'As We May Think'. Ted Nelson took up the challenge in the 1960s with his still unfinished 'xanadu' software project which, nonetheless, became the model for more modest projects such as Apple's Hypercard and Tim Berners-Lee's vision of the WorldWideWeb. Hypertext, or hyperlinked text encompasses the linking of material with documents, across a range of formats, that can expand aspects of the text through 'clickable' words or images that take the reader to other documents. The prefix 'hyper', from the Greek 'υπερ', means to go beyond, over and above, to expand. This describes well the potential of hyperlinked documents. The implications of this are that people will be able to enter a document at, for example, a general overview level, and navigate (a further spatialisation) to more detailed material on specific topics. These expansions can be further down a document, in the manner that a contents page leads deeper into a book through page markers, or they can be links to totally different documents by other authors with information held in a computer next door or halfway around the world in the manner of footnotes or references.

Conceptually, this represents a shift in the author–reader relationship. With hypertext, readers construct their own narrative sequence, bringing together the functions of author and reader in ways that go far beyond the reader skipping chapters in a book. The structure of texts on line is different from the linearity of books. Writing in short 'chunks' provides efficient and concise access to information with gestures outward to other texts online. In this sense, hypertext provides content for the 'space between the words'. Because readers may choose their own path through a text, each will encounter different texts in the same work. The modernist notion of an *œuvre* will no longer apply in the same way as it did for printed works. Moreover the originary (power) relation between author and reader becomes transformed in hypertext works in terms that tend to undermine the hierarchy between author and reader, sender and receiver.

Each information technology embodies its own rules and conditions of operation. Each embodies a world-view, and each is at least subtly different from each other. Both the material conditions under which information technologies work, and the limitations of each information technology, articulate an underlying philosophical basis which determines the outlook of a culture, as seen in its cultural practices. We have seen that these cultural practices are an inherent aspect of a culture's identity. They are an essential part of the way a culture construes the sense of Self as against the Other. Ultimately this may be the crucial difference between the wired and the unwired. Not only are there issues of access to information, but also there are issues of access to a way of thinking, a world-view, a philosophical outlook, that will forever distinguish those who articulate a proactive view of the world as a set of processes, and those who articulate a passive view of the world as a set of objects.

As we saw in the discussion in earlier chapters, this has important implications for the structure and even the existence of states, not only between first and developing worlds, but also for socio-economic survival within the industrialised world. The increasingly global spread of the Internet is set to bring changes at least as great as the shift from print to radio and television. Perhaps it will bring a philosophically more important change: from an economy of objects to an economy of signs, and from a philosophical world of nouns, to one of verbs. Already the distinctions are blurring within language, as verbs become nominalised, and nouns are transformed into verbs. We 'email' each other, 'satellite-in' the news, become 'informationalised', 'cycle' to work, or 'network'.

Hypertext is a mode of constructing documents such that the *relations* between documents become a significant part of the meaning of the text, the way the relationship between words produces meaning in a printed text. This was in part the idea behind Vannevar Bush's 'memex' machine which provided some of the foundation of the idea behind the development of hypertext itself. Woolley (1993: 158) concludes his chapter on hypertext with the rather cryptic remark to the effect that the Internet makes everyone an author and that therefore no one would be. He suggests that the distinction upon which the term author rests, in opposition to 'reader', disappears. This is of course a binarist way of looking at the issue. There will still be readers and authors, but there will no longer be 'simply' readers and authors. This is the point Derrida raises in suggesting that

> we could . . . take up all the coupled oppositions on which philosophy is constructed, and from which our language lives, not in order to see opposition vanish, but to see the emergence of a necessity such that one of the two terms appears as the *différance* of the other.
>
> (Derrida 1976: xxix)

Derrida interprets *différance* here as a conflation of the French words for 'difference' and 'deferment'. That is to say that language depends on terms differing from each other, while at the same time consideration of one term defers, or postpones consideration of the other. What we are dealing with, in other words, is not a destruction of difference but a deconstruction – that is, a reconstrual – of the relationship between the two terms. We are seeing a shift in how we conceive of the nature of meaning, away from originary or essentialist views of meaning, towards a view of meaning as a contextual process in which meaning emerges from the relationships set up between the terms rather than from an absolute standpoint. This underlines the importance of the move in recent years away from prescriptive grammars to descriptive grammars. What emerges from this is an analysis of how language is functioning at the moment, rather than how it 'should' function according to some more or less arbitrary set of rules.

But let me be clear on this point. I am not suggesting that we have no rules. Nor am I suggesting that there is no meaning, rather, that meaning is historically contingent and essentially contested. It always acts in relation to other established ways of reading, rather than some absolute and universal regime of meaning. Landow (1994: 14) suffers a similar confusion in his discussion of hypertext, suggesting that a defining feature of hypertext is that readers can write their responses to the text and thereby collapse the difference between authors and readers. What he is actually saying is that readers can also become authors. This has always been true, but does not stop authors from reading other works, or readers from writing things, acting as different identities in different situations. We all take on a range of roles, but that does not make any other role less meaningful. Landow missed the crucial point raised by Bush, Englebart, Nelson, van Dam and others (see van Dam 1996), that readers of hypertexts are active in the production of meaning insofar as they determine the narrative sequence, whereas in the print media, authors (more properly writers) establish the narrative sequence. This is what is meant by a blurring of the distinction between reader and author in hypertexts.

Moreover, the concept of writing becomes extended to include the ability to add links or 'bookmarks' which enable the reader to retrace steps along the narrative sequence. In graphical browsers, such as Netscape or Internet Explorer, the program keeps a limited track of the sequence in which sites are visited, enabling the user to go back to any of these sites in whatever sequence is desired. Derrida and Foucault both addressed this question in slightly different, if complementary ways. Derrida (1985) revisited the scene of writing by examining the relation between speech and writing. Classical philosophers have tended to consider speech to have priority over writing, as speech was seen as somehow 'closer' to the origin of the utterance. This is the source of Socrates' concerns in Plato's discussion of the dangers of writing – and hence the dangers of other information technologies, as we have seen in earlier chapters. Derrida suggests that we need to examine the locus of meaning – the site at which meaning making takes place. If the reader is actively engaged in the process of 'decoding' the utterance, then the reader is effectively producing meaning in a way that counters the hierarchy of writing seen as a poor reflection of speech. In other words the reader is in fact engaged in a form of writing. This reader–response theory has considerable resonance with the way in which hypertexts operate to engage the reader in the active process of producing meaning. Foucault (1979), in his paper 'What is an Author?', argues that authorship is always a multiplicity. If we look for originary sources, we have to look beyond the person who put pen to paper or hands to keyboard, out into the culture which provided the conditions under which certain meanings could be expressed in a certain way at a certain time, within certain institutional parameters and within certain relations of power. When we read a work, we are reading the culture that enabled the work to be written at that moment in time. This also has considerable resonance with the idea of hypertext. In the former case we have readers engaged actively in making meaning from the work by establishing their own narrative sequence, while in the latter case we see something of the nature of hypertext always already linked outward into the culture that enabled its production. The 'work' in this sense is always plural, but then so too is the reading subject – the person engaged in the reading. In a sense the development of hypertext provided a concrete expression of a philosophical idea about the nature of the way we make meaning through signs. And it provides us with a concrete expression of the way in which the old order hierarchies are systematically breaking down and transforming into new structures as these ideas find expression in ever wider fields.

While this may seem to some an unnecessarily lengthy excursus into what may appear to be a trivial arena, it may be worth recalling that language shapes the way we look at the world. It provides us with the conceptual tools with which to comprehend the world. Language influences the way we come to conceive of ourselves – our identity – and, as we have seen, identity is at the seat of power, politics and the global economy. So an information technology that changes the terms by which we see the world is also a technology that shapes the way we structure the world. People without access to such technologies will find themselves less able to deal with, and comprehend, the nature of the current and emerging changes within the global economy. Such people stand the risk of becoming effectively disenfranchised. The same holds true for states in the developing world insofar as they risk new forms of colonisation.

The world we are facing today is a world of haves versus have-nots. It is a world of considerable social inequalities. It is a world divided by power politics made more complex with the end of the Cold War. It is a world where the nature of identity is being contested between pre-modern states, such as Rwanda, Burundi, Cambodia, Laos and Burma; modern states such as Bosnia, former Yugoslavia, former Soviet Union, Singapore, Malaysia, Latin America and South Africa; and postmodern states such as those in the European Union, the US and other OECD countries. In some cases we see open and armed conflict, while in others we see the identity struggle being played out in terms of modernisation, tariff and trade boundaries.

As physical boundaries become ever more permeable to the passage of information – financial transaction flows, investment, the boundary-making practices that produce identity will continue to be played out in terms of regulation, censorship and cryptography. Moreover these will be played out in national governments through the passage of legislation and through the imposition of connection standards, and through the competitive provision of infrastructure.

Moreover, people within national boundaries are increasingly articulating their identity in terms of common interest groups spread throughout the world. Such groups can range from fans of soap operas and Barbie dolls to human rights organisations on the lookout for political prisoners and human rights violations. Dissident political groups can now have a voice that is very difficult for governments to silence. Such groups have been able to mobilise support in order to facilitate dialogue between such groups and their governments, such as happened, for example, between the Sendero Luminoso (Shining Path) and the Peruvian government. We are beginning to look at our world in new ways when school children in a single-teacher school in Mid-West US can have real dialogue with a single-teacher school in outback Australia. The Internet will not produce a world society, much less a world government, but rather a world that recognises and perhaps celebrates its diversity as well as its moments of recognition. Some will see the Internet as a continuing threat to our moral values, our education system, our security, our identities as members of nation-states. Perhaps there is potential for the Internet to be all these things. But, as with telephone and telegraph, the Internet will be there only for some people. It will be there for the privileged minority, whether the privileged minority of nation-states, or the privileged minority within privileged nation-states. The rest will remain the great unwired.

To bring us back to earth, it is worth noting that the co-dependent developments of ideas, and the technologies with which they become concretised, have widespread implications for daily life in the developed, and consequently in the developing world. The philosophy and the technology provide in tandem the software and hardware for an emerging era. From this arise a number of practical and ethical questions that have yet to be resolved. Just as Renaissance architects and painters began to sign their works and bring about the legal mechanisms to protect intellectual property rights, the Internet poses challenges for intellectual property where the 'work' is a conscious *bricolage* of other people's texts. In the same way postmodernism challenged the modernist notion that intellectual works were the unitary products of 'great men'. Indeed many of the concerns raised about the Internet at the personal and at the national level are at least in part issues of identity formation and boundary maintenance.

The issue of identity is not merely one of philosophical importance, it is also of immense practical importance for the conduct of states. For example, the issue of the 'authentic' author is an aspect not only of intellectual property rights, but also of authentication for business transactions. Am I the purchaser that I am representing myself as? Are you a genuine business to whom I can submit my credit card number? Will a third party intercept my credit card details? All these are questions of identity. Is the visitor to an adult site of legal age to receive sexual information? Are you, the person I am flirting with, really the person you are presenting yourself as? Am I the person you think you are flirting with on a chat room? Does it matter? Perhaps in this last instance it matters if either a law is being broken or if fixed identities 'really' matter to me. Perhaps it is all harmless chat, or good clean fun. Perhaps the Internet provides a 'safe' opportunity for me to try out other versions of myself that I would never dream of doing in physical life.

Questions of identity are also at stake in any debate about censorship or about privacy, both in simplistic ways about the way I see myself, and, in more complex ways, about the boundaries between public and private, between individual and state. In the print and broadcast media, myths abound concerning the nature of the Net and what is available on it, or what it can do to you or your home computer system. These myths are also about identity. They are about the identity of the Internet as against other forms of information technology. They are about the distinction between the wired and the unwired. And always there is the fear of the unknown. Conspiracy theorists and other alarmist commentators on the Net will always build up the Other to seem more powerful than it is. If we do not know the extent or limitations of the Net, or of the government, or of hackers, it is easy to build visions of dark forces, rather than of a few concerned individuals. But identities do have limits, just as the technology of the Net has limitations, just as criminals have limits. They are merely different because, like all identities, they are works in progress.

But to come back to the opening of this chapter, the Internet is less 'about' a technology of communication, than a way of looking at the world. If anything will mark out a net user it is that the idea of the 'local' has acquired new meanings. It has become extended to include those of common interest wherever they are situated in physical space. It produces, if one can generalise, an identity that is comfortable with the idea of networks, or teams. It produces an identity that is comfortable with its own plurality.

For businesses it can mean enormously enhanced flexibility, through the coming together of disparate groups to form limited joint ventures, or 'virtual corporations' that have far greater flexibility than fixed companies. Small flexible networked businesses can wield considerably more power in strategic areas than large inflexible organisations. This too is an attitude, or way of looking at the world that can identify one kind of business over another.

For nation-states it can provide challenges in terms of a state's ability to establish an effective line between being borderless, thereby losing sales taxation revenue because people can buy items cheaper via the Internet, and being an identity structure that helps set the conditions for prosperity among the domestic polity. These issues will never be fully resolved. If they were, then identity structures such as states could perhaps fade away as some naive pundits are saying. Identity is about the narratives we continue to tell about ourselves, always multifaceted, always told with the mythic simplicity appropriate to the situation. Identity is about boundaries. The big boundary with the Internet is not about the technology but about expanded horizons and a new way of looking at the world. As for states? Personally, I think states will remain a part of our lives for as long as we continue to engage in identity making practices that construct communities of 'us' versus the rest, or 'them'. It is a never-ending story.

Summary

- The Internet is a cultural artefact. As such it encodes within its structures, its technology and the language surounding it, a world-view or philosophical outlook. New habits of thought emerge from the way the Internet structures information.

- The Internet is anarchic, but not chaotic, so while it supports a philosophy of self-government, which can appear chaotic, it nonetheless supports its own structures.

- The Internet reflects the classical Greek and Latin roots of the language used to describe it, from cyberspace to hypertext.

- The spatial element of cyberspace is particularly important insofar as it depicts a complex interplay of surfaces. This chapter argues that the interplay of surfaces is what produces a mythos or 'grand narrative' of identity. Rather than criticising the Internet for its lack of depth, perhaps we need to consider questioning the mythical origins of depth.

- Cyberspace will soon have global coverage, if not global penetration. People will be able to access the Internet from any point on the globe, but not everyone will be able to access the Internet.

- The interplay of surfaces will lead to new forms of literacy which will stress multimedia literacy, or semiotic literacy over linear textual forms. This is a shift in mode rather than a decline in level of educational standards. Effective education will stress intertextuality over linearity.

- Hypertext represents a shift in the author/reader hierarchy, such that readers will increasingly set their own narrative sequence – a role formerly reserved for the author. In addition, the reader becomes the focus for the production of meaning, thus the author/reader distinction will become increasingly blurred, as it has already done in contemporary literary philosophy.

- The distinction between haves and have-nots in the information economy will be only in part a distinction of access to specific items of information. Rather the distinction will be one of access to a way of looking at the world. People without access to such technologies will find themselves increasingly less able comprehend and to deal with the emerging changes in global economy.

- The co-dependent developments of ideas and the technologies in which they find expression have widespread implications for daily life in the developed world, the developing world, and between individuals and states. There are practical and ethical questions yet to be resolved. The exploration of these questions is an important aspect of the process of boundary making, from which identity emerges as a by-product.

- The difficulty in establishing state structures in cyberspace stem not from ontological differences between cyberspace and geographical states, but rather from the virtual nature of states themselves.

Bibliography

Note: while it is accepted practice in some quarters to separate journals, books and online material, in some cases the work cited may be found in more than one format and for this reason the bibliography has been cast in an aggregated form.

Air Power Studies Centre (APSC) (1996) *Military Information Operations in a Conventional Warfare Environment, APSC paper no. 47*
http://www.adfa.oz.au/DOD/apsc/paper47.htm

Allison, G. (1976) *Remaking Foreign Policy: The Organisational Connection*, New York: Basic Books.

Anonymous (1997) *Liberty or Tyranny*
http://www.pobox.com/~rene/liberty/

Aronowitz, S. (ed.) (1996) *Technoscience and Cyberculture*, London: Routledge.

Aronson, J. (1996) 'The Consequences of Free Trade in Information Flows', *International Affairs*, 72(2), 311–328.

Arquilla, J. (1994) 'The Strategic Implications of Information Dominance', *Strategic Review*, 3(summer), 24–30.

Arquilla, J. and Ronfeldt, D. (1993) 'Cyberwar is Coming!', *Comparative Strategy*, 12(2), 141–165 also available at
http://www.stl.nps.navy.mil/c4i/cyberwar.html

Arquilla, J. and Ronfeldt, D. (1995) *Cyberwar and Netwar: New Modes, Old Concepts of Conflict*
http://www.rand.org/publications/RRR/RRR.fall95.cyber/cyberwar.html

Austin, J. L. (1975) *How to Do Things with Words*, Oxford and New York: Oxford University Press.

AW&ST (1994) 'EW Expands Information Warfare, Electronic Warfare', *Aviation Week and Space Technology* 10 October, 47–48.

Bakhtin, M. (1981) *The Dialogic Imagination*, Austin, TX: Texas University Press.

Bannister, D., Capello, R. and Nijkamp, P. (eds) (1995) *European Transport and Communications Networks*, Chichester: Wiley.

Baran, P. (1962) *On Distributed Communications Networks (RAND AF 49(638) – 700) (1964 version)*
http://www.rand.org/publications/RM/RM3420/

Baran, P. (1965) *Security, Secrecy and Tamper-free Considerations*
http://www.rand.org/publications/RM/RM3765/

Barbrook, R. (1995) 'Electronic Power to the People', *New Scientist*, 29 July, 46–47.

Barry, A. (1991) 'On the Problem of Long Distance Control: Territory, Communication and Speed', in *History of the Present*, unpublished paper, London School of Economics.

Baudrillard, J. (1988) *The Ecstasy of Communication*, New York: Semiotext(e).

Baudrillard, J. (1995) *The Gulf War Did Not Take Place*, Sydney: Power Publications.

BBN (1995) *BBN Timeline*
http://www.bbn.com/customer_connection/timeline.htm

Benedikt, M. (Ed.) (1991) *Cyberspace: First Steps*, Cambridge, MA: MIT Press.

Biddle, S. and Zirkle, R. (1996) 'Technology, Civil–Military Relations and Warfare in the Developing World', *Journal of Strategic Studies*, 19(2), 171–212.

Brockman, J. (1997) *Digerati: Encounters with the Cyber Elite*, London: Orion Business.

Brown, D. (1997) *Cybertrends: Chaos, Power and Accountability in the Information Age*, London: Viking.

Bull, H. (1977) *The Anarchical Society: A Study in Order in World Politics*, London: Macmillan.

Burchell, G., Gordon, C. and Miller, P. (eds) (1991) *The Foucault Effect: Studies in Governmentality*, London: Harvester/Wheatsheaf.

Bush, V. (1945) 'As We May Think', *New Atlantic Quarterly*, July
http://www.isg.sfu.ca/~duchier/misc/vbush/vbush-all.shtml

Campbell, T. (1998) *The First Email Message*
http://www.pretext.com/mar98/features/story2.htm

Casper, L., Halter, I., Powers, E., Selva, P., Steffens, T. and Willis, T. L. (1996) *Knowledge-Based Warfare: A Security Strategy for the Next Century, Joint Forces Quarterly Autumn 1996*
http://www.dtic.mil/doctrine/jel/jfq_pubs/1813.pdf

Castells, M. (1996) *The Rise of the Network Society*, London: Blackwell.

Castells, M. (1997) *The Power of Identity*, London: Blackwell.

Cerf, V. (1996) *How the Internet Came to Be*
http://www.geocities.com/SiliconValley/2260/cerf1.html

Clausewitz, C. von (1987) *On War*, Harmondsworth: Penguin.

Cobb, A. (1997) *Re: SCADA Technologies*, in personal communication with the author acobb@coombs.anu.edu.au.

Crawford, G. (1996) *New Roles for Information Systems in Military Operations*
http://www.cdsar.af.mil/cc/crawford.html

Cruttwell, P. (1995) *History Out of Control: Confronting Global Anarchy*, Foxhole, Devon: Resurgence.

Dawson, W. and Turner, J. (1989) *When She Goes to Work She Stays at Home*, Canberra: Women's Research amd Employment Initiatives Program, Department of Education, Employment and Youth Affairs.

Deleuze, G. (1992) 'Postscript on the Societies of Control', *October* 59, 3–7
ftp://etext.umich.edu/pub/Politics/Spunk/anarchy_texts/misc/Spunk962.txt

Deleuze, G. and Guattari, F. (1983) *On the Line*, New York: Semiotext(e).

Deleuze, G., and Guattari, F. (1986) Nomadology: The War Machine NY: Semiotext(e).

Della-Giacoma, J. (1996) 'Asia: Internet an Active Player in Indonesian Politics', *Reuters*, 18 August, news wire.

Della-Giacoma, J. (1997) 'Asia: Indonesia Planning Controls on Internet Access', *Reuters*, 18 June, news wire.

Derrida, J. (1976) *Of Grammatology*, Baltimore, MD: Johns Hopkins University Press.

Derrida, J. (1985) 'Freud and the Scene of Writing', in his *Writing and Difference*, London: Routledge & Kegan Paul.

Dery, M. (Ed.) (1994) *Flame Wars: The Discourse of Cyberculture*, Durham, NC, and London: Duke University Press.

Deutsch, J. M. (1996) *Foreign Information Warfare Programs and Capabilities, Congressional Testimony 25 June 1996*
http://www.odci.gov/cia/public_affairs/speeches/dci_testimony-062596.html

Dillon, G. M. (Ed.) (1988) *Defence Policy Making: A Comparative Analysis*, Leicester: Leicester University Press.

Dillon, G. (1995) 'Sovereignty and Governmentality: From the Problematics of the "New World Order" to the Ethical Problematic of the World Order', *Alternatives*, 20(3), 323–368.

Dillon, G. and Everard, J. (1992) 'Stat[e]ing Australia: Squid Jigging and the Masque of State', *Alternatives*, 17(3), 281–312.

Doan, N. T. (1996) 'Regulation of Internet Connections', *Hanoi Courier*, 1–7 September, 7.

Dobrez, L. (ed.) (1994) *Identifying Australia in Postmodern Times*, Canberra: Australian National University.

Economist (1993) 'Telecommunications: Economist Survey', *The Economist*, 23 October, 1–18.

Economist (1995a) 'The Accidental Superhighway: Economist Survey', *The Economist*, 1 July, 3–26.

Economist (1995b) 'The Myth of the Powerless State', *The Economist*, 7 October, 15–16.

Economist (1996) 'The Economics of the Internet: Too Cheap to Meter?' *The Economist*, 19 October, 21–24.

Elmer-DeWitt, P. (1994) 'Battle for the Soul of the Internet', *Time Magazine*, 25 July, 50–56.

Elshtain, J. B. (1987) *Women and War*, Brighton: Harvester Press.

Emerson, T. (1995) 'Opening the Windows, Keeping Out the Flies: Cyberdissidents Worry Some Asian Nations', *Newsweek*, 25 December 1995–1 January 1996, 27.

Evans, C. (1979) *The Mighty Macro: The Impact of the Computer Revolution*, London: Victor Gollancz.

Everard, J. (1994) 'Re: Constituting Australia – The Differend, The (Re)Public and the Proper Name', in L. Dobrez (Ed.) *Identifying Australia in Postmodern Times*, Canberra: Australian National University.

Fogleman, G. R. R. (1995) *Information Operations: The Fifth Dimension of Warfare*
http://www.dtic.dia.mil/defenselink/pubs/di-index.html

Fogleman, R. R. and Widnall, S. E. (1995) *Cornerstones of Information Warfare*
http://www.infowar.com/mil_c4i/mil_c4ia.html-ssi.

Foucault, M. (1970) *The Order of Things*, London: Tavistock.

Foucault, M. (1977) *The Archaeology of Knowledge*, London: Tavistock.

Foucault, M. (1979) 'What is an Author?', in J. V. Harari (ed.) *Textual Strategies: Perspectives in Post-Structuralist Criticism*, London: Methuen.

Foucault, M. (1980) *Power/Knowledge*, ed. Colin Gordon, New York: Pantheon.

Foucault, M. (1984) *The History of Sexuality: An Introduction*, Harmondsworth: Penguin.

Gajjala, R. (1996) *Cyborg Diaspora and Virtual Imagined Community: Studying SAWNET*
http://www.pitt.edu/~gajjala/sanov.html

Galluzzi, P. (1996) *Renaissance Engineers from Brunelleschi to Leonardo da Vinci*, Florence: Instituto e Museo di Storia della Scienza.

Gatens, M. (1996) *Imaginary Bodies*, London: Routledge.

Gibson, W. (1984) *Neuromancer*, New York: Ace.

Giddens, A. (1987) *The Nation-State and Violence*, Berkeley, CA: University of California Press.

Gilmore, J. (1997) http://www.toad.com/gnu/index.html

Goldstuck, A. (1995) *The Hitchhiker's Guide to the Internet: A South African Handbook*, Johannesburg: Zebra Press.

Goodman, S. E. (1996) 'War, Information Technologies, and International Asymmetries', *Communications of the ACM*, 39(12), 11–15.

Granger, J. V. (1979) *Technology and International Relations*, San Francisco: W. H. Freeman.

Gray, C. H. (Ed.)(1995) *The Cyborg Handbook*, London: Routledge.

Gray, C. (1996) 'A Rejoinder to Martin Libicki', *Orbis*, 40(2), 274–276.

Greenleaf, G. (1996) 'An Emerging Law of Cyberspace?' in *Computers and Law Conference*, unpublished papers, Melbourne and Sydney.

Gregston, B. (1996) 'The European Picture: The Net is Conquering the Old World', *Internet World*, December, 52–55.

Harari, J. V. (Ed.) (1979) *Textual Strategies: Perspectives in Post-Structuralist Perspectives*, London: Methuen.

Haraway, D. J. (1991) *Simians, Cyborgs, and Women: The Reinvention of Nature*, London: Free Association Press.

Hardy, H. E. (1993) *The History of the Net* (unpublished masters thesis) ftp://ummc.umich.edu/pub/seraphim/doc/nethist8.txt

Hazlett, J. (1995) *Just-In-Time Warfare* http://www.ndu.edu/ndu/inss/books/dbk/dbkch08.html

Heidegger, M. (1969) *Identity and Difference*, trans. J. Stambaugh, New York: Harper and Row.

Held, D. (Ed.) (1991) *Political Theory Today*, Cambridge: Polity.

Herzfeld, C. (1995) 'The Immaterial World', *Scientific American*, September, 171.

Hiebert, M., Jayasankaran, S., Miller, M. and Tiglao, R. (1997) 'Future Shock: Malaysia', *Far Eastern Economic Review*, 27 February, 44–47.

Hobbes, T. (1987) *Leviathan*, Harmondsworth: Penguin.

Horace (1997) *The Complete Odes and Epodes*, trans. D. West, Oxford: Oxford University Press.

Horner, D. and Reeve, I. (1991) *Telecottages: The Potential for Rural Australia*, Department of Primary Industry and Energy, Canberra: Australian Government Publication Service.

Howard, J. D. (1997) *An Analysis of Security Incidents on the Internet 1989–1995* (PhD thesis) http://www.cert.org/research/JHThesis/index.html

Hudson, D. (1997) *Rewired: A Brief (and Opinionated) Net History*, Indianapolis, in: Macmillan Technical Publishing.

I*M (1997) *INFO 2000 and Harmful Content on the Internet. EU Document* http://www2.echo.lu/legal/en/Internet/presrel.html

Jakobson, F. (1996) 'The Internet: A South African Experience', in *Cybermind96*, Perth, Western Australia.

Jameson, F. (1991) *Postmodernism or the Cultural Logic of Late Capitalism*, London: Verso.

Jayasankaran, S. (1997) 'Field of Dreams: Malaysia is Building it – Will the World Come?', *Far Eastern Economic Review*, 27 February, 49–50.

Jervis, R. (1970) *The Logic of Images in International Relations*, Princeton, NJ: Princeton University Press.

Johnson, S., and Libicki, M. (1995) *Dominant Battlespace Awareness*, Washington, DC: NDU Press
http://www.ndu.edu/ndu/inss/books/dbk/dbk1.html

Kennedy, P. (1989) *The Rise and Fall of the Great Powers*, New York: Vintage.

Koestler, A. (1970) *The Ghost in the Machine*, London: Pan.

Kristeva, J. (1986) 'Revolution in Poetic Language', in T. Moi (ed.) *The Kristeva Reader*, Oxford: Basil Blackwell.

Lacan, J. (1982) *Ecrits: A Selection*, London: Tavistock.

Landow, G. P. (Ed.) (1994) *Hyper/Text/Theory*, Baltimore, MD: Johns Hopkins University Press.

Leiner, B., Cerf, V., Clark, D., Kahn, R., Kleinrock, L., Lynch, D., Postel, J., Roberts, L. and Wolff, S. (1997) *A Brief History of the Internet*
http://www.isoc.org/Internet_history/

Lemmon, L. T. and Reis, M. J. (eds) (1965) *Russian Formalist Criticism: Four Essays*, Lincoln, NB: Nebraska University Press.

Lever, R. (1996) 'US: US Prepares Defences for "Electronic Pearl Harbor"', *Agence France-Presse*, 3 March, news wire service.

Lévi-Strauss, C. (1966) *The Savage Mind*, Chicago: University of Chicago Press.

Levy, S. (1995) 'The Year of the Internet', *Newsweek*, 25 December 1995 – 1 January 1996, 17–26.

Libicki, M. (1995) *What is Information Warfare?*
http://www.ndu.edu/ndu/inss/actpubs/act003/a003cont.html

Libicki, M. J. (1996) 'The Emerging Primacy of Information', *Orbis*, 40/2 (spring), 261–276.

Lubar, S. (1993) *Infoculture: The Smithsonian Book of Information Age Inventions*, Boston, MA: Houghton Mifflin.

Lykke, N. and Braidotti, R. (eds) (1996) *Between Monsters, Goddesses and Cyborgs*, London: Zed.

Lyotard, J-F. (1984) *The Postmodern Condition: A Report on Knowledge*, Manchester: Manchester University Press.

Lyotard, J-F. (1988) *The Différend: Phrases in Dispute*, Manchester: Manchester University Press.

Machiavelli, N. (1986) *The Prince*, Harmondsworth: Penguin.

Magsig, D. (1995) *Information Warfare in the Information Age*
http://www.seas.gwu.edu/student/dmagsig/infowar.html

Mann, P. (1996) 'Cyber Threat Expands with Unchecked Speed', *Aviation Week and Space Technology*, 8 July, 63.

Mansell, R. (1993) *The New Telecommunications: A Political Economy of Network Evolution*, London: Sage.

Markley, R. (Ed.) (1996) *Virtual Realities and their Discontents*, Baltimore, MD: Johns Hopkins University Press.

Martin, J. and Norman, A. (1973) *The Computerized Society*, Harmondsworth: Penguin.

Martin, L., Gutman, H., and Hutton, P. (eds) (1988) *Technologies of the Self*, London: Tavistock.

Mehler, M. (1996) *To Surf or Not to Surf*
http://www.beyondcomputingmag.com/9-96/connect.html

Mesher, G. (1996) 'The Internet in Asia: Modern Countries Move Ahead', *Internet World*, December, 56–57.

Mikkelson, B. and Mikkelson, D. (1997) *Faxlore/Netlore*
http://www.snopes.com/spoons/faxlore/lighthse.htm

Miller, L. (1995) 'Fear of net.sex.', *Wired*, November, 43.

Minihan, K. (1997) 'Interview', *Aviation Week and Space Technology*, 10 February, 148.

Mitchell, W. J. (1996) *City of Bits: Space, Time and the Infobahn*, Cambridge, MA: MIT Press.

Moi, T. (1985) *Sexual/Textual Politics: Feminist Literary Theory*, London: Routledge.

Morgan, M. L. (1997) *What is SCADA?*
http://www.ezl.com/~nuevo/scada.html

Morley, D. and Robins, K. (1995) *Spaces of Identity: Global Media, Electronic Landscapes and Cultural Boundaries*, London: Routledge.

Morrison, P. and Morrison, E. (eds) (1961) *Charles Babbage: On the Principles and Development of the Calculator*, New York: Dover.

Mumford, L. (1934) *Technics and Civilisation*, London: G. Routledge.

Neel, J. (1988) *Plato, Derrida and Writing*, Carbondale, IL: Southern Illinois Press.

Negroponte, N. (1996) *Being Digital*, London: Hodder & Stoughton.

Nua (1996) *Nua Internet Surveys: 1996 Review*
http://www.nua.ie/surveys/1996review.html

Nye, J. and Owens, W. A. (1996) 'America's Information Edge', *Foreign Affairs*, 75(2), 20–36.

OECD (1990) 'Cities and New Technologies', in OECD, *Cities and New Technologies*, Paris: OECD.

OECD (1996a) *Globalisation of Industry: Overview and Sector Reports*, Paris: OECD.

OECD (1996b) *OECD Draft Guidelines for Cryptography Policy*
http://193.154.75.3/Netzeil/OECD/oecd_09.htm

OECD (1997a) *IT Outlook: Current Issues Relating to Information Technologies* ·
http://www.oecd.org/dsti/itblurb.html

OECD (1997b) *Information Technology and Information Policy*
http://www.oecd.org/puma/gvrnance/it/

Offe, C. (1996) *Modernity and the State: East, West*, Cambridge: Polity.

Ohmae, K. (1995) *The End of the Nation-state*, London: HarperCollins.

Pacey, A. (1983) *The Culture of Technology*, Oxford: Blackwell.

Panos (1995) *The Internet and the South: Superhighway or Dirt Track?*
http://www.oneworld.org/panos/panos_Internet_press.html

Petre, D. and Harrington, D. (1996) *The Clever Country? Australia's Digital Future*, Sydney: Macmillan.

Phillips, D. L. (1977) *Wittgenstein and Scientific Knowledge: A Sociological Perspective*, London: Macmillan.

Plato (1973) *Phaedrus and Letters VII and VIII*, Harmondsworth: Penguin Classics.

Plato (1992) *The Republic*, New York: Quality Paperback Book Club.

RAND (1995) *Information Warfare: A Two-Edged Sword*
http://www.rand.org/publications/RRR/RRR.fall95.cyber/infor_war.html

Reinert, E. S. (1995) 'Catching-up from Way Behind: A Third World Perspective on First World History', in J. Fagerberg, B. Verspagen and N. v. Tunzelmann (eds) *The Dynamics of Technology, Trade and Growth*, Aldershot: Edward Elgar.

Rheingold, H. (1992) *Virtual Reality*, London: Mandarin.

Rheingold, H. (1994) *The Virtual Community: Finding Connections in a Computerized World*, London: Secker & Warburg.

Rice, P. and Waugh, P. (eds) (1991) *Modern Literary Theory: A Reader*, London: Edward Arnold.

Robertson, G. (1989) *Freedom, the Individual and the Law*, 6th edn, Harmondsworth: Penguin.

Rosecrance, R. (1986) *The Rise of the Trading State*, New York: Basic Books.

Rousseau, J-J. (1986) *The Social Contract*, Harmondsworth: Penguin.

Rucker, R., Sirius, R. U. and Mu, Q. (1993) *Mondo 2000: A User's Guide to The New Edge*, London: Thames & Hudson.

Rushkoff, D. (1994) *Cyberia: Life in the Trenches of Hyperspace*, London: HarperCollins.

Salomon, J-J., Sagasti, F. and Sachs-Jeantet, C. (eds) (1994) *The Uncertain Quest: Science, Technology, and Development*, Tokyo: United Nations University Press.

Schelling, T. (1968) 'Bargaining, Communication and Limited War', in M. E. Smith and C. J. Johns (eds) *American Defense Policy*, 2nd edn, Baltimore, MD: Johns Hopkins University Press.

Schenk-Sandbergen, L. and Choulamany-Khamphoui (1995) *Women in Rice Fields and Offices: Irrigation in Laos-Gender-Specific Cases in Four Villages*, Amsterdam: Het Spinhaus. See also
http://www.sara.nl./spinhaus/

Schrage, M. (1990) *Shared Minds: The New Technologies of Collaboration*, New York: Random House.

Schwartau, W. (1994) *Information Warfare: Chaos on the Electronic Superhighway*, New York: Thunder's Mouth Press.

Sellers, S. (Ed.) (1994) *The Hélène Cixous Reader*, London: Routledge.

Senft, T. N. (Ed.) (1997) *Sexuality and Cyberspace: Performing the Digital Body*, New York: Women and Performance Journal.

Simpson, E. S. (1994) *The Developing World – An Introduction*, Harlow: Longman.

Smith, A. (1993) *Books to Bytes: Knowledge and Information in the Postmodern Era*, London: British Film Institute.

Smith, M. and Johns, C. I. (eds) (1968) *American Defense Policy*, Baltimore, MD: Johns Hopkins University Press.

Soroos, M. (1986) *Beyond Sovereignty: The Challenge of Global Policy*, Columbia, SC: University of South Carolina Press.

South, A. (1996) *Preparing for the 21st Century* (White Paper), Johannesburg: Department of Arts, Culture, Science and Technology.

Spender, D. (1995) *Nattering on the Net: Women Power and Cyberspace*, Melbourne: Spinifex.

Stein, G. J. (1995) *Information War*
http://www.usafe.af.mil/direct/sc/stein.htm

Stein, G. J. (1996) *Information War – Cyberwar – Netwar*
http://www.cdsar.af.mil/apj/stein.htm

Stephenson, N. (1995) *The Diamond Age*, London: Viking.

Sterling, B. (1993a) *The Hacker Crackdown*, New York: Bantam.

Sterling, B. (1993b) 'Internet', *Fantasy and Science Fiction*, 44(February), 99–107.

Stoll, C. (1996) *Silicon Snake Oil: Second Thoughts on the Information Highway*, London: Pan.

Strange, S. (1994) *States and Markets*, London: Pinter.

Swade, D. (1991) *Charles Babbage and his Calculating Machines*, London: Science Museum.

Swett, C. (1996) *Strategic Assessment: The Internet*
  http://www.fas.org/cp/swett.html
Szafranski, C. R. (1996) *Theory of IW*
  http://www.cdsar.af.mil/apj/szfran.html
Tapscott, D. (1996) *The Digital Economy: Promise and Peril in the Age of Networked Intelligence*, New York: McGraw-Hill.
Thompson, J. B. and Held, D. (eds) (1982) *Habermas: Critical Debates*, London: Macmillan.
Toffler, A. (1981) *The Third Wave*, London: Pan.
Toffler, A. (1995) *The I-Bomb BBC Documentary Discussion*
  http://helios.njit.edu/1994/cgi-bin/contrib/interdependence/ibomb.htm
Toffler, A. and Toffler, H. (1993) *War and Anti-War: Survival at the Dawn of the 21st Century*, Boston, MA: Little, Brown.
Turkle, S. (1996) *Life on the Screen*, London: Weidenfeld & Nicolson.
Tzu, Sun (1994) *The Art of War*, Hertfordshire: Wordsworth Reference.
US General Accounting Office (1996) *Information Security: Computer Attacks at Department of Defense Pose Increasing Risks* (no. GAO/AIMD-96–84), General Accounting Office.
van Dam, A. (1996) 'Hypertext-87 Keynote Address'
  http://www.cs.brown.edu/memex/HT_87_Keynote_Address.html
Venkatesh, A. (1996) 'Computers and Other Interactive Technologies for the Home', *Communications of the ACM*, 39(12), 47–54.
Virilio, P. (1986) *Speed and Politics*, New York: Semiotext(e).
W3C (1997) *W3C Activities related to the 'Global Information Networks' Ministerial Conference Meeting in Bonn, Germany 6–8 July 1997*
  http://www12.w3.org/TR/NOTE-eu-conf-970711
Wales, E. and Hilvert, J. (1997) 'Europe, US at War over Net Domain Name Issue', *The Australian*, 6 May, 40.
Walker, R. (1991) 'Ethics, Modernity and the Theory of International Relations', in R. Higgott and J. Richardson (eds) *International Relations: Global and Australian Perspectives on an Evolving Discipline*, Canberra: Australian National University.
Waller, D. (1995) 'Onward Cyber Soldiers', *Time Magazine*, 21 August, 43–50.
Waters, M. (1995) *Globalization*, London: Routledge.
Weber, S. (1996) *Mass Mediauras: Form, Technics, Media*, Sydney: Power Publications.
Weizenbaum, J. (1984) *Computer Power and Human Reason: From Judgement to Calculation*, Harmondsworth: Penguin.
Whitaker, R. (1996a) *IW: Questing Power via Cyberspace (a bibliography)*
  http://www.informatik.umu.se/~rwhit/IWBib.html
Whitaker, R. (1996b) *Information Warfare Glossary*
  http://www.i-war.com/glossary.html
Widnall, S., and Fogleman, G. R. R. (1995) *Cornerstones of Information Warfare*
  http://www.infowar.com/mil_c4i/mil_c4ia.html
Wittgenstein, L. (1983) *Philosophical Investigations*, Oxford: Blackwell.
Woolley, B. (1993) *Virtual Worlds*, Harmondsworth: Penguin.
Yonekura, H. (1995) 'Institutional Arrangements of Asian Agriculture under Market Incompleteness: Theoretical Framework and Implications', *Developing Economies*, XXXIII(4), 369–373.

Index